Milton

Milton

Stevie Davies

HARVESTER
WHEATSHEAF

New York   London   Toronto   Sydney   Tokyo   Singapore

First published 1991 by
Harvester Wheatsheaf
66 Wood Lane End, Hemel Hempstead
Hertfordshire HP2 4RG
A division of
Simon & Schuster International Group

Typeset in 11/13pt Goudy
by Cambridge Composing (UK) Ltd, Cambridge

Printed and bound in Great Britain by
Billing and Sons Ltd, Worcester

British Library Cataloguing in Publication Data

Davies, Dr Stevie
    Milton. — (Harvester new readings)
    I. Title II. Series
    821.8

    ISBN 0-7108-1355-4
    ISBN 0-7450-1045-8 pbk

1 2 3 4 5   95 94 93 92 91

To Katherine
for your journey

Harvester New Readings

This established paperback series offers a range of important new critical introductions to English writers, responsive to new bearings which have recently emerged in literary analysis. Its aim is to make more widely current and available the perspectives of contemporary literary theory, by applying these to a selection of the most widely read and studied English authors.

The range of issues covered varies with each author under survey. The series as a whole resists the adoption of general theoretical principles, in favour of the candid and original application of the ciritical and theoretical models found most appropriate to the survey of each individual author. The series resists the representation of any single either traditionally or radically dominant discourse, working rather with the complex of issues which emerge from a close and widely informed reading of the author in question in his or her social, political and historical context.

The perspectives offered by these lucid and accessible introductory books should be invaluable to students seeking an understanding of the full range and complexity of the concerns of key canonical writers. The major concerns of each author are critically examined and sympathetically and lucidly reassessed, providing indispensable handbooks to the work of major English authors seen from new perspectives.

HARVESTER NEW READINGS

David Aers	*Chaucer*
James Boooth	*Larkin*
Joseph Bristow	*Robert Browning*
Angus Calder	*T. S. Eliot*
Brian Cummings	*Donne*
Alexander Davis	*Ted Hughes*
Steve Davies	*Milton*
Simon Dentith	*George Eliot*
Kate Flint	*Dickens*
Paul Hamilton	*Wordsworth*
Brean Hammond	*Pope*
Bernard O'Donoghue	*Heaney*
Adrian Poole	*Henry James*
Kiernan Ryan	*Shakespeare*
Simon Shepherd	*Spenser*
Nigel Wood	*Swift*

Contents

Acknowledgements and Bibliographical Note

This book has its roots in an Extra-Mural class on Milton which I led at Manchester University from October 1988 to April 1989: it was a profound experience of reading together and listening to one another, which I shall never forget. I thank Susi and Simon Barber, Beth Brownhill, Barbara Cockburn, Eileen Edwards, Irene Walton, Mary and Simmel Goldberg, Ann Hart, Moira Harris, Chris Heywood, Ann Long and Frank Regan for all they gave to me. I mention separately Joan Mills who will always be my idea of 'the true wayfaring Christian', and Jack Payne, whose extraordinary brilliance qualifies him as *the uncommon reader*. I thank also Professor William B. Hunter, Emeritus Professor of English Literature at the University of Houston, who visited us to share his unequalled knowledge of Milton and whose generosity furnished me not only with information and suggestions but also with many of the texts I needed in order to write this book.

I owe a great debt of thanks to my friend and fellow-scholar, Andrew Howdle, for years of shared Renaissance thought and talk, and to Rosalie Wilkins for her loving friendship. Finally I thank my husband, Frank Regan, whose love and thoughtfulness sustained me throughout the writing of the book.

ACKNOWLEDGEMENTS

The text of Milton's poems used throughout is John Carey's and Alastair Fowler's edition of *The Poems of John Milton* (London and New York, 1968); the Bible is cited in the Authorised Version.

S. Davies

Introduction: Towards a Holistic Reading Practice

When I take down a copy of Milton's *Paradise Lost* from my bookshelf, lay the book open at Book One, Line One, and begin to read:

> Of man's first disobedience, and the fruit
> Of that forbidden tree . . .
>
> (I. 1–2)

my hands and eyes repeat verbatim the action of countless other readers unknown to myself over a period of three centuries. But my mind as I scan the words on the page can never reproduce with exactitude that more intimate, subtly various mental process which takes place in the recess of the individual mind and remains as nearly unknowable to others as the human self. For most of us, though not for all (including Milton who was blind for the last twenty years of his life), the act of reading rests on a primary act of seeing. The print on the page encodes significant sounds which we translate upon recognition through the eye into meaningful messages. But the primacy of the eye can exert an unsettling effect on the meaning of what is read. The same words can look oddly different in different texts and contexts: the last paragraph of *Paradise Lost*, displayed on the London underground between the maps and the advertisements, scribbled out on rough paper in longhand, taken down in shorthand, inscribed in an

1

antiquarian book or a Penguin paperback – all may hit the eye of the mind at different angles. We and our language are nervously at the mercy of conditions. Milton's first readers, opening the poem in 1667, *saw* a somewhat different text on the page:

> OF Mans First Disobedience, and the Fruit
> Of that Forbidden Tree, whose mortal tast
> Brought Death into the World, and all our woe,
> With loss of *Eden* . . .

> (I. 1–4)

The opening 'O' in OF was printed as an ornamental letter in a square five lines deep, a convention persisting from the illuminated manuscripts of the medieval period. Five out of the seven words in the first line begin with capital letters, making a sort of compositorial flourish as if to set a secondary title within the text itself. This corresponds to conventions of the time, whereby it was becoming standard to capitalise all nouns: but two nouns in the first lines open with lower case letters: 'tast' and 'woe'. Each of these degraded words stands last in the order of its line and each signals the fall to come: 'tast' its cause and 'woe' its effect. The capitalisation of 'Death' at line 3 (omitted in the modern text) may remind a careful reader that Death in *Paradise Lost* is a character as well as a condition. Minor though these differences are, they are many, and not absolutely superficial – as the slight variations and nuances of expression on a stranger's face which we seek to 'read' may seem significant in the moment of perception.

Reading, then, must somehow take the face of the page into account; insight be dependent on an initial act of sight. But the despotism of the optic nerve when it comes to matters of understanding (we say *I see* when we feel we have read someone's meaning aright) reminds us that the experience of the author of *Paradise Lost* was shorn of the visual dimension. The poet saw neither the manuscript of his poem nor the printed book:

> But cloud in stead and ever-during dark
> Surrounds me, from the cheerful ways of men
> Cut off, and for the book of knowledge fair
> Presented with a universal blank

Of nature's works to me expunged and razed,
And wisdom at one entrance quite shut out.
(III. 45–50)

To have suffered blindness is to have been visited by a terrible censor. The visible creation is represented as an encyclopaedia of divinely authorised wisdom, written out in the handwriting of God: 'the book of knowledge fair'. Milton's diction is bibliographical and technical: a *blank* (associated with French *blanc*, white) is an unprinted page in *nature's works* signifying the Creation but also with the suggested meaning of literary works, *opera omnia; expunged* (from Latin *expungere*, to prick out) is a term used in censorship meaning to erase undesired matter and, by fortuitous sound-similarity, was often confused with the licencer's *sponge; razed* repeats the idea of deletion, with the suggestion of scratching out. Just as in his poignant 'Sonnet: On His Blindness', Milton sees himself as violated in his sacred duty of writing ('that one talent which is death to hide / Lodged with me useless'), so in *Paradise Lost* he presents himself as violated in his Christian profession of reading. The concept of the world as a great book (amplified by Bacon in his *Advancement of Learning*), handwritten by the Creator, in which each phenomenon bears some emblematic meaning in relation to the whole composition, makes the art of reading profoundly and crucially significant. We come into the world expressly to read. The Bible, inspired directly by God, is the key text for interpreting the hieroglyphics inscribed in the Book of Knowledge. As literate and literary beings, we cultivate reading skills which serve a double function: divulging meanings in the words on a page and decoding the language of the universe whose rich eloquence was pronounced 'in the beginning' by God's creating Word. The community of the faithful is thus, pre-eminently, a readership. It is against this luminous and (to the student of learning) comforting equation of literary arts with the art of living that we read the desolation imprinted on the sight-censored Milton by the white page of Nature's *universal blank*. He presents to our eyes a poem hidden from his own, whose words existed in his mind's ear and mind's eye alone, his method of composition being a threefold process of early-morning composition, committing to memory and dictation to a secretary:

And hee waking early (as is the use of temperate men) had commonly a good Stock of Verses ready against his Amanuensis came; which if it happend to bee later than ordinary, hee would complain, Saying *hee wanted to bee milked.*[1]

Milton's blindness is as inseparable from our reading of his later poetry as the fact of his gender or his place in history. It may help to explain the peculiar inwardness of his expression, together with its extraordinary memorability, as if his blind compositions carried traces of that mnemonic art characteristic of oral poetry, with its concise rhythmic intensities and sound-patternings.

What Milton 'intended' by his poetry, together with its precise meaning to other readers, critical theory in the modern period has warned us to doubt whether we can know or should wish to enquire – insisting that language itself is an unstable, fluently suggestive medium, self-reflexively in pursuit of a conclusiveness which forever eludes it; meaning not an objective presence ascertainable to the studious or intuitive eye somewhere 'behind' the text; the author, in Foucault's words, 'not a regulator of the fictive' but an oppressive fiction, from whose parsimonious constraints the polysemous texts must be set free to be composed, decomposed and recomposed by the active reader.[2] My reading of Milton takes advantage of modern reader-theory, with its emphasis on the active completion of the text by the process of reading; it is indebted to modern insistence on the disrupted, ambivalent, displaced and insecure condition of literary language, for its perception of fluid insecurity (of life and of language) as a major subject of Milton's poetry. But my reading, in extending a welcome to plurality of meanings and the authority of readers, also willingly embraces the matrix or root-system of the poem in a conjectured and reconstructed person who was its source. The history, thoughts, desires and idiolect of the author, in so far as these can be comprehended or guessed out, are taken into account in this book, not to limit or determine meaning but to allow the author to participate in widening the parameters of possible meaning to the fullest extent. I do this in the interests of a holistic interpretation. Like every philosophy or *Weltanschauung* claiming objective and forensic status, our literary theories also present an unacknowledged symptomatology of desire. Literary theory has immemorially served the function of clearing a free space in which we can say what we want to say about literature with impunity, establishing an area which is a sanctuary for cherished insights. Like artists, literary critics are imaginers: their work is to reimagine what has already been imagined, and it is perhaps in part because so many of us are would-be or failed artists ourselves that we itch to marginalise or evacuate the author from his own work, appropriating it as our own.

For me, there is a need to clear space sufficient to engage, if not the whole self, at least as much of the self as can be summoned, in dialogue with other reading selves, including the voice of the author: the amplest space must be secured for the critical act. Modern criticism emphasises, with justice, the embattled intelligence in relation to the self-conflicting text. There is much talk of 'interrogating the text'. But we also need to 'interrogate' our own metaphors, in the light of George Eliot's pregnant reminder that we all get our thoughts entangled in metaphors, and act fatally on the strength of them. We present our symptoms in the form of metaphor. If literary language is polysemous, bearing telltale news of authorial stratagems and repressed drives, so also critical terminology (which pretends to authoritative technical status and arrogates the privilege of pedagogy) is polysemous, metaphor-brimming, and gives us away at every turn. *Is* the text a political dissident or suspect spy that we should insist so cantankerously on 'interrogating' it? We could with equal value meditate on it, reflect on it, even listen to it. *Is* the author always such a bogey that he must have all his 'privileges' confiscated? Many of the critical metaphors now in current usage bear, to my eye, the marks of a patriarchal aggressiveness which is less than true to the common experience of reading. Reading is a deeply inward process in which we seem to share a mind – to be temporarily of one mind – with the book's creator: full enjoyment involves a listening receptiveness as well as an interrogative alertness. The contours of our loneliness dissolve as the author's 'I' is assimilated to my 'I' or yours, in a dissolution of boundaries as 'I' (a woman) become through mimetic reiteration 'him' (Milton) who has himself through the literary impersonation of her speech become 'her' (Eve). The act of reading creates a complex sensation of union, mingling assent and dissent, but resembling at least as much as a power-relationship, a love-relationship which includes, for the time being, another mind as part of the self.

My book attempts to avoid what I see as the fundamentally

patriarchal weakness of endlessly running for father, the constant appeal to the authority of the big guns – 'As Derrida/Lacan/Freud/Marx/Barthes says . . .', together with the equally patriarchal bullying tactics which seek to empower a discourse founded on (often justifiably) preferred metaphors by presenting its insights as authoritative doctrine, with the warrant of the *Imprimatur*. Barthes' description of the plural text presents a handy instance of this passing-off of metaphor as licensed doctrine:

> The Text is not coexistence of meanings but passage, traversal; thus it answers not to an interpretation, liberal though it may be, but to an explosion, a dissemination. The Text's plurality does not depend on the ambiguity of its contents, but rather on what could be called the *stereographic plurality* of the signifiers that weave it (etymologically the text is a cloth; *textus*, from which text derives, means 'woven').[3]

The vitality of this text, together with the heat generated as private language becomes public discourse, is due to its thrusting-out of metaphors. 'Coexistence' (living together in amity) is discarded in favour of 'traversal' (dynamic inter-penetration); 'interpretation' (exposition) gives way to 'explosion . . . dissemination'. This literary-critical explosion of seed suggests nothing as arrestingly as the experience of male orgasm: a privileged discourse indeed.

A holistic reading practice must also resist the privileging of the academic readership over the common reader, by refraining from the excesses of an élite, technocratic jargon. As a reader who has shared Milton with fellow common readers as well as with academics, I seek a mutually accessible language. The wide gap between the lexis and project of the professionals and readers within the community is regrettable. It is solved neither by the sanguine paternalism which hails the general public as at last 'ready' for re-education, nor by the verbal fiat that abolishes the problem by denying the existence of a common reader, since all twentieth-century readers are held to be a product of the education system.[4] My reading of Milton aims, as far as possible, to respect and integrate the practices of those specialists whose living is literature and those who read purely for love. For the latter, the discarnate voice of Milton is an urgent presence in his poems, as a real illusion rather than an oppressive dictator. We 'hear'

him in the passionately committed lyric voice that is as authentic a
presence as a stranger on a telephone or a voice on radio. The author
of *Lycidas* and *Paradise Lost* will never in practice lie down and die:

> This traditional quarry of criticism is always a phantom – not merely elusive
> and probably illusory, but also dead. The author's intended meaning died in
> the moment that the text came into being, and the text is necessarily more
> than the author conceived or knew.[5]

There is a deep but narrow truth in the embargo on intentionality as
index to interpretation. The dead author cannot legislate for the living
text and the living reader. Yet the processes of composition and
readers' reactions to an imagined 'Milton' whose stresses, biases, hopes,
wishes and fears they detect in the text, not only should not but
cannot be censored from reading practice. In a holistic criticism, such
material has an auxiliary rather than a dictatorial function.

Reactions to *Paradise Lost* through time have been powerfully
charged with emotion. Often responses have been disturbed or self-
contradictory, both because it is a poem which registers an internal
clash between revolutionary and reactionary, ancient and modern, the
dictates of theology and the affiliations of the human heart, and
because its subject matter arouses nervous energy and a sort of
combative self-defensiveness in readers. The world of reading is a field
of change. Readers endlessly give place to one another through the
cycle of the generations: they reshelve the book and turn away into
the night. The individual reader himself or herself may change, year
by year, in response to circumstances and events, the ageing process,
joy or affliction. We read with new eyes at each encounter with
Paradise Lost: the meanings the text yields are often those we have
cried out to find, or alternately hoped to evade. Just as the lens in
jaundice yellows the objects of vision, so we see green in envy, red in
anger, and all vision is black in melancholy. Unbending prejudice and
intemperate assumption rigidify the structure of words, and repeated
readings can deaden our attentiveness to nuance and colour. But the
more characteristic effect of *Paradise Lost* has been to awaken, irritate,
goad or arouse the imagination and susceptibilities of its readers. The
history of *Paradise Lost* criticism is also, in a unique way, the passionate
history of the tribe. Its ideological militancy aggravates opposing

attitudes and awakens dormant feelings of anger with authority, release from oppression, or (confusingly) both. For over three centuries it has been getting under the skin of its readers, sparking heated arguments, frequently of great hostility and volatility of temper, and setting man against man and woman against man. The poem is a war of words, composed in the wake of the English Civil Wars and concerning the War in Heaven. The author of *Paradise Lost* was an inveterate self-defender and apologist for radical causes, the author of the *Defence of Himself* (1655) and two *Defences of the English People* (1651, 1654). The pen with which he wrote was a blade with a cutting edge, in a period when Renaissance traditions of rhetoric still identified literature as a branch of armed struggle. A. L. Rowse's vituperative *Milton the Puritan* is still retaliating against the Puritans: 'liars as they were', 'self-righteous and self-satisfied, self-confident and self-laudatory, arrogant and aggressive . . . a nasty spirit' in the person of their champion, Milton, in whom 'rigid obstinacy of an almost psychotic kind' pre-vailed; in the other camp, a Revolutionary Milton-criticism is still cheering Milton on, as the protagonist of a universal struggle.[6] The war of words in his poetry and prose is experienced by participating readers as the testament of an emergency occupying us in an eternal present.

During the 1650s, the decade in which *Paradise Lost* was begun, Milton's voice articulated the militant Protestant Commonwealth of England. To his antagonists he was:

'A monster horrible, deformed, huge, and sightless.' Though, to be sure, he is not huge; nothing is more weak, more bloodless, more shrivelled than little animals such as he, who the harder they fight, the less harmful they are . . .

. . . John Milton. Who he was and where he came from was in doubt, whether a man, or a worm voided lately from the dungpit.

the vile Milton . . . this gallows-bird . . . That Foul Rascal JOHN MILTON . . . you dung-heap, you blockhead . . .[7]

It is a bizarre and provocative experience for a modern reader, leafing through the bitter pages of the pamphlet wars of the 1650s, to come

upon that name whose monumentality in relation to the course of
literary history stands almost as cause to effect, sunk in such linguistic
mire. The coarse dialect of the regicide dispute – whether in barracks
Latin or gutter English – reminds us that there is a soldiery of the pen,
and that Milton himself served as such a soldier. The Commonwealth,
which had been established by force of arms, Milton would 'as the
next highest deed, defend by another kind of arms against envy and
calumny, forces against which the steel and the equipment of war are
powerless'.[8] Hence he placed himself at the centre of ideological
struggle, where language is both weapon and barricade. He justified his
party, his nation, his God and himself, seeing such militancy as an
epic and sacred calling, the equivalent vocation in the realm of the
vita activa to the writing of an *Arthuriad* in the *vita contemplativa*. In
the poems postdating the defeat of his Good Old Cause, he maintains
those ideals in a state of crisis, stress and breakdown, so that we witness
at once a self-justifying, self-challenging ideology which makes the
heart of *Paradise Lost* not certainty but a maelstrom of conflict.
Outnumbered, he looks to a God of Wrath to vindicate him against
the 'many foes' who laugh him to scorn, saying:

> No help for him in God there lies.
>   . . . Of many millions
>   The populous rout
>   I fear not though encamping round about
> They pitch against me their pavilions.
> Rise Lord, save me my God for thou
>   Hast smote ere now
>   On the cheek-bone all my foes,
>   Of men abhorred
>   Hast broke the teeth. This help was from the Lord
> Thy blessing on thy people flows.
>   (Psalm III; 9 August 1653)

Paradise Lost is a violent poem and the product of a violent period of
history, exposing the scar-tissue of unhealable war wounds, asking the
impossible questions raised by God's apparent desertion of the saints.
The tooth-splintering Deity of Psalm III had inexplicably allowed the
encamping pavilions of the ungodly to overrun the sacred places of his
chosen people. The poet remains immutably the champion of the

Almighty, but disquietly so: his poem is a force-field of contending assertions of Divine Justice (Adam's 'Him after all disputes / Forced I absolve' – X. 828–9) and turbulent questionings of that Justice (Adam's 'Inexplicable / Thy justice seems' – X. 754–5). At other times the poem quarrels with its own combativeness. Its voice can be inexpressibly gentle and tender. It is an amatory epic, a nature poem and a song of praise, whose narrative voice declares a constitutional antagonism to the bellicosities of its own material: 'Not sedulous by nature to indite / Wars . . .' (IX. 27–8). The Miltonic 'voice' has been traditionally equated with the sublime and heroic. Modern reading methods may teach us a listening art which detects many – often irreconcilable – voices in the one poem, the total meaning not being understood as a resolution of those antiphonic voices which sing so intensely against one another but as the complexity of their vital contradiction. In this respect, the principle of the 'dialogic' imagination enunciated by Bakhtin,[9] in which the work of art is heard as a many-centred polyphony of voices, challenging rather than reinforcing ideology, has an acute relevance to *Paradise Lost*; as (in the context of current neo-Saussurian linguistic theories which stress the inscrutable self-reflexiveness of language, together with the Derridean emphasis on its polysemous openness) is Bakhtin's awareness of the multiplicity of languages at work within the linguistic community. Living discourse is always in flux, defying its own rules: every one of us speaks a foreign tongue, so that to catch another's meaning is to visit the very boundaries of the self, in the effort to translate. The dynamic of irreconcilable tonalities is obviously heard far more insistently in some works than others: *Paradise Regained* is the most rigorous ('monologic') plainsong as against the powerful polyphony of *Paradise Lost*, whose clashing keys and unexpected modulations betwen major and minor came down to us over the centuries like a final poetic justification of the Renaissance theory of music as *concordia discors* or *discordia concors*. Discordancy and contradiction are as intrinsic to artistic pattern as they are to the visible world to which the Christian faith attributed an underlying divine harmony.

The musical analogy is important in bringing us to an understanding of poetic 'voice' in Milton, and its growing complexity as his life developed. Milton was the son of a scrivener who was also a practising musician and a published composer: as Aubrey tells us, 'he was an ingeniose man, delighted in Musiq. composed many Songs now in print especially that of Oriana.'[10] The family's living was therefore secured by a literary trade but when Milton's father retired on the proceeds, it probably was to cultivate his addiction to music. This combined inheritance of literature and music seems to this reader to have given an unusual quality of intensity to Milton's commitment to the familiar equation of poetry with music. He calls *Paradise Lost* 'heroic *song*' (IX. 25) and, composing in his blindness before the rest of the world is awake, reminds himself of the nightingale:

> Then feed on thoughts, that voluntary move
> Harmonious numbers, as the wakeful bird
> Sings darkling, and in shadiest covert hid
> Tunes her nocturnal note.
>
> (III. 37–40)

Remembering Ovid's story of Philomela, the raped girl whose tongue is cut out and who is metamorphosed into the nightingale, Milton haunts his reader with an account of the composition of the words he offers as song welling from an experience of deep pain and violation, physical and mental. Remedial beauty, by a divine paradox, pours from the rift opened in the spirit by savage impairment – Philomela's loss of human tongue is compensated by the wordless glory of a sentient music. Excision of eyesight and estrangement from the human community liberate from Milton in the dead of night an unprecedented fluency of articulation which cannot be written down in that obscurity but plays like a tune in his mind until morning light brings the amanuensis and he is freed of its burden. The primacy of rhythm, with its power to soothe and animate into the composition of 'Harmonious numbers', is implied in the nightingale passage, together with an experience of language as 'voice', exiled from its body in the visible words on a page and existing as something heard rather than viewed. The Philomela analogy for the blind poet, *persona non grata* in his own country after the Restoration, is suggestive in a number of ways. Not far from the sharp sense it mediates of being shamefully violated at the core of the self is a motif recurrently appearing as a vague fear in the earlier poetry but making a grand theme of the later works: a sense of emasculation, gelding and loss of caste in the patriarchal world, which swells to a climax of purgative rage and grief in *Samson Agonistes*:

> . . . why was the sight
> To such a tender ball as the eye confined?
> So obvious and so easy to be quenched . . .?
>
> (93–5)

> Then swoll'n with pride into the snare I fell
> Of fair fallacious looks, venereal trains,
> Softened with pleasure and voluptuous life;
> At length to lay my head and hallowed pledge
> Of all my strength in the lascivious lap
> Of a deceitful concubine who shore me
> Like a tame wether, all my precious fleece,
> Then turned me out ridiculous, despoiled,
> Shaven, and disarmed among my enemies.
>
> (532–40)

The *tender ball* of the eye wincingly connotes the vulnerability of the sensitive human optic to casual but fatal damage: we remember perhaps the gouging-out of Gloucester's eyes in *King Lear*: 'Out, vile jelly! / Where is thy lustre now?'[11] The second of my quotations connotes the vulnerability of the male sexual organs, and the mortification of virility by the very apparatus on which it stakes its pride (a *wether* is a ram, especially a castrated ram, a term used metaphorically for a eunuch). The complex, bitter lyricism of Milton's later poetry is grounded in male mortification and the recognition of a kind of impotence which breeds a compensatory song of great power from its own stigma and disempowering. Many strange contradictions came into play in this music. Phallic pride is on its knees and must occupy the same low ground as the female it needs to look down upon; autonomy gives way to dependency for the very functions of life to be performed. The poet of *Paradise Lost* figures himself as a female bird singing her sexual violation, and knows the loss of security and grace as Eve knows it. Perhaps something of this emotional complexity made it possible for women readers to feel that *Paradise Lost* was peculiarly *their* poem, despite its surface misogyny.

Passionately divergent reactions to *Paradise Lost* have been the rule amongst readers, whose interpretations have been vertiginously at odds with one another. An eighteenth-century black woman reader found *Paradise Lost* 'no king's book, but instead a book through which slaves could win their freedom'.[12] White women in the same period record their experience of reading *Paradise Lost* as a liberating, empowering one.[13] Gilbert and Gubar, in their influential *The Madwoman in the Attic* (1979), identify Milton as the 'bogey' of the writing daughters, firing their imaginations with inspirations that destroy their creative confidence, so that they must wrestle with his tyrannous influence rather than have their free say.[14] The Romantic poets acclaimed Milton as a revolutionary hero:

> Would *he* adore a sultan, *he* obey
> The intellectual eunuch Castlereagh?

>   He died,
> Who was the Sire of an immortal strain,
> Blind, old, and lonely, when his country's pride,
> The priest, the slave, and the liberticide
> Trampled and mocked with many a loathèd rite
> Of lust and blood; he went, unterrified . . .[15]

They read their Milton in the light of the French Revolution and the Greek War of Independence. During the Second World War, a generation of critics reading *Paradise Lost* by the light of the embattled British monarchy pitted against the German Fiend, interpreted the hieroglyphs to signify that the poet was 'really' a Royalist: hence the title of M. M. Ross's *Milton's Royalism*.[16] In 1977, Christopher Hill's Marxist study *Milton and the English Revolution* read the epic as a Puritan and Republican document.[17] Jesuits have read *Paradise Lost* with satisfaction, and Roman Catholic priests and laymen have testified to their conviction that the poem has nothing to say that should be obnoxious to the ears of a Christian of their persuasion. It was Blake's opinion that the poem had a subliminal content, such that Milton was 'of the Devil's party without knowing it'.[18] Nonagenarians and prodigious children, kings and workers, black female slaves and white Caucasian male slave-owners have recorded their appropriation of the poem.[19] One aim of my book is to seek out something of the source of this multiplicity of response, beyond the well-attested observation that poetry tends to mirror the meanings which we bring to it and presents to our designing eyes the illusions of answers to the questions we feel constrained to address. Beyond this, are there special qualities in Milton's vision and voice which might beget such discrepant interpretations?

*　　　　*　　　　*

In liberating a text from the privileged reading imposed by the author and appropriating it to a reader-dominated interpretation, the gain in freedom may be offset by the blocking-out of light by readerly egoism which mistakes its own wildly gesticulating shadow for reality. To read a poem *in vacuo*, isolated from what we know or infer about the conception and generation of the work in the life, treating it as a self-referring structure of words, can increase that tendency. The present study seeks to temper flights of hermeneutic fancy by respect for a matrix in the complexities of an individual, conceived of as a self-articulator as well as a nexus in history. Like the psychoanalytic schools of criticism (whose greatest Miltonic exponent is William Kerrigan in his *The Sacred Complex*)[20] my approach is alive to that inscrutable but fascinating transition from the inner complexity of the creative process to emergent poetic form. Mine is a holistic approach in which all that precedes and surrounds the act of writing is of legitimate interest, though not of equivalent importance. Intentionality is not derided as unknowable but rather conjured as imaginable; and the projections of unintended meanings from the subconscious mind are also given place. The poetry is viewed as a structuring of the psychic life of the author, and may be attributed with conscious and unconscious meanings. I understand the work of criticism as a supplying of one reader's concentrated imaginative capacities to the poem and its readers. Language is above all a teemingly multitudinous body of (often buried) images, and the logic of art, like dream, is deeply-rooted in image and symbol; often all the critic can do – though he frequently claims a more exalted function – is to supply his own images to shed light on the imagery generated by the poet. My book reimagines the process of Milton's poetic career, taking into account selections from the superabundant documentary evidence concerning his life and thoughts, and guessing into the dark of his imaginative processes with the tentative faith rather than aggressive certainty which belongs to the prudent interpreter of another human life. We know that we know nothing; but we have found that we can imagine much.

Sexuality is a major theme of the present book because it is an intense emotional and political preoccupation of Milton's poetry. My feminist approach is based on a perception that Milton at once identified himself with and vehemently disowned something female which was experienced as part of the self. The psychosexual history of the poetry from *Comus* to *Samson Agonistes* is a turbulent, angry and yearning struggle with this identification. My psychological bearings are taken on the one hand from the Jungian theory of the androgynous integration of *animus* and *anima*, and on the other from the modern post-Freudian pyschologists like Chodorow and Winnicott who view male development as a costly process of division from female origins in the primary union with the mother's breast which is at once identified as part of the self and is progressively dissociated and excised from the identity of the self as the child is appropriated by the patriarchal tribe.[21] That first experience of shared being, with its wordless rapture and oneness, the famous 'oceanic' feeling, is a Paradise lost to the male of the species. To love well is to make a tender and adjusted re-accommodation to source: each poem by Milton declares in a differently angled emotion the longing for such access and the invincible difficulty of attaining it in view of the abdication of maternal values required of every boy as the price of caste. Mother-loss, the sense of betrayal, the odd intuition of the 'woman-within', charge Milton's poetry with conflict, as it moves from the suspended animation and withheld passion of the poetry of the 1630s (and its strong identification with the Lady in *Comus*) through the profound eroticism of *Paradise Lost* to the sexual rage and humiliation of *Samson Agonistes*.

Each poem by Milton was a radical experiment, so that it is possible to feel that there exist not one but many Miltons, whose poetry lives in a state of constant self-renewal. It exposes, challenges and questions every dogma it assimilates and every genre it touches, evolving a medley of styles and attitudes to language. The reader of this book will therefore find a somewhat different reading-method applied to each poem. The revolutionary voice of an author who could never construe any word as final or any knowledge as conclusive calls for an arduous and adaptable reader; rather than reading in comfort at our desks, we are asked to read as it were in flight or in fall, insecurely. The idea of unity in art is especially challenged: unity is a complex idea, based on conflict, and from first to last Milton's poetry will be seen as taking its dynamic from the irresoluble oppositions the poet encountered within himself, society, tradition, history and language. Experiments in Puritan plain English, such as *Paradise Regained*, only generate more subtle stress in the anatomy of repression.

The eye is central to my treatment of the poet and his development. It is impossible, as one reads Milton's poetry, with its powerful autobiographical drive, to forget the darkened, maladaptive eye which obstructed or strangely and numinously refracted the consensus version of reality agreed upon by the safely sighted, which passes among us for 'reality'. Such 'reality' became unavailable to the poet of *Paradise Lost*, *Paradise Regained* and *Samson Agonistes*. The poetry became as potently compensatory as dream in creating radiant bursts of interior light such as are never dreamt of by the sighted because we never need to dream them, common daylight being the medium which we lackadaisically take for granted as a given norm. This daylight 'reality' came into doubt for the poet: it was a fiction agreed upon by the half-awake majority, based upon contingent observations proportioned to its unquestioning eye. Milton's maladaptive eye became the light by which he saw, measured and affirmed a new Heaven and a new Earth. Its data confirmed the findings of the new relativistic astronomy and optics, and of the modern baroque schools of art and architecture, producing the deviant and problematic perspectives which we recognise as modern. His poetry revolutionised eyeline and criticised perception. The light with which his poetry flooded and delighted his consciousness in the process of composition was generated by words. The eye and the word (means of perception and system of linguistic articulation) are intimately and intrinsically one for Milton; and both eye and word are primary subjects of his poetry.

Today a new puritanism admonishes us to abstain from reading Milton's sonnet 'Methought I saw my late espoused saint' in the knowledge that the author was himself blind: the poem should stand on its own as an autonomous text.[22] This is just in maintaining the right priorities, but it is over-severely prescriptive. We are not such self-censoring machines as to be able to unknow what we know. We cannot become innocent by repressing information, and to suggest that we should attempt it implies not only perverse resistance to the facts of the average reading consciousness which will slyly supply the information to the text anyway, but a denial of the human and emotional richness which the imagining mind of the reader receives in the poet's personal testament. My book is as responsive to the personal element in the art-work as it is respectful of the practices and feelings of someone who can still be called the 'common reader'. On an intellectual level, Milton's experience of blindness presents a sort of optical gloss on the perspectivist manner of *Paradise Lost*. In September 1654, Milton wrote a detailed account of the progress of the symptoms of his disease over a ten-year period to Leonard Philaras, who had undertaken to consult a Paris physician on his account. This visual testimony has enabled modern ophthalmologists to diagnose Milton's illness as glaucoma (or, possibly, detached retina);[23] but that is a side-issue. The account gives us entrance into Milton's journey into hell. Confined day and night to the inferno of a violently anomalous vision which was in constant process of flux and degeneration, this matter-of-fact document makes us feel as if the birth and death of the cosmos had been played upon his optic nerve, a primal brew of being and an eschatological bitter end. What Milton 'sees' is a deviant and aberrant, uncorroborated challenge to every norm and assumption:

as often as I looked at a lamp, a sort of rainbow seemed to obscure it. Soon a mist appearing in the left part of the left eye . . . removed from my sight everything on that side. Objects further forward too seemed smaller if I chanced to close my right eye. The other eye also failing slowly and gradually over a period of almost three years, some months before my sight was completely destroyed, everything which I distinguished when I myself was still seemed to swim, now to the right, now to the left. Certain permanent vapours seem to have settled upon my entire forehead and temples, which press and oppress my eyes with a sort of sleepy heaviness, especially from mealtime to evening, so that I often think of the Salmydessian seer Phineus in the *Argonauts*,

> All round him then there grew
> A purple thickness; and he thought the earth
> Whirling beneath his feet, and so he sank,
> Speechless at length, into a feeble sleep.

But I must not omit that, while considerable sight still remained, when I would first go to bed and lie on one side or the other, abundant light would

dart from my closed eyes; then, as sight daily diminished, colors proportion-
ately darker would burst forth with violence and a sort of crash from within;
but now, pure black, marked as if with extinguished or ashy light, and as if
interwoven with it, pours forth. Yet the mist which always hovers before
my eyes both night and day seems always to be approaching white rather
than black; and upon the eyes turning, it admits a minute quantity of light
as if through a crack.

(CPW. IV. ii. 869–70)

To quote at length affords the reader imaginative entrance into a
phantasmagorical world of kaleidoscopically changing illusions which
either suffuse and veil the field of vision; alter its relative dimensions
and proportions; block out some of the view; colour the lens; produce
the impression of aberrant motion; inaugurate effects like firework
displays. Extreme vertigo (a condition of the fall in *Paradise Lost*)
accompanies this maelstrom. The vessel of the eye is experienced not
as passive recipient of extrinsic light but as light- and dark-generating,
exploding colour into the mind to the accompaniment of sounds ('a
sort of crash'), abolishing the safe boundaries between the senses.
Finally, the eyesight becomes completely veiled ('white rather than
black') like the 'universal blank' or unwritten page of *Paradise Lost*,
Book III (see page 2 above), with only an occasional 'crack' opening
to admit a tantalising sliver of light in to the shrouded self.

How much do any of us really see, while we have the chance?
Perhaps a 'crack of light' is all that ever penetrates through to our
terminally inattentive selves from the outside world, until it is too
late. For the Milton of *Paradise Lost* it was too late – and that condition
of dereliction was the occasion of creative freedom and tragic solace.
The abolition of the perceptual world was compensated by the release
of power to give himself symbolic rebirth through a light-conceiving
language. The 'blank' page becomes an open invitation rather than a
prohibition: empty of inscription, the external universe lost its dominance of his inner world, subsiding into the passive quarto on which
he might inscribe his own active story. The testament of *Paradise Lost*
is a record of the vertiginous freedom of blindness, in violation of the
givens of perception, to reconstruct according to the vagrant forms of
the imagination the dimensions of inner space.

1

The Schismatic Word

Milton wrote his mature poems at a time of maximum instability and stress, not only in the political world but in the fields of scientific, theological and linguistic change. He is often identified as the last great Renaissance humanist scholar-poet in the Tudor and Jacobean tradition, but of course his life postdated that of the last of the Tudors and he wrote in and of an age in which modern science had succeeded in changing the world-view of intellectuals from the stable cosmology of the Ptolemaic system towards the heliocentric view, or to an adaptation of the Copernican system to the old model such as that offered by Tycho de Brahe, for whom the sun and moon were earth-centred but the planets circled the sun.[1] Alongside this compromise model, which seems not to have appealed to Milton, both models were, incompatibly, current, and it is significant that in Book VIII of *Paradise Lost*, when Adam asks Raphael for astronomical information, the visiting Archangel propounds both views and is archly unwilling to decide between the two. His speech proceeds on the *what if?* principle:

> What if the sun
> Be centre to the world, and other stars,
> By his attractive virtue and their own
> Incited, dance about him various rounds?
> ....

What if that light
Sent from her through the wide transpicuous air,
To the terrestrial moon be as a star . . .
(VIII. 122–5; 140–2)

Here is an acknowledged stress in the poem's dictation of Divine Truth. We naturally wonder why Milton hedged his bets? His hesitation is understandable if we reflect that the sole advantages of the Copernican over the Ptolemaic astronomy were then that it was simpler (hardly proof) and that the latter made motions in the sky impossibly fast after Galileo revealed with his telescope the vast distances involved. On the Ptolemaic side was the absolute testimony of the biblical report of Joshua telling the sun and moon to stand still. Yet Milton had visited the blind Galileo in Florence 'grown old, a prisner to the Inquisition, for thinking in Astronomy otherwise then the Franciscan and Dominican licencers thought' (Areopagitica, CPW. II. 538). The blind astronomer (a contradiction in terms surely as blackly ironic as the stigma of blind poet or deaf composer, for the astronomer's profession depends on vision) is twice mentioned in Paradise Lost. The first and most startlingly vivid occasion is in the epic simile which compares Satan's shield in Book I with

the moon, whose orb
Through optic glass the Tuscan artist views
At evening from the top of Fesole,
Or in Valdarno, to descry new lands,
Rivers or mountains in her spotty globe.
(I. 287–91)

Paradise Lost as it stands could not have been written before the invention of the telescope. After the telescope, the universe was a changed place, its proportions deranged from the standardised dimensions declared normative by the unaccommodated human eye. Perspectivism was, of course, a favourite theme of Renaissance art and thought: what you see depends on where you stand, and the relative eye-beam determines the field of vision. But telescopic vision is a drastic step on from such relativism, and we shall see the influence of the new optical sciences on the radical complexities of Milton's art (see pages 115 ff. below). Through the telescope's revelatory lens, the universe magnifies and dilates to an extraordinary degree: the moon, for instance, is called into our ken, swelling to fill the horizon of vision while, however, space beyond (beginning to imply vistas of open infinity rather than concentric fixity) sweeps away into previously unguessed immensities of expansion. In *Paradise Lost* Milton supplies a number of lenses. Galileo is spied by Milton and Milton's reader through an imaginative telescope which draws the tiny figure of the stargazer into momentary focus. We see from England to Italy. We see also across time, for of course when Milton was writing Book I towards the end of the 1650s, Galileo had been dead for about fifteen years. The landscape contracts; the individual figure expands, through the magnifying eye of the poem. The 'Tuscan artist' is clearly something of a projection for the Miltonic persona whose subject is the cosmos and the penetration of the secrets of God. Milton's sympathies must, we feel, have been on the side of the heliocentric and modern, the empirical and experimental vision. Yet Milton cannot or will not in *Paradise Lost* state this allegiance unequivocally. His soul is with the old God of Genesis – the Ancient of Days – and with the old philosophers – the Pythagorean–Platonic music of the spheres. Milton plays the modern against the ancient. He whirls the new ideas of a relativistic, problematic mathematics against the moral and cosmographical arithmetic learnt in childhood and carrying for him (as indeed it did for the physicist, Kepler) the poignant beauty of order, fixity, harmonious and meaningful number. *Paradise Lost* is an account of this contradiction. The poet is at once sure and unsure; the poem, calmly and monumentally certain of its bearings and an agitated flux of radical and modern uncertainty.

As with cosmology, so in the field of linguistic theory, all was unstable. Milton looks to an immutable language, implying a coherent identity between word and thing represented, hoping in the medium of English to mime the creating Word and to tell a truth which, as a believing reader of the Bible, he understands to be objective and intelligible:

> what in me is dark
> Illumine, what is low raise and support;
> That to the highth of this great argument

> I may assert eternal providence,
> And justify the ways of God to men.
>
> (I. 22–6)

But to transmit these truths he is bound to the unstable, changeful and unregulated medium of language, in which meaning is always potentially ambiguous. The philosophy of language in the seventeenth century was developing a critique of language itself, as Milton knew. Bacon in his *Novum Organum* speaks of words as prime misleaders. There are, for instance, words for things which do not exist, no words for things that do, and multitudes of words in common currency which are so ambiguous as to mean nothing:

> words absolutely force the understanding, put all things in confusion, and lead men away to idle controversies and subtleties, without number . . .

> Words are generally imposed according to vulgar conceptions, and divide things by lines that are most apparent to the understandings of the multitude: and, when a more acute understanding or a more careful observation would point out these lines, to place them according to nature, words cry out and forbid it. And hence it happens, that great and serious disputes of learned men frequently terminate in controversies about words and terms, which it were better to begin with, according to the prudent method of the Mathematicians, and reduce them to order by definitions. But in natural and material things, even these definitions themselves cannot remedy the evil; because definitions themselves consist of words, and words generate words, so that, of necessity, recourse must be had to particular instances.[2]

For Bacon, words exhibit a mindless, anarchic life of their own, constitutionally resistant to meaningful discrimination, and attached not to an extrinsic reality but self-reflexive to one another. Later, Hobbes (to whom, on political grounds, Milton maintained a respectful aversion) listed in *Leviathan* (1651) four abuses of language: self-deceiving linguistic ambiguity; metaphorical use of words to deceive others; lying; use of language to grieve others. He is scathing about self-contradictory phrases like *incorporeal substance* which means the equivalent of *bodiless body* (see page 171 below).[3] In addition, the rise of empirical science was working towards a plain style in order to escape the delusory suggestiveness of language, and an artificial 'philosophical language' (prefiguring Esperanto) which would free speakers from limitations on clear thought and communication was under discussion. The possibility of a universal language in which symbols would stand for ideas was widespread in the 1630s and continued until about 1670. In 1668, John Wilkins published *An Essay Toward a Real Character and a Philosophical Language* under the auspices of the Royal Society. The comparative study of language and philology was also developing in the period.[4] These developments are all well within Milton's lifetime, and indeed he was personally acquainted at crucial stages of his life with some of the figures eminent in the new attitudes to language. He attended St Paul's School and was taught by Alexander Gil, the spelling reformer.[5]

I shall suggest that Milton's affinities, linguistic as well as political and social, were at once profoundly conservative and avant-garde. While he manifested no Hobbesian anxiety about such contradictions in terms as the theological *incorporeal substance* (indeed his treatise *Christian Doctrine* concerns itself painstakingly with just such mysterious intangibles), his greatest works show considerable concern about the possibility of 'Erroneous wandering' (*Paradise Lost*, VII. 20) as a result of the vagrant character of man and his language. In his tract *Of Education* (1644), Milton distinguishes between two kinds of discourse, that proper to logic and that of poetry: the latter 'as being lesse suttle and fine, but more simple, sensuous and passionate' (*CPW*. II. 403). In other words he contrasts a language of analytic exactitude with an affective discourse which speaks to the emotions, beautifully and arousingly. Linguistic studies emerge from *Of Education* as the core of Milton's ideal curriculum, in helping the student to achieve the aim of education, which is 'to repair the ruins of our first parents by regaining to know God aright' (*ibid.*, 366–7). But he emphasises that in our fallen condition of life in the body, our understanding is necessarily limited by 'sensible things', that is, sensory experience, upon which all knowledge and hence all language is founded:

> And though a linguist should pride himselfe to have all the tongues that Babel cleft the world into, yet, if he have not studied the solid things in them as well as the words and lexicons, he were nothing so much to be

23

esteem'd a learned man, as any yeoman or tradesman competently wise in his mother dialect only.

(*ibid.*, 368; 369–70)

The meanings denoted by languages must be significant and adapted to the understanding of the student: linguistic knowledge consists not just in the technical mastery of verbal and grammatical forms but in the 'solid things' denoted. This concern for the coherent strength of the link between the verbal sign and the object it denotes is fundamental to the Miltonic scrupulosity with language throughout his poetic career – his hunt after the *exactly* right term and not an approximation, because of his certainty (it is an article of Christian faith and an assumption of the humanist tradition in which he lies) that there is an objective Truth to be denoted, and that it is the obligation of the Christian poet to seek this identification. At the same time, he is of the modern world in recognising the mendacious slipperiness intrinsic in the words available.

Milton was a polyglot. In this he stood at the end of the humanist bibliographical tradition of concern for the establishment and transmission in vernacular languages of authentic original ancient texts, as well as standing at the centre of the Protestant insistence on accurate biblical translation: both of these movements led directly into the movements of modern philology and comparative linguistic studies which were young in Milton's day. His nephew Edward Phillips records the languages which Milton introduced to his pupils as an essential part of their education:

> Nor did the time thus Studiously imployed in conquering the *Greek* and *Latin* Tongues, hinder the attaining to the chief Oriental Languages, *viz.* The *Hebrew, Caldee* and *Syriac*, so far as to go through the *Pentateuch*, or Five Books of *Moses* in *Hebrew*, to make a good entrance into the *Targum*, or *Chaldee* Paraphrase, and to understand several Chapters of St. *Matthew* in the *Syriac* Testament . . . and into the *Italian* and *French* Tongues . . .[6]

The emphasis on knowing ancient and especially sacred texts in the original rather than through translation, even if it comes to a question of perfecting oneself in Ancient Chaldean, is a sign of the emphasis of Protestantism on the individual's right and duty to judge for himself, by the twin lights of divine inspiration and reason, rather than to rely upon any human middleman, whether translator or interpreter. The original meaning of the Scriptures is primary, and such meanings are incorporated in the original Greek and Hebrew Scriptures. Textual criticism was a tool at once theologically radical and politically revolutionary. This double implication was demonstrated by the scathing irony of John Selden at the Westminster Assembly in 1643. Arguing against the deductions from Scripture made by the Presbyterians who wished to impose their form of church government upon England, he said contemptuously, 'It may read so in your little pocket bibles with the gilt leaves, but the Hebrew reads thus – .'[7] Linguistic competence is therefore to be equated with the clarification of divine light. The middleman becomes a censor to which the reader ignorant of the original tongue has no choice but to submit.

Milton's urge is always back to origins, to what occurred 'in the beginning', the primal scene, the primitive church, the root meanings of words and the language of God in its original communication. If we can grasp origins, we can understand ourselves now and determine what our actions ought to be. His poetry is fascinated with beginnings, initiations. On The Morning of Christ's Nativity, written shortly after his coming of age, inaugurates a new life by recapitulating the birth of Christ. Paradise Lost, elaborating Genesis, the first Book of the Bible, concerns 'man's first disobedience' and turns for inspiration to the Holy Spirit, the creative force that won life from Chaos:

> thou from the first
> Wast present, and with mighty wings outspread
> Dove-like sat'st brooding on the vast abyss
> And mad'st it pregnant . . .
>
> (I. 19–22)

Paradise Lost fabricates a language of men and of angels in its original purity and charts the fall of that language into a linguistic field of ambiguity, double entendre, pun, innuendo, self-deception and rancorous abuse. Paradise Regained adopts a plain-speaking austerity of manner, bereft of elaboration, to relate Christ's initiation into his understanding of his role as Son of God, and by extension our roles as

25

younger sons. *Samson Agonistes*, ostensibly dramatising the closing day of a life, actually records a movement from lifelong shadow into late spiritual light, the peremptory growth of vision in 'inward eyes illuminated' (1689) as the Chorus phrases it.

This fascination with origins is equally evident in Milton's attentiveness to original texts in the original languages. Milton was a competent Hebraist of his day.[8] He was a Latinist of distinction. His love of Greek is attested in the virulent Sonnet XI, which contrasts the present age of barbarous linguistic ignorance, exemplified in the market-place in which booksellers have reduced books to a casual browser's paradise of trashy merchandise, with the great age of Reformation learning represented by the Greek scholar Sir John Cheke, tutor to Edward VI:

> A book was writ of late called *Tetrachordon*;
>> And woven close, both matter, form, and style;
>> The subject new: it walked the town awhile,
>> Numbering good intellects; now seldom pored on.
> Cries the stall-reader, Bless us! what a word on
>> A title-page is this! And some in file
>> Stand spelling false, while one might walk to Mile-
>> End Green. Why is it harder sirs then *Gordon*,
> *Colkitto*, or *Macdonnel*, or *Galasp*?
>> Those rugged names to our like mouths grow sleek
>> That would have made Quintillian stare and gasp.
> Thy age, like ours, O soul of Sir John Cheke,
>> Hated not learning worse than toad or asp,
>> When thou taught'st Cambridge, and King Edward Greek.

Milton's love of Greek exceeds, at this indignant hour, his distrust of kings: the world of Edward's Reformation court is preferable to the godless, Greekless market-place of parliamentary London in the mid-1640s.[9] This asperity and disgust at a situation in which the noble profession of humane letters has degenerated into the buying and selling of ephemera to feed a population of fools comes close to Dryden's satire in *Mac Flecknoe* thirty-odd years later:

> From dusty shops neglected Authors come,
> Martyrs of Pies, and Reliques of the Bum.[10]

Disbound books are sold off by the stationers for wrapping pies or wiping bottoms: the unsavoury residue of this desecration is tossed as litter on the public streets. *Tetrachordon*, the title of a tract advocating divorce – much vilified by the Presbyterians – is the Greek musical term for a four-note scale which was the basis of Greek harmony. Milton in his excoriated pride, mimes the public's gaping ignorance both of Greek and of harmony (integral concepts in his mind) by taking the last two syllables of the Greek word as the octet's controlling rhyme, and playing off a dire four-note tune of an English usage at once barbarous and uncouth: *Tetrachordon, pored on, word on, Gordon.* The poem is an act of furious mimicry. It delivers to us the voices Milton heard around him every day from a bourgeoisie he learnt to despise, though he shared their origins. The vulgarity of the feminine rhymes deriving from *Tetrachordon* ventriloquises the modern blankness to all but surface meaning: the provincialism of Londoners deaf to the beauty of the timeless Greek. The rhyme-scheme is the sign for the degeneration of tongues which Milton hears on the literary market-place. Animosity and hurt pride were all his life powerful spurs to poetic creativity: anger was inspirational to him. It burns at the heart of the tender, regretful *Lycidas* in the attack upon the corrupt clergy (113–31); *Samson* is almost all anger, moving from impure to pure rage in the destruction of the Philistines. The sonnet consciously 'spells false' as the Londoners do: the book-buying public which inanely leafs through a volume ('Bless us! what a word on / A title-page is this!') and cannot get its mouth round the foreign-seeming matter. The poem is in part a discussion of language and its social and moral implications, and specifically of loan-words, addressing similar issues to those raised by the inkhorn controversy of the sixteenth century, over the allowability of imported vocabulary to replenish the English tongue where the vernacular had no word for the thing designated, or to enrich the language with near-synonyms on the principle that *copie* (copiousness of vocabulary) is a root of linguistic eloquence.[11] It is also a class-oriented poem, appealing to an élite of the Protestant intelligentsia and to nationalistic prejudice to erect two languages (Greek and Latin) over another (Scottish English). London at this time being full of Covenanting Scots Presbyterians (to whom Milton's views on divorce were odious, as the church government which they wished to settle on the English church was odious to him), Milton jeers at the importation of Scots names like *Gordon, Colkitto, Macdonnel* and finally, usurping *Tetrachordon* to become the controlling rhyme for the sestet, the outlandish *Galasp*, from which he derives the open-mouthed stupefaction of the Roman rhetorician Quintillian's *gasp* and the forked tongue of *asp*. The linguistic élitism displayed by the sonnet is a deeply-felt prejudice sustained throughout Milton's career. When Edward Phillips chronicles his uncle's appointment to the office of Latin Secretary to the Counsel of State, he explains that:

> they stuck to this Noble and Generous Resolution, not to write to any, or receive Answers from them, but in a Language most proper to maintain a Correspondence among the Learned of all Nations in this part of the World; scorning to carry on their Affairs in the Wheedling, Lisping Jargon of the Cringing *French*, especially having a Minister of State able to cope with the ablest any Prince or State could imploy for the *Latin* tongue . . .[12]

Latin as the international language of scholarship and statesmanship had in fact undergone attack by the mid-seventeenth century, in view of the rising prestige of the European vernaculars. Milton's classicism is an index of his allegiance to the humanist and Erasmian heritage; his contempt for 'the Wheedling, Lisping Jargon of the Cringing *French*' is an aspect of his anti-Royalism and anti-Catholicism (the Stuarts found refuge in France) but also of his Anglo-Saxon nationalism, for Norman French had been, since the Conquest, the language of government and law in Britain, a badge of the free English nation's 'ancient slavery', 'norman gibbrish', as Milton noted, and associated with the Norman Yoke, a myth essential to the Puritan radicalism of the seventeenth century.[13]

It was Milton's epic task to free the English language not only from the Norman Yoke but also from the Latin Yoke and from subordination to every other language that might claim precedence over it. The English language had for him a moral, spiritual and political being just as real as that of the nation and its laws: if England was the Chosen nation (as seemed the unavoidable implication of events in the 1640s), then God had chosen to speak to the modern world in the English tongue. In *Areopagitica*, Milton wrote a book about books, the native language, the author, the writer and the readership, and the relation of the whole to the civil and ecclesiastical authorities. Here he declares the sacred right of a free citizen to publish his own testament, on his own warrant, to be read by his fellow citizen in the form in which it had been originally cast: the inquisitorial censorship of the Roman church violated the bond between author and reader:

> Sometimes 5 *Imprimaturs* are seen together dialogue-wise in the Piatza of one Title page, complementing and ducking each to other with their shav'n reverences, whether the Author, who stands by in perplexity at the foot of his Epistle, shall to the Presse or to the spunge. These are the prety responsories, these are the deare Antiphonies that so bewitcht of late our Prelats, and their Chaplains with the goodly Eccho they made; and besotted us to the gay imitation of a lordly *Imprimatur*, one from Lambeth house, another from the West end of *Pauls*; so apishly Romanizing, that the word of command still was set down in Latine; as if the learned Grammaticall pen that wrote it, would cast no ink without Latine: or perhaps, as they thought, because no vulgar tongue was worthy to expresse the pure conceit of an *Imprimatur*; but rather, as I hope, for that our English, the language of men ever famous, and formost in the atchievements of liberty, will not easily finde servile letters anow to spell such a dictatorie presumption English.
>
> (CPW. II. 504–5)

The first sentence seems to inhabit equally the rectangle of a title-page and the piazza of an ecclesiastical palace in Rome. Its subject is the marks on a page left by an author (his name appended to the Preface) and by the censors ('It is passed', *Imprimatur*). But the passage erects the dried ink marks of the pen into personifications of the men who held the pen, the piously bald holders of Vatican offices with their oleaginous mutual civilities ('complementing and ducking'); the name of the author is an anxious bystander in his own book, awaiting his fate. The effect of looking over the sentence is one of comic *trompe-l'œil*: where are we? On the title-page of a book or in Rome amongst the 'glutton friars'? We get comic release of our virtuously English and Protestant indignation by being granted a bird's-eye view of St Peter's Square, imprinted on an innocent page where the shady dealings of the priestly licencers are disclosed to the eye of day in the light of the folly of their hairstyles combined with the unEnglishness of their behaviour and their language. The author of *Areopagitica* enacts a war of words on his page: English against Latin. At the same time he

29

makes free with language to blur a distinction language insists on making: a man is not actually a piece of writing; a man is not a book. This act of blurring is a – perhaps, *the* – major premiss of *Areopagitica*, which brazenly insists that a book *is* a man, and that the same laws apply:

> as good almost kill a Man as kill a good Book; who kills a Man kills a reasonable creature, Gods Image; but hee who destroyes a good Booke, kills reason it selfe, kills the Image of God, as it were in the eye. Many a man lives a burden to the Earth; but a good Booke is the pretious life-blood of a master spirit, imbalm'd and treasur'd up on purpose to a life beyond life.
>
> (*CPW*. II. 492–3)

The passage goes on to argue, preposterously, that censorship is a kind of 'homicide', 'martyrdom', and indeed 'massacre'. Metaphor is established as, by sleight of hand, *the* rhetorical procedure on which the logic of *Areopagitica* will stand, and on the dynamic potency of Milton's image-breeding faculty the text's conviction is founded.

In the '*Imprimatur*' passage, the English prelatical censors are said to be 'apishly Romanizing'. 'Romanizing' bears a double satiric sense: it implicates the Roman Catholic Church and the Latin language appropriated by the Church in the service of militant power-politics. You can 'Romanize' in a number of ways: by scandalously arrogating the powers to murder a good book, as the Archbishop of Canterbury and Bishop of London did by right of the infamous *Decree of Starre-Chamber, Concerning Printing* (1637); by writing in Latin rather than in your native English as did these censors when expurgating texts; by writing English as if it were only the sum of its Latin loan-words minus the pith and heart of its native Anglo-Saxon, as Milton satirically does here. The passage is sensitive to a high degree to the etymological roots of English and their political implications. It sets off charges of derisive Anglo-Saxon against the imperialist invasive Latin, arraying what it presents as the sturdy, sterling down-to-earth plainness of English root words against the Latinate mannerisms of the prelates, their mouths rudely inflated with polysyllabic hot air: a binary opposition which it exploits to oxymoronic effect.[14]

Latin-derived	*Anglo-Saxon or Norman-French vulgar usage*
complementing	ducking
reverences	shav'n
responsories	pretty
antiphonies	dear
romanizing	apishly
dictatory presumption	English

The Anglo-Saxon halves of the pairings represent for the Milton of *Areopagitica* the 'free' words – words of the people – which are not part of the 'dictatory presumption' of Roman imperialism. Milton's use of the word *dictatory* is suggestive to us as readers. It is the first recorded coinage of the adjective from the noun *dictator*, a derivative of the Latin signifying a political absolutist, and related integrally to the Latin verb *dictare*, which can mean equally dictating words to be set down as said, and the making of dictatorial prescriptive pronouncements. In glancing at the root meanings of the word we can come to share a sense of Milton's feeling for the politics of language. The obfuscations of Latin practised by the priesthood held a twofold threat: they authorised and prescribed the language which was allowable to use in a sacred context. They intervened between the Englishman and his vernacular Bible; they made the author's pen an instrument of dictation. This forcing of the conscience of language was an act of dictation in the other sense: arbitrary power, exercised over free spirits. Hence the *dictatory* behaviour is also *presumption* (from Old French *presumer* and Latin *praesumere*, to take for granted before the fact and without warrant.) Presumption is the sin of Lucifer, in *Paradise Lost*. Thus Milton enrolls his native tongue in the cause of revolutionary Protestantism. He presents it as an insidious home guard making sharp guerrilla raids on the self-exposing follies of church Latin: the priests 'complementing and ducking each to other with their shav'n reverences' make vain faces in the mirror of their mutual Latin: they *compliment* each other and greet one another as *Your Reverence*. The English *ducking* comments upon the compliments and *shav'n* advises us how to see the reverences. Anglo-Saxon root words are used to give

31

pictorial realism, carrying a clear-sighted, sardonic system of value-judgements. They skew the self-gratifying picture the priests have of themselves, cartooning and burlesquing their manners and appearance. In *Lear*, Shakespeare had offered a similar confrontation of low-register English with high-register Norman in the image of the 'twenty silly-ducking observants' derided by Kent (II. ii. 100): the French arrays, the English denudes. Church Latin is revealed by Milton as an absurd farrago of affectations which, when confronted by the forthright Anglo-Saxon, dissolves into the thin air of ritualised pride and pretension (*reverences, responsories, antiphonies*). The muscular, imagistic Anglo-Saxon words chase the precious and effete Latin diction all around the page.

In *Areopagitica*, Milton embraced the lower class of Anglo-Saxon and sought to purge it of its colonisation by Latin: he did so in the name of liberty. But *liberty* is itself a Latin-derived word. When Cromwell and the New Model Army undertook to 'free' Parliament of the reactionary Presbyterian element in 1648, he was constrained to station Colonel Pride, equipped with a list of names and a company of soldiers, at the doors of Westminster to exclude the undesired MPs by force: 'Pride's Purge' issued in the undemocratic 'Rump' Parliament which claimed to legislate on behalf of the 'free people of England'.[15] Cromwell and the Army grandees felt compelled to ensure liberty by violence. Milton's 'free' native English would have constituted just such a linguistic 'Rump'. A mass evacuation of the undesired elements would also have had to be achieved by violence – a pride's purge in the parliament of letters which would have issued in a republic as fictitious as that original England proclaimed by the radical theory of the 'Norman Yoke'. Such experiments had in fact been made during the Renaissance by linguistic purists like Sir John Cheke and Ralph Lever, determined to write 'our own tung . . . cleane and pure, unmixt and unmangeled with borowing of other tunges'.[16] Cheke's translation of Matthew's Gospel uses forms like *biwordes* for *parables*, *hunderder* for *centurion*, *onwriting* for *superscription*, *gainrising* for *resurrection*. Lever, in *The Arte of Reason, rightly termed, Witcraft*, invented technical terms for logic 'compounded of true english words': *ifsay* (*propositio condition-alis*), *naysay* (*negatio*), *saywhat*, *shewsay*, *yeasay*. Lever appeals both to patriotic sentiment and to democratic comprehensibility. The purist movement continued in the seventeenth century, influencing students of Anglo-Saxon like Richard Verstegen and antiquarians like John Selden, the latter greatly respected by Milton and cited in his *Commonplace Book* and *Areopagitica*.

Milton was never a purist in this sense. In *Areopagitica* he argued for the inseparability of good and evil in this world: 'It was from out the rinde of one apple tasted, that the knowledge of good and evill, as two twins cleaving together leapt forth into the World' (*CPW*. II. 514). He assented joyfully to complexity as a condition and constraint of language. The very richness of the language which he inherited and used for this poetry was the result of the flexible hospitality of the language to foreign forms, structures and usages. As a humanist scholar of Greek and Latin literature, Milton was profoundly sensitive to the past history of language, its archaeology of meaning whose buried strata might dextrously be brought to light by the provision of a revelatory syntactic context. If *Paradise Lost* is an Anglo-Saxonist's poem,[17] yet simultaneously – and connectedly – it is a Latinist's poem. It connects the island of English with the mainland of European languages through this exposure of a root source common to the Western community of languages. Jonathan Richardson, the latest of Milton's early biographers, saw with penetrating insight that Milton had amplified English in the direction of an international language:

> *Milton's* Language is English, but 'tis *Milton's* English; 'tis Latin, 'tis Greek English; not only the Words, the Phraseology, the Transpositions, but the Ancient Idiom is seen in All he Writes, So that a Learned Foreigner will think *Milton* the Easiest to be Understood of All the English Writers.[18]

Words are sites of change, designations of history and recapitulations of the fall. In tracing mankind's history back to origins in prelapsarian Paradise, *Paradise Lost* traces language back to source: the meaning of a word before it changed (or, in Ricks' analysis, 'fell')[19] is salvaged and returned to modern usage. The linguistic mode is therefore recuperative and redemptive, as Ricks believed, but this recuperation is a further problematising factor, since adverse meanings wrestle in the individual word, irreconcilably, or grammatical expansions mime the unimaginable. A revolutionary grammatical innovatoriness rescues, for instance, the Latin root from the verb *ruin* by using it in an alien intransitive rather than a familiar transitive mood:

> Hell heard the unsufferable noise, hell saw
> Heaven ruining from heaven and would have fled
> Affrighted . . .
>
> (VI. 867–9)

The polarities of the Miltonic universe are shaken to their foundations by the fall of the angels. It is literally unimaginable to the human mind, and outside the range of his discourse, to propose and analyse a departure of heaven from heaven. Linguistic form is also shaken to its foundations by its duty to give an integrated account of a disintegrative process which confounds the systems language is committed to expressing. Heaven by its nature cannot part company with heaven. Angels cannot fall and yet be angels. But Scripture maintains they did. Milton's language records events we cannot conceive and for which our word-system does not allow: the birth of evil from a good design; disorder the product of order. Primitive animism is called into play to express this explosive parturition – father sun and mother earth; hell a creature with compulsions, desires and energies. *Hell* and *heaven* are the Anglo-Saxon *hel* and *heofon*; but *ruining* derives from the Latin *ruinare* (to fall down), a rare intransitive usage in English which, corresponding rather to the Latin than the English usage, implies a kind of falling-apart not only of the thing denoted (the split-second appearance of disintegration in the sound, firm heart of the cosmos itself) but also a breakdown of grammatical relations. A *ruin* becomes *to ruin*: noun becomes verb, overflowing its contours of stable containment into a state of process, change and destabilisation signalled by the grammatical function of a verb. Our linguistic systems are attempts to bring into a rational comprehensive order that which, nakedly experienced, may be irrational or emotionally and intellectually confounding. Words in grammatical structures can be palliatives, anodyne against the unease generated by the indeterminacy or riddlingness of a truth that lies utterly beyond their reach. Milton was no more free of the temptation to bridge the void of doubt and ignorance with words-on-paper than any other language-user skilled at his craft and with all the traditional tricks of the trade at his disposal. But he was also deeply attracted by temperament to heretical questionings and to playing upon areas of doubt and discrepancy. The Miltonic language is adapted to a strenuous declaration of that which is *unsufferable* both to human reason and to the logic of grammatical relations. Tender places in the mind are sensitive to conflict and incompatibility, and tend naturally to slide over unsufferable issues: the Miltonic language tends in the opposite direction, drawing attention to and aggravating these sore areas of conflict and insoluble debate.

Milton's evolution of an English which lays bare its debt to foreign languages makes it possible for us to read the language of *Paradise Lost* as an innovation running parallel to the seventeenth-century search for a 'universal language', a 'philosophical language' prefiguring Esperanto (see page 23 above). But the assimilated languages refuse to lie down quietly together in solution: the total effect is one of complexity and self-contradiction rather than resolution. In this capacity to call in to his poetry a world of languages and to explore the diversity of foreign relations within a single national tongue, Milton is both of the Renaissance and of the modern world. His linguistic experiments imply a search for integration and synthesis: what they more often reveal is vital discordancy, a multiplicity within apparent unity which maintains memorable life because it maintains difference and dispute. His Renaissance predecessors had a Platonistic fondness for the idea and the practice of synthesis. Humanism attempted to reconcile apparent incompatibles: the classics with Christianity, man with the gods, art with life, by supplying refracting lenses in theology, philosophy, the occult sciences and literature which would demonstrate to the informed eye that All was really One, seen truly. This predeliction found its voice in concepts such as the *coincidentia oppositorum*, the identity of opposites; the androgynous motifs in the alchemists' experiments and in Hermetic occult philosophy; musicologists' theories of *concordia discors*.[20] The Spenserian reconciliation of the eternal with the mutable in the Garden of Adonis:

> All be he subject to mortalitie,
> Yet is eterne in mutabilitie,
> And by succession made perpetuall . . .

and of male with female oppositions in the androgynous image of

> that faire *Hermaphrodite*,
> Which that rich *Romane* of white marble wrought,

And in his costly Bath causd to bee site:
So seemd those two, as growne together quite . . .[21]

is the most intensely felt expression of this ideal in English literature. Milton at once shared this partiality and constitutionally disowned it. *Paradise Lost*, which theoretically adds up to a justification of the One God, actually (in the experience of many readers) breaks down upon itself in a complex of fascinating ways. The Renaissance intellect which seeks to dissolve differences in images of cosmic harmony gives way in Milton, developing in response to the events of history, to a schismatic intelligence, which relishes variables and thrives on provoc- ative irony, syntactic disjunction, and complexity or contradictoriness of implication. Milton composed three divorce tracts; not three tracts in favour of marriage. On occasion he rather tends to celebrate than regret divorce. In the 1644 edition of *The Doctrine and Discipline of Divorce*, he presents God's Creation of the universe as an act of divorce:

> God and nature signifies and lectures to us not onely by those recited decrees, but ev'n by the first and last of all his visible works; when by his divorcing command the world first rose out of Chaos, nor can be renew'd again out of confusion but by the separating of unmeet consorts.
>
> (CPW. II. 273)

The conventional representation of the Creation as an act of integra- tion is reversed and praised as an act of quickening *dis*integration. Birth breaks the unity and safe dormancy of self-sealed custom: in *Paradise Lost*, Book VII, the birds break from their confining eggs 'with kindly rupture' (419). *Paradise Lost* highlights the concept of Adam's and Eve's *felix culpa* to a degree little less than heretical: man's breaking of allegiance to God is re-angled as a polarisation between man and God which gives human nature space to develop a new 'paradise with thee, *happier far*' (XII. 587, emphases added) – an explicit critique of the initial closed world of the fertile, womb-like Garden – and God a chance to develop the idea of love by becoming man and ultimately laying aside his attributes of power in favour of that love: 'For regal sceptre then no more shall need, / God shall be all in all' (III. 340–1). The fall is ultimately interpreted as a birth into greater individuation, full of pain but meaningful as pilgrimage.

In this light, the linguistic variousness and the rich blend of foreign and vernacular elements in Milton's poems, with his tendency to neologise and to transform grammatical usages (zero morpheme derivation), may be read not as a neo-Spenserian resolution of discordancies but as a powerful invocation of discordancy in language as part of our birthright after the fall, regrettable perhaps in itself but a vital condition of life, and a source of struggle and self-discovery. Milton is known to have liked argument. He argued vehemently and on little provocation. Aubrey records his social behaviour as being 'Extreme pleasant . . . but Satyricall'.[22] With Cromwell and Vane, and their fellow Independents, his support for the liberty of the individual conscience was the most binding practical ethic, in theological, political and literary affairs. This was the one premiss which did not change throughout his life (although he refused tolerance to Roman Catholics as being themselves forcers of conscience, and history edged him, unsettlingly, into filling the very place of Licenser – to Parliament – that he had scorned in earlier years). Because of the pre-eminence of the idea of liberty of conscience, he severed his allegiance from one party after another – King, Church of England, Presbyterian-dominated Parliament, Protectorate – becoming after the Restoration able to tolerate alienation and estrangement from almost the whole community by establishing himself as a church of one, entirely his own (because entirely God's) person. The centrality of reading to this singular stance cannot be over-estimated. Freedom of conscience for Milton rested on the twin facts that there existed a God-given text to read together with the God-made light within which made the individual competent to read and interpret the Word. Each light – even one's own, which the ego is naturally blinded by – being only partial, it follows that readers both of the Scriptures and the Book of Nature and history, need to exchange interpretations in order to achieve maximum understanding. During the period of 1641–60, the stringent laws of censorship were relaxed to an unprecedented degree: singular views and eccentric perspectives found their way into print, through presses which were cheap and portable, serving a public whose appetite for radical discussion was aroused and whose literacy was much improved.[23] The climate, especially in the second half of the 1640s, was schismatic and sectarian. Where each man's, or even woman's, voice might be the vehicle of divine inspiration, the right to speak and be heard becomes not only desirable but also politically expedient. Preparing for the trial of Charles I, the Council of the Army twice paused in its deliberations to hear the divine revelations of a woman from Abingdon, Elizabeth Pool, a prophetess: such testaments might have the authority to change the course of history.[24]

In *Areopagitica*, under the reimposition of censorship, Milton raised his voice in favour not just of tolerating but of welcoming public disagreement. The volatile and unsteady state of affairs in which all matters had been opened out for reassessment, with no consensus reached, did not perturb him. Certain words have been immemorially productive of fear and apprehension, both politically and in more intimate and personal terms. One group of such words is that implying division and separation, which can evoke a most primitive terror as well as a corporate reflex of self-defensive banding-together, as people fly for the safety of tradition and assumption. Division and separation connote doubt and uncertainty, and especially political instability. Censorship is an attempt to enforce unity and preserve the status quo. In *Areopagitica*, Milton presents his generation with a revaluation of division, attaching to it connotations of multiple search integrated by a common aim: in its revised form it becomes a ground of security rather than insecurity. The word which he undertakes to purge of its frightening connotations is *schism*: 'There be who perpetually complain of schisms and sects, and make it such a calamity that any man dissents from their maxims' (*CPW*. II. 550). Dissidence is named as a creative good, and is furthermore defined as intrinsic to the state of things in the fallen world. We are all different; we know things differently and see along discrepant eye-beams. At the centre of Milton's argument is an acceptance of the many-sidedness of truth, symbolised in the building of Solomon's Temple:

> Yet these are the men cry'd out against for schismaticks and sectaries; as if, while the Temple of the Lord was building, some cutting, some squaring the marble, others hewing the cedars, there should be a sort of irrationall men who could not consider there must be many schisms and many dissections made in the quarry and in the timber, ere the house of God can be built. And when every stone is laid artfully together, it cannot be united into a continuity, it can but be contiguous in this world, neither can every peece of the building be of one form; nay rather the perfection consists in

this, that out of many moderat varieties and brotherly dissimilitudes that are not vastly disproportionall arises the goodly and gracefull symmetry that commends the whole pile and structure.

(CPW. II. 555)

By the change of a single letter, the idealistic *continuity* becomes the realistic *contiguity*. The building of the Temple by the English must take place 'in this world' where perfection is limited by the capacities of the workmen and the nature of the raw materials available. But by an artful manoeuvre, multiple discrepancy of detail to detail may result in a sort of balance in the whole, so that realism adjusts itself towards a new idealism through the antithetical phrasing of *dissimilitudes that are not vastly disproportionall.* Thus *schism* is commended as integral to unity. The nation can have unity on the basis of dissident opinions. A sacred art-work can have unity though its parts may not perfectly fit together. I shall read *Paradise Lost* in the light of the subjective relativism Milton licenses here: appraising it as a Temple whose 'goodly and gracefull symmetry' rests upon its balance of contradictions, its many-angled perspectivism. Milton is profoundly modern in his willingness to allow that a coherent 'spirituall architecture' may be made out of incoherencies. In *Paradise Lost*, written during and after the dereliction and sack of the Temple, he presents a baroque vision of multiple perspectives, in which no one vantage-point is stable where the whole universe becomes the theatre of action. Subjectivism and the individual's vantage (or disadvantage) point dominate the poem, with its introspective speeches, questionings of bearings, insecure emotions and fluid situations. The arbitrating narrative voice strives towards fixity in its attempt to emulate or reproduce the divine language: but even the narrative voice (especially in the four beautiful Invocations) admits its partiality and subjectness to delusion. This great poem of faith is miraculously built on many doubts and uncertainties. William Blake inaugurated the school of Milton criticism which holds that Milton was 'of the Devil's party without knowing it' (see page 13 above): his conscious allegiance to God the Father was subverted by his subconscious sympathy with Satan the errant son. This attribution to the text of a rebellious subconscious has become a commonplace in our thinking about *Paradise Lost*, and it corresponds to an experience to which many readers testify: a feeling of deep and unacknowledged rift and fissure in the work, seething energies which rise indignantly and exaltedly against its own most hallowed tenet of obedience to and trust in the paternal God, as Milton rose against Charles with his fellow free-thinking Puritans; implosive rage and doubt as God turned against his saints and utterly demolished and demoralised their armies. Christopher Hill astutely moved on from Blake in 1971 to claim that the peculiar tension of the contradictions in *Paradise Lost* came of the fact that Milton was indeed of the Devil's party (as were numerous of his radical contemporaries in the English Civil War, believing that most Christians worshipped a wicked God) but that *Milton partly knew it.*[25] Something of the brilliant pain transmitted by the poem to its readers is explained by this emphasis on Milton as a radical heretic who remained in constant dialogue not only with history, God and his own conscience but also with Levellers, Quakers (his friends after the Restoration) Familists and Ranters. Milton believed that he had sacrificed his eyes in the service of God's cause: then God had sacrificed him. On the basis of this daily, yearly shock – never absorbed, always renewed as he opened 'these eyes, that roll in vain / To find thy piercing ray, and find no dawn' (*PL.* III. 23–4) – he built the temple of his late poems, *Paradise Lost, Paradise Regained, Samson Agonistes*, out of materials not continuous but contiguous.

Reading Milton is always a powerful and potentially unnerving experience because it represents a destabilising wrestle with the language which is ours in common with him. Milton (with Shakespeare) has in some sense constructed us as readers. He was an embodied revolution who unmade and remade the language of literature – though not, as Shakespeare did, enriching the language with neo-colloquialisms and new minted proverbs, axioms and felicitous images. There are two periods of literary English: Before Milton and After Milton. Whether for good or ill, later generations have been affected or afflicted by what Milton did for English and revealed of its possibilities. The tyranny of Milton over the imaginations of the eighteenth-century poetry of the sublime and the Augustan satirists is well documented; so is the Romantic debt. Wordsworth's *Prelude* is by *Paradise Lost* out of *Paradise Regained*. Shelley's *Adonais* is from Bion's *Lament for Moschus* through *Lycidas*. Byron's *Cain* and *Heaven and Hell* are so evidently the progeny of *Genesis* through *Paradise Lost* that

Byron felt bound to deny that he had read a word of Milton for over a decade, fleeing his debts. In the nineteenth century, Emily Brontë's *Wuthering Heights* is a wicked inversion of Miltonic myth, and George Eliot's Mr Casaubon exhibited the face of Milton seen in a spoon. Milton therefore became to English literature a god: the kind of god you have to fight. He himself taught the principles of such rebellion. One of Milton's regicide tracts is entitled *Eikonoklastes*, the Image-breaker: an answer to the popular work of meditations and self-exoneration attributed to Charles I, *Eikon Basiliké*, the Image of the King.

> For which reason this answer also is intitl'd *Iconoclastes*, the famous surname of many Greek Emperors, who in thir zeal to the command of God, after long tradition of Idolatry in the Church, took courage, and broke all superstitious Images to peeces.
>
> (*CPW*. III. 343)

The Puritan soldiery too were self-licensing image-breakers, smashing formalism in the shape of altar-rails, costly art-works, bells and statues. At Worcester in 1642, they sacked the Cathedral and tore down its sweet-toned organ. At Colchester, Puritans smashed glass and ornaments in the Lucas family private chapel, broke open the family tombs and scattered the bones of the dead.[26] Milton undertook the desecration of linguistic traditions which reinforced value-systems and power-structures which were considered venerable for no better reason than that they were old. To the language he received from European tradition, Milton stands as *Eikonoklastes*. One of the most fundamental qualities of his mature poetry is its thrust and impulsion, the stress of violent rhythmic energies retarded and released in complex units of syntax. The reader of Milton's great verse paragraphs must take deep breaths and be prepared for strenuous negotiation with the grammatical processes of what he reads. This is partly because the stable grammatical forms of English have been broken down and subjected to rules normative in other languages or rare in our own – varying, especially, word order after the fashion of inflected languages like Latin or Old English. He does this only just within the rules of the English language, and in so doing exposes the laws of English in an extraordinarily naked way, like the rippling vertebrae of a backbone beneath the flesh. The laws only just hold under the stress of Milton's vital experiment.

41

But they do hold. The poem is perceived by many readers as monumental, architectural, massively well-founded as a structure; simultaneously as fluid, shifting, free-moving. Milton breaks the accustomed formalities but not the basic forms of English. He can through this wrestle with language throw the whole linguistic code out of the realm of easy assumption and into the area of the questionable and problematic. To vary word and clause order, for instance, can bring into question the grammatical status and function of individual words or phrases (since in English word order rather than inflected forms tends to define logic of grammar) to the degree that a reader may not know how to parse a sentence. Meaning flies loose from grammatical fixities. A clause may, in Miltonic usage, appear to be attached either to its predecessor or successor: again the reader experiences the significance as under a question. Nouns may be used as verbs, verbs as nouns; adjectives stand as nouns; verbs may be withdrawn altogether, or disagree with their subjects ('both Death and I / Am found eternal' – X. 815–16); ablative absolutes and gerundiums are mimed by English fabrications. Language is subjected to truly seismic stress, not on the basis of a handful of verbal tricks but through the application of an anatomising intelligence to the chemistry of the mind in a state of passion, and the simultaneous generation of a language capable of miming this inner drama. In Book I of *Paradise Lost*, Satan turns to Beelzebub:

> If thou beest he; but O how fallen! how changed 84
> From him, who in the happy realms of light
> Clothed with transcendent brightness didst outshine 86
> Myriads though bright: if he whom mutual league,
> United thoughts and counsels, equal hope 88
> And hazard in the glorious enterprise,
> Joined with me once, now misery hath joined 90
> In equal ruin: into what pit thou seest
> From what highth fallen, so much the stronger proved 92
> He with his thunder, and till then who knew
> The force of those dire arms? . . . 94

This is a language of utter bafflement, ungrounded in known laws, bereft of assurance that anything can be known: a grammar vertiginously liberated from the safety of fixed rules. It begins as conditional address, expressive of uncertainty as to the fact to be articulated. Satan is not sure to whom he is speaking: the vocative breaks down over the need to distinguish *thou* from *him*, present appearance from past reality. The attempt to address the putative Beelzebub is almost immediately riven by a highly-charged exclamation of regret – O *how fall'n, how chang'd.* The direction of the sentence has been completely lost at the outset under the surge of disarraying emotions, a disjunction reflecting the condition of things in a world of phantasmagoria, where all experience is at once hypothetical and contingent. It is a self-abdicating grammar of acute anxiety, mapping bursts of inward alarm, detours of bright memory, a nervous sense of utter schism between past and present. Within the fight for coherency, a reader feels the conscious will of the speaker striving against nearly insuperable odds to gain control. At line 87, the originating *if* is picked up again as if to stabilise the rocking grammar of disjunction. But *if* is itself unstable, needing something firm to depend on. It precipitates a new turn of thought, hoping to proceed by a backward-looking survey of past usage. Satan brings forth a roll-call of self-affirming phrases which had proved inspirational in heaven: they march along two by two, adjective plus noun – *mutual league, united thoughts, equal hope, glorious enterprise* – with the purpose both of comforting and arousing, stressing shared endeavour and seeking therapy against the desolating isolation of Hell. But the stable union of adjective and noun falters, and grammatical hold is lost at the inchoate juncture of past and present (*once, now,* line 90), where an intense compression of thought and feeling has relinquished explicit clausal connections. The reader is now staggering in a mire of grammatical turbulence, without bearings, registering the protagonist's agony of shock and incomprehension, by being forced to struggle himself in the tensions of the sentence, with their contrary drags like tidal ebb and flow. A reader conscious of his own mental and optical procedures whilst reading might find his eye searching forward for grammatical satisfaction and, not finding it, a recurrent recoil, as the eye flicks back through the lines in the irritated or uneasy wish to align the parts of the sentence in a rational relationship – to complete the pattern and 'close' the sentence. We are aroused but not rewarded by the sentence; given the pleasure of a riddle without the satisfaction of a key. This is one reason why it is never possible to close the book of *Paradise Lost*. Milton presents us here with the queasy grammatical equivalent of Satan's attempt to find *terra firma* on the burning lake. Lines 91–4 achieve near-complete anarchy. The hollow vaunting insistence on the old verbal patterns of heroic rhetoric (*into what . . . From what*) picks up the balancing exclamations of the first line (*how fallen! how changed*) and throws the repeated words into a temporarily equivocal status midway between the exclamatory and the interrogative. *What* and *how* are words denoting the absence of knowledge. At this stage the sentence could be (but, as it turns out, is not – yet) turning into a question. Its status has to be left hanging while the eye takes in and tries to fix the *so much* clause. But this clause is totally dependent on the foregoing problematic clause for its intelligibility. Upon the loose conjunction *and* (which seems to imply leaps of thought which have been going on inarticulately under the surface of the quoted utterance) the sentence falls limply into a helplessly self-apologetic rhetorical question.

This, of course, is an extreme case of linguistic disruption and readerly vertigo. But *Paradise Lost*, fluctuating between Heaven and Hell, the certain and the indefinite, meaningfulness and the 'vast vacuity', is full of extreme cases. The total effect is one of restlessly vociferous energy, an urgent grammar of quest, which intensely arouses its reader to the *pursuit* of meaning – meaning as process, much as *Areopagitica* had understood Truth as an evolutionary matter, to be come at over time through much disputing and searching in strange places and the sincere engagement in 'strong and healthfull commotions' (*CPW*. II. 566). Milton, who stood 'ever in my great task-master's eye', (Sonnet VII), also demands a working reader, to perform a co-operative shared act of deducing complex harmonies from the shifting firmament of language. Meaning in *Paradise Lost* is a process of becoming, not something located as already in being. The poem tests its language against the unknown, the imponderable, that which cannot be said, and queries indeed whether there are things which we trespass in trying to say at all: 'May I express thee unblamed?' (III. 3). This great epic poem travels with its imaginative eye the limits of the imaginable universe. As an odyssey of language it flies to the extreme limits of language too, divining areas of deeper meaning which language is helpless to define, but towards which it can gesture by feats of implication. In the end, the meaning is off the page, reposing in the silence beyond our wordy, self-mirroring disclosures: 'The meaning, not the name I call' (VII. 5).

Most readers carry away in memory the poetry of Hell rather than of Heaven. Perhaps this is because of the sharply human and recognisable quality of Milton's Hell. We speak of our pains as 'hellish', of 'being in hell', of 'hell on earth' and of sufferers as 'poor devils'. We know exactly what is meant by such figures of speech because all of us have been there. The theory that hell should not be seen as a geographical place of sulphurous fires in which sinners are roasted to eternity, but as a psychological state, was well-known in Milton's day. Marlowe's Mephistophelis' 'where we are is hell' (*Dr Faustus*, II. i. 125) leads directly to Milton's Satan's 'my self am hell' (IV. 75). During the Civil Wars and Interregnum, many radicals began to deny the reality of any heaven and hell beyond our experience in this world. Hell is poverty and oppression. Hell is when we are in pain or sorrow; heaven when we laugh. Hell is an invention of the haves to keep down the have-nots by terrifying them. A good God would certainly not damn his children eternally for their venial misdemeanours. Hill quotes John Boggis of Great Yarmouth, who asked in January 1646, 'Where is your God, in heaven or in earth, aloft or below, or doth he sit in the clouds, or where doth he sit with his arse?'[27] *Paradise Lost* attempts to answer this question. Hell is constraint, exile, impotence. It is being laughed to scorn by God. It is being cut off from one's Father and having one's name excised from the book of memory. Hell is political defeat. There is a hell of self-questioning: the most hellish form of speech being soliloquy. It is the lonely core of the mind where one cannot be touched, nor can impulses of love and cherishing arise. Most profoundly it is life without sexual love and the peace, security and excitement of loving touch. The inmost heaven of *Paradise Lost* is the bower within Eden where Adam and Eve make love and sleep together. The converse of this blessedness is the hell of sexual frustration and sexual jealousy; the blind, stupid aggression of hurt sexuality, for the tenderest place is also the most vulnerable. Woman's hell is man's misogyny. The poet's hell is blindness. The language of *Paradise Lost* at once expresses this hellish pain, and atones for it by transforming a passive sensation into an active discharge of energy. Fictive language puts up a fight with what it submits to communicating:

> hell scarce holds the wild uproar,
> As when Alcides from Oechalia crowned
> With conquest, felt the envenomed robe, and tore
> Through pain up by the roots Thessalian pines . . .
>
> (II. 541–4)

Hercules in Thessaly, seared by the poisoned shirt, discharges his pain as enraged energy. This is the kind of sheer, frantic pain which is experienced over all the nerve-endings as intimately as a garment on naked skin. It issues in retaliatory effort which seeks to throw inner pain on to the outside world. As Hercules dismembers the natural world, so Milton's linguistic mime scrambles the rational flow of normative English word order. An expected word order for the final line might be: 'through pain Hercules tore up Thessalian pines by the roots.' In Milton's verb-founded discourse, the *act* dominates. *Tore* hangs precipitously at the end of the previous line reaching out for its object. The object is delayed until the conclusion of the last line, as the purgation of Hercules' violent pain is infinitely deferred. The sensation *through pain* crowds in between the verb and its adverb *up*; the adverb is raised into suspension, as with monumental effort; *by the roots* now reveals the parting of the object from its foundation in the solid earth, and some of the pain of the action is also recorded in this participial phrase, as if *hair* were being torn up by the roots (we do not know the object of the sentence yet, and microcosm and macrocosm intensely mirror one another); finally the withheld object, *Thessalian pines*, is revealed, beautiful slender and lofty, beyond human imaginative reach to dislodge. This is a pain so disproportionate to the sufferer that it cannot be kept in. It is discharged in staccato rhythms of self-rending utterance like a series of cries. The lines tell us much of the psychology of pain: its almost unavoidable articulation as senseless acts of violence, such that violent acts may seem a language through which the observer must read the otherwise incommunicable testimony of profound inward agony. The effect of the line is somewhat reminiscent of the legendary mandrake, whose roots were said to scream in pain when pulled up.

In Milton man wrestles with his conditions and the creature with his Creator; likewise the poet wrestles with his language. The spirit of the poetry reminds us of Jacob's famous wrestle with God in *Genesis*:

And Jacob was left alone; and there wrestled a man with him until the breaking of the day.

And he said, Thy name shall be called no more Jacob, but Israel: for as a prince hast thou power with God and with men, and hast prevailed.

(Genesis 32:24, 28)

Milton had used the image of a wrestling-match in *Areopagitica* to declare his confidence in the expression rather than the repression of divergent opinions:

And now the time in speciall is, by priviledge to write and speak what may help to the furder discussing of matters in agitation. The Temple of *Janus* with his two *controversal* faces might now not unsignificantly be set open. And though all the windes of doctrin were let loose to play upon the earth, so Truth be in the field, we do injuriously by licencing and prohibiting to misdoubt her strength. Let her and Falshood grapple; who ever knew Truth put to the wors, in a free and open encounter.

(CPW. II. 561)

We can see Milton here evolving a radical vocabulary, taking words calculated to arouse insecurity in the conservative and propertied; setting them out plainly and boldly in a matrix of positivism and inviting his reader to confront them and see whether these words (together with the things they represent) can actually hurt them, or whether they will not rather do us good as a community. *Agitation* is one such word: *Janus* and *controversal* others. *Agitation* had a complex of mutually implicating meanings. One was debating; another involved delegation and acting for others (the radical agents for the private soldiers in the New Model Army from 1647–9 would be called *Agitators*, and the term obviously prefigures the corrupted usage of political agitator with its implication of trouble-maker); a third carried the modern implication of perturbation and excitement. Milton's usage alludes to debate (the most innocuous meaning) but the whole context ties in the image of turbulence, the ruffling of the waters of thought, hitherto kept smooth only by state repression. His procedure is to use the innocuous meaning to salvage the suspect, with the implication that *agitation*, with all its ramifications and possible issues, is a genuine social good, if we understand it aright. *Janus*, the two-faced Roman god, keeper of doors (giving us our word *janitor*) had long been invoked as a symbol of hypocrisy, but could equally well be interpreted as a sign for openness, freedom from the constraints of prejudice, the meaningful complexity of truth. In time of war, his Temple in Rome stood open; in peacetime it was shut. The Civil War, Milton implies, gave opportunity for productive controversy. The term *controversal* had three current meanings, of which Milton here apparently elects for the most superficial and innocuous: turned in opposite ways at once, but again, with that rhetorical craft which is equally notable in the prose works and in *Paradise Lost*, Milton so angles the word as to arouse the other meanings – subject to dispute, and pertaining to controversy, polemical. This verbal manipulativeness uses the semantic richness of English – the many-nuanced meanings and values of key words – to imply a paradox which readers of *Paradise Lost* and *Samson* will recognise as central to the Miltonic vision: only at the heart of the battle are we truly safe, if Truth is with us; only in blindness can we see; the bewildering multiplicity of counter-meanings in language will yield a weighty assurance if we embrace them inclusively; alienation is the condition of extraordinary security:

> More safe I sing with mortal voice, unchanged
> To hoarse or mute, though fallen on evil days,
> On evil days though fallen; and evil tongues;
> In darkness, and with dangers compassed round,
> And solitude; yet not alone . . .
>
> > (*PL*. VII. 24–8)

*　　　　　*　　　　　*

The living immediacy of Milton's schismatic language was generated by the Revolution and its defeat, together with radical changes occurring in the status of the published word during that period, and complicated by the exigencies of writing in subjection to a severe Court censor during the Restoration. *Paradise Lost, Paradise Regained* and *Samson Agonistes* were subversive texts by an author who was a suspect person in Restoration society, disgraced for his allegiance to the republican cause and his public defences of the execution of Charles I. We who read his poetry in the privacy of a study or library, need to remember the status of the printed word in the mid-seventeenth

48

century, in order to recognise what we have in our hands – what political weapon, dissident's autobiography or testament of continuing resistance. We read with calm eyes a language that was not composed in tranquillity: Milton's lines have settled back into the stylisation of ink-on-paper, domesticated and tamed by time. They were not written thus, but composed at white heat and in the urgency of the moment.

There are three major periods of Milton's poetic career before the English Revolution: 1624 (the date of his first recorded poem) to 1640, including *On the Morning of Christ's Nativity*, *L'Allegro* and *Il Penseroso*, *Comus* and *Lycidas*; 1641 to 1660, the period of the Civil Wars, the Commonwealth and Protectorate, when he composed little poetry save occasional sonnets and versified translations of the Psalms (mainly of political significance); 1660 (more accurately 1658, believed to be the year in which he began *Paradise Lost* to 1673, the period of *Paradise Lost*, *Paradise Regained* and *Samson Agonistes*. Although the central period is that in which Milton abstained from writing poetry, throwing his whole effort into revolutionary public service, this transitional period is the most important for establishing the status of the written word in his personal and public history. The time of intense stress and flux changed him radically. From an author who was emerging before the war as a graceful humanist, with debts to Spenser, Shakespeare and Jonson, he became a participant in the whole national life, committing himself to engage his energies and talents with those of the common people, the Army and the Independents in expectation of a new world. During this period the written word to which Milton committed himself took on violent political efficacy. From the eloquence of the *vita contemplativa* (exemplified perhaps in the pensive onlooker's stance of the persona or personae of *L'Allegro* and *Il Penseroso*, essentially standing outside life), Milton turned to the public eloquence of the *vita activa*. From poetry he turned to prose; from a timeless engagement with art, using ancient aristocratic traditions of poetry where the poem is a transparency through which we read its generic predecessors – Theocritus, Bion, Moschus, Virgil through *Lycidas* – Milton moves to a moment-by-moment dispute with the present. Conflict and dialogue become central to his writing-style: energy and dynamic struggle intrinsic to the momentum of his thought. Milton's prose is free-ranging, vituperative, frequently off-beat, tumultuously imagistic, an active response to a changing and changeable

49

situation. Through language he hopes to transform the world. The later poetry is the linguistic inheritor of Milton's prose. His freely-moving and idiosyncratic blank verse derives from his prose rhythms not only its rhetorical and polemical effects but also its display of zeal and immanent participation in a war between good and evil which is not the embellished transcription of ancient records of what is essentially over and done, but an emergency experience in the here-and-now. The Bible was experienced by Milton and his generation as a contemporary text. It was an open book, subject to daily or hourly reinterpretation in the light of events. One could own a copy of one's own for 3s 2d in 1649 (not prohibitive at current book prices); later the price dropped to 2s. Handy pocket editions were available which could be carried around and consulted in churches or ale-houses. The contemporary relevance of the Bible is attested by the Welsh Puritan polemicist, Arise Evans in An Eccho to the Voice of Heaven (1653): 'Afore I looked upon the Scripture as a history of things that passed in other countries, pertaining to other persons; but now I looked upon it as a mystery to be opened at this time, belonging also to us.'[28] The soldiers of the New Model Army sang Psalms before they stormed a city's fortifications or engaged Prince Rupert's Cavaliers. Milton translated Psalms in the urgent and dubious moments of the 1650s, calling down God's wrath upon his enemies with David's voice: 'An open grave their throat, their tongue they smooth / God, find them guilty, let them fall' (Psalm V. 28–9; 12 August 1653). The English Milton writing on the twelfth day of August 1653, and the Hebrew Psalmist David composing 2000 years before are one in Milton's adaptation of the Psalm to articulate and answer his own personal needs in relation to the stress of history.

Milton's development in the 1640s follows a path of enthusiastic engagement with the issues of practical politics – disestablishment of the Church, divorce, freedom of speech and of the press, rights of the subject against the Crown – moving to a growing disillusion with the mass of the people as a mob incapable of using liberty, and with its leaders, to almost complete withdrawal from public politics towards the end of the 1650s. But in the earlier years of the 1640s, Milton threw in his lot decisively with the revolutionary population of England.[29] Before 1641, Milton was an ageing scholarly young man of promise, author of several richly musical and complex poems in

English, Latin and Italian: but dilatory, oddly retentive and lacking in self-confidence for one of such high-achieving ambitions. The earlier poems were mainly called from him by persons or circumstances – occasional poems in response to invitations. But after 1641, as a result of his commitment to historical dialogue rather than to poetic isolation, anxiety about productivity and uncertainty about his own identity seem to have passed away. Disaster in the forms of a bad marriage, the death of his only son, his blindness in 1652 and political disillusion only bred fluency and self-affirmation. Before the Revolution, Milton could dedicate Latin poems to Bishops (*Elegia tertia: On the death of the Bishop of Winchester; In obitum Praesulis: On the death of the Bishop of Ely*) and to a female member of the aristocracy ('An Epitaph on the Marchioness of Winchester'). During the Revolution, the episcopacy became 'the serpent's egg that will hatch an Antichrist', associated in his tract *Of Reformation* (1641) with deformity, disease, scum on a pot, anatomical grossness, greed, the lower animals, alcohol, perverted sexuality and predators. The devotion of the bishops 'gives a Vomit to GOD himself' (*CPW.* I. 537). The well-relished crudity of the gutter vocabulary which Milton shared with every itinerant priest-hating pedlar, millenarian Ranter and propertyless Levelling squatter in the country, brings Milton down from the high horse of poetry, with its aristocratic lineage and tradition of patronage, into another élite – the élite who were God's elect and might be found at the lowest level of the social hierarchy. For a few excited and transforming years, Milton's humanistic class-bound pretensions were set aside in favour of an uncharacteristic alliance with the English common people – however mean and uneducated – as fellow-readers of God's Word:

The very essence of Truth is plainnesse and brightnes; the darknes and crookednesse is our own. The *Wisdome* of God created *understanding*, fit and proportionable to Truth the object, and end of it, as the eye to the thing visible. If our understanding have a film of ignorance over it, or be blear with gazing on other false glisterings, what is that to Truth? If we will but purge with sovrain eyesalve that intellectual ray which *God* hath planted in us, then we would beleeve the Scriptures protesting their own plainnes, and perspicuity, calling to them to be instructed, not only the *wise*, and *learned*, but the *simple*, the *poor*, the *babes*, foretelling an extraordinary effusion of *Gods* Spirit upon every age and sexe, attributing to all men, and requiring

> from them the ability of searching, trying, examining all things, and by the
> Spirit discerning that which is good . . .
>
> (CPW. I. 566)

Milton here enrolls himself with what we might call the English
common reader, a large and inclusive readership as against an academic
élite of theologically-trained cognoscenti. The priesthood of all believ-
ers and the plainness of truth become cardinal and linked precepts
which draw the constitutionally solitary Milton into the totality of the
human race, 'all men' searching 'all things'.

His language in the tracts extended itself to impersonate the
linguistic habits of a social world in which native Anglo-Saxon formed
the base for a vivid, fertile and concrete register of address: a language
of the body rather than the soul. The pamphlets move between the
higher scholarly discourse of ratiocination and a language characterised
by comic deflation, colloquial idiom, vigorous irony and imagery and
conceits drawn from common life – the language of the streets, fields
and market-place. In *Areopagitica*, talking of the arrogance of the hacks
who are chosen as censors, he breaks out:

> When every acute reader upon the first sight of a pedantick licence, will be
> ready with these like words to ding the book a coits distance from him, I
> hate a pupil teacher, I endure not an instructer that comes to me under the
> wardship of an overseeing fist.
>
> (CPW. II. 533)

The irascible gesture of the self-respecting reader who slings the book
across the room takes its comic precision from the fact that it is thrown
like a quoit: we can see the action and imaginatively follow the violent
trajectory of the book because the image instructs us how to visualise
its flight path. It is thrown contemptuously sideways from the hand.
The Anglo-Saxon verb *ding* is a splenetic colloquialism reinforcing the
violence of the sudden action. As the man bursts out, 'I hate a pupil
teacher' the sense of justified indignation in a comically realistic setting
is reinforced, but the comedy darkens as the sentence proceeds to its
rhetorically powerful conclusion in the revelatory plain-speaking
Anglo-Saxon of the *overseeing fist*. Milton's low-register language is a
combative reply to the institutionalised violence practised by the

licensing state. The prose oscillates between playful and grave, sardonic and oratorical, bursts of short sharp Anglo-Saxon monosyllables and perspicacious and excogitative Latin polysyllables. There is something joyous about *Areopagitica*: a spree of words, warm from the pen, fountains onto the page with the passion of total commitment. The extravagant play or antagonism between high and low register, Latin and vernacular, articulates a sense of freedom in an exuberant choice of diction. There is a superabundance in his lexis, so that he can choose from riches of vocabulary which seem to extend in every direction. Milton's language in the tracts is characteristically voluminous and copious. It has an air of the impromptu and is headily versatile, like a musician improvising through the full range of the instrument. His prose works through elaboration and embellishment, and a constant thrust of the abstract towards the pictorial, single images towards populous conceits. The language has a choiceful character, exhibiting permutations of inventiveness as if to dramatise in print the qualities he attributes to the people of England in 1643: 'a Nation not slow and dull, but of a quick, ingenious and piercing spirit, acute to invent, sutle and sinewy in discourse, not beneath the reach of any point the highest that human capacity can soar to' (*CPW*. II. 551). The tract celebrates pleasure and enjoyment, experience-within-the-moment, refusing a cantankerous sobriety in favour of music and beauty, 'recreations and pastimes, all that is delightfull to man', arguing from a view of virtue that has dug its root deep into the good earth of happiness: 'Wherefore did he creat passions within us, pleasures round about us, but that these rightly temper'd are the very ingredients of vertu' (*CPW*. II. 523, 527)?

From the transcendent brooding mind of the earlier poems, Milton moves to the immanence of life in the body, in the here-and-now, in the prose works. The genre of the popular Puritan tract, fully established by the mid-seventeenth century (its best-known early protagonist being Marprelate), already included these features of colloquial English, which are surely a source of the thrusting blank verse of his later poetry. Through prose he broke the gracious confinement of rhyme, octosyllabic and decasyllabic couplet art, the sonnet and even his own neo-Shakespearean blank verse of *Comus*, releasing his energies into the unregulated measures of prose. Rhetorically, of course, the prose tracts tend to be decorously structured according to the fivefold classical laws of composition known in that era to every schoolboy (*introductio, narratio, probatio, refutatio, conclusio*); but within these constraints the author is free to produce vagrant rhythms, elaborations of sentence structure (sometimes, as in Sir Thomas Browne and Burton as well as Milton, a single sentence pages long), or to catch on the page the urgent modulations of a speaking voice. This 'speaking voice' – or voices – reinforced by the use of dramatic dialogue in A *Treatise of Civil Power* (1659; *CPW*. VII. rev. edn, 264, 250) were passed on to *Paradise Lost*. The growling sarcasms of the anti-Prelatical tracts:

> they would request us to indure still the rustling of their Silken Cassocks, and that we would burst our *midriffes* rather than laugh to see them under Sayl in all their Lawn and Sarcenet, their shrouds and tackle, with a *geometricall rhomboides* upon their heads. . . . They pray us that it would please us to let them still hale us, and worrey with their bandogs and Pursivants; and that it would please the *Parliament* that they may yet have the whipping, fleecing and fleaing of us in their diabolical courts . . .
>
> (*Of Reformation in England, CPW*. I. 611–12)

lead into the withering satire of the Paradise of Fools:

> Embryos and idiots, eremites and friars
> White, black and gray, with all their trumpery
> ....
> then might ye see
> Cowls, hoods and habits with their wearers tossed
> And fluttered into rags, then relics, beads,
> Indulgences, dispenses, pardons, bulls,
> The sport of winds.
>
> (*PL*. III. 474–5; 489–93)

Of course Milton had satirised the corrupt clergy in *Lycidas*, using the trenchant and biting Anglo-Saxon vocabulary of plain-spoken Protestant satire: the clergy 'scramble at the shearers' feast, / And shove away the worthy bidden guest' (117–18). The uncouth verbs *scramble* and *shove* put down the mighty from their seats and exalt the humble and meek: high and mighty churchmen violate the good manners of the Beatitudes, elbowing out those who are 'worthy' by election and 'bidden' as at the wedding feast in Matthew's Gospel, where the king invited alternative guests from 'the highways' (22:1–14). But the satire in *Lycidas* is properly speaking an interpolation, on the model of the anti-ecclesiastical satire expected in pastoral and exemplified by Spenser's practice in *The Shepheardes Calender*.[30] What the composition of the anti-prelatical tracts seems to have done for Milton's satiric style is to endorse and accentuate the Miltonic tendency to that figure of speech (and the associated caste of mind) known by Puttenham as 'Micterismus. Or, the fleering Frumpe'.[31] To 'fleer' is to make a wry, contemptuous face; a 'frump' is a derisive snort. Milton brought these verbal gestures in his prose and poetry to the condition of a proto-Swiftian high art. The priests are surely not human. They are a peculiar kind of boat, rigged 'with shroud and tackle' and topped incomprehensibly with '*a geometricall rhomboides* on their heads': it hurts our midriffs to hold in our laughter (the dispensation of our saving commonsense) as they sail past us. This putting down of pretension and iniquity by generating collusive laughter at its mad dress looks forward not only to the whirling nonsenses of the Catholic trumpery in the Paradise of Fools in a windy corner of the universe of *Paradise Lost* but also to the cold-faced satiric incomprehension of the Chorus in *Samson Agonistes* as it reports the phenomenon of Dalila approaching her husband:

> But who is this, what thing of sea or land?
> Female of sex it seems,
> That so bedecked, ornate, and gay,
> Comes this way sailing
> Like a stately ship
> Of Tarsus, bound for th' isles
> Of Javan or Gadire
> With all her bravery on, and tackle trim,
> Sails filling, and streamers waving . . .
> (710–18)

What '*thing*' is this? Start from the beginning, it is suggested, and do not assume anything about the nature and status of what hits your eyes on this earth – and you will see more clearly. We turn ourselves from God's rational creatures into exotic artefacts, sartorially insane in our exhibitionism, as if we meant to put out to sea in a high wind.

55

Contempt for costume and display informs both Milton's hatred of the clergy and his distaste for (and fascination with, for it is a complex attitude) female sumptuousness. Perhaps we could see the satiric line of vision generated by Milton's prose period as vernacular perspective, a view obtained by angling a clarifying beam of light from reality as it registers itself in the vulgar tongue (the naked body of language) to its appearance in the full dress regalia of fashionable foreign terms.

Before the Civil Wars, Milton composed some poems in Latin, in the academic traditions of humanist poetry; after 1660, the poetry is steadfastly English. Before 1641, Milton wrote a masque, *Comus*, a notoriously Royalist genre, traditionally involving expensive display and associated with, or implicated in, the fulsome adulation practised by courtier-poets around the person of the monarch. Milton's use of the form represents a purging of its extravagances: it is a literary masque rather than an exhibition piece, moving around the 'sober dictates of spare Temperance' and praising a chastity which is linked with an argument in favour of fair distribution of wealth (see pages 71 ff. below). Nevertheless, the idea of a 'Puritan masque' is well-nigh oxymoronic. Milton in *Paradise Lost* would come to speak witheringly of 'Mixed dance, or wanton masque, or midnight ball' (IV. 768), where 'wanton', with its erotic implications, is used almost as a constituent of the generic title. The Satanic stage effects in *Paradise Lost* and *Paradise Regained* are evidently masque-derived (e.g. II. 1–10; X. 441–52)[32] and intended to show the glittering spuriousness of Satan's pretensions. But in 1634, the 26-year-old Milton, pleased with patronage, was willing to dedicate his pen to the Earl of Bridgwater at his inauguration as Lord President of Wales, as earlier he had composed the shorter *Arcades* in honour of the Countess Dowager of Derby at Harefield, dedicatee of Spenser. The Civil Wars and Interregnum changed Milton almost beyond recognition. His proposed readership had included bishops, the aristocracy, fellow-academics, the Continental Protestant-humanist intelligentsia. After 1641, his readership widened dramatically to include, for a few years, the whole company of the English Protestant literate, governing, middle and (at least potentially) lower classes.

In December 1641, the whole of London seemed to be out on the streets shouting 'No Bishops!' Apprentices, mariners and dock-hands, hawkers and journeymen were joined by substantial citizens in coaches in daily mass demonstrations to Westminster:

> The oyster-women locked their fish up
> And trudg'd away to cry 'No Bishop'.[33]

A petition to exclude from the House of Lords all bishops and Popish peers was being prepared, rumoured to be 24 yards long and containing 15,000–20,000 signatures. Workers, vagrants, MPs, burghers, capitalists and scholars made up a teeming national unanimity of protest. During the years 1641–2, Milton published five anti-prelatical tracts. We need to hear the shouts in the streets as a background noise to Milton's vituperations of clergy and state, in order to apprehend the immediacy of Milton's language, and the extent to which, learned and sophisticated as it was, it also ventriloquised a popular voice and integrated Milton for the first and last time in his life with the broad mass of his countrymen. The concord of property-owning classes and the landless may have been short-lived and based on partial delusion as to one another's interests, but it was intensely real in the moment of experience. In the 1640s, the status, uses and capabilities of the written language changed: Milton was part of that change, both impelled by it and contributing to it. Very suddenly, the written word became immediate and accessible, on a mass basis. Milton's father was a London scrivener, a trade which combined writing with capitalism, and which generated the considerable profits which enabled the father to retire from active engagement in business and the son to enjoy his seven studious years at Hammersmith and Horton preparing himself for poetry. Milton was therefore born into a middle-class profession whose income derived from the sale of writing skills as a utility. The political implications of such trades become manifest when we consider that Parliament had employed scriveners to compile manuscript summaries of debates. When the Star Chamber was abolished, printers, relieved of fear of political prosecution, began to issue copies of MPs' speeches, then weekly bulletins of events at Westminster. Within a week rival news-sheets appeared (*Diurnall Occurrences*, *True Diurnall Occurrences*, a number of *Mercuries*).[34] The birth of the English press occurred precipitately in the year that Milton took to pamphleteering. At the same time, and contributing to the near-simultaneity of the written word with the events recorded, a form of shorthand came into public use, known as stenography or tachygraphy. Shorthand had been known to the Greeks and Romans, and was current in the Middle Ages, but during the revolutionary years of the seventeenth century in England it came to play a crucial part in the dissemination of current news to a mass readership. Parliamentary proceedings, King Charles I's trial and the famous 'Putney Debates' of the New Model Army in 1647, were taken down verbatim in shorthand.[35] Taking at dictation, a procedure which serves as a metaphor in *Areopagitica* for Roman Catholic indoctrination (see page 31 above), is however presented in *Paradise Lost* as the process by which he receives the poem from his Muse who 'dictates to me slumbering, or inspires / Easy my unpremeditated verse' (IX. 23–4). Milton becomes the passive scrivener to his active Muse, the vehicle rather than the source of his poem's truth – responsible to his God as the pen is responsible to the hand that guides it. The vivid immediacy and luminous ease of the experience of receiving fully formed, authoritative messages from his unconscious mind are wonderfully captured in the image of 'dictation'. The blind poet then coded the message in his memory until he could in turn dictate it to an amanuensis. During the Civil Wars and Interregnum, the taking-down and dissemination of events in writing had given modern-seeming centrality to words-in-print, and at the same time closed the gap between language on the tongue, with its fluent openness to variant possibilities, and language on the page in its immutable definiteness. Speech is language on the wing, a process of becoming; Milton's mature poetry impresses readers with its artful mimesis of the urgent immediacy of the unfinished verbal and historical event. Kerrigan speaks of *Paradise Lost* as a poem always coming into existence now, suspended between origin and end, a universal prolepsis, the promise of everything.[36] This immediacy was first generated by a prose reaction to the flux and instability of the 1640s, the age of the ratification of the ephemeral moment in the news-sheets, pamphlets and shorthand transcriptions. Shorthand fixed the indecipherable, unstable moment; it transcribed a riddle. When King Charles escaped from Oxford in April 1646, his armies beaten, in disguise as a serving man, John Cleveland the Cavalier poet lamented: 'Oh the accurst Stenographie of fate! / The Princely Eagle shrunke into a Bat.'[37] Moment-by-moment the world changed, often absurdly and grotesquely, inverting ancient norms and the codes which accounted for them. God's handwriting on the universe had taken on for the generation of the 1640s a volatile inscrutability which writers on both sides wrestled to clarify.

Finally there remains the question of secret codes.[38] Writing can be a means of passing secret messages between members of a given group whilst at the same time concealing them from others. As a privileged, initiated form of communication, it can so angle itself as to transmit to an elect readership what it hides from, confuses or leaves open for others. This is the 'stenographie' of Charles I's disguise in Cleveland's poem, hiding his royal emblem as eagle under the camouflaging sign of an anonymous 'lower' creature that flies by night. In the Civil Wars and the intrigue-riven years of the Restoration, secret codes became a norm of political discourse; in the personal sphere, Pepys used short-hand in the Diaries as a private code. One of his correspondents, Dr Vincent, perfected an invention for the message so secret that it vanishes: 'a way of writing which can never be deciphered. It beares the reading, but a very few Minutes, and then its characters vanish . . . by which meanes the writer is secured . . . against Curiosity, sawciness or Accidental discoveries'[39] Milton's later poems also manifest 'a way of writing which can never be deciphered', not by means of vanishing hieroglyphs but because his inscriptions have been purposefully blurred by the author so as to allow for political readings which however are never actively endorsed or legitimised. *Paradise Lost, Paradise Regained* and *Samson Agonistes* are open and mysterious poems partly because they were written as an underground literature by a member of a suppressed and silenced resistance under Restoration persecution. To insinuate a political message through the severe censorship, Milton was constrained to adopt a cryptic and enigmatic code and to refrain from supplying an adequate key. One of Milton's biographers, John Toland, claimed that the first edition came near to being suppressed:

> I must not forget that we had like to be eternally depriv'd of this Treasure by the Ignorance or Malice of the Licenser; who, among other frivolous Exceptions, would needs suppress the whole Poem for imaginary Treason in the following lines.
>   –As, when the Sun new risen
>   Looks thro the Horizontal misty Air

> Shorn of his Beams, or from behind the Moon
> In dim Eclipse disastrous Twilight sheds
> On half the Nations, and with fear of change
> Perplexes Monarchs.[40]

In the passage Toland quotes, the court censor must have smelt an oblique reference to the regicide. Surely it rang an alarm bell in his mind because it expressed so exquisitely the unease that generates censorship in the first place ('fear of change'), together with the state of mind in which the censor must grapple with coded threats likely to be implied in a literature of multiple meaning ('perplexity'), whose militant under-meanings might ignite the fuse of a combustible readership in a world which has demonstrated the practical efficacy of words to shadow events in 'dim Eclipse'. An underground writer is suspected to be addressing an underground readership.

Such a mode of writing naturally widens the parameters of interpretation while it narrows the possibility of ascribing definitive meaning to the whole or its parts. It opens the poems to radical interpretation by the choice of apocalyptic stories whose narrative conflicts structure party battles leading to punitive denouements such as the fall of Satan in *Paradise Regained* and the demolition of the Philistine Temple in *Samson Agonistes*, catastrophes in which 'we' (an alliance of narrative or choric voice, protagonist and reader) trounce 'them' (representatives of the ruling élite apparently victorious in this world). It further solicits radical interpretation by inviting the reader to make specific application of large general principles such as the attacks on kings and the credulous, self-interested common people in *Paradise Lost* and *Paradise Regained*, as well as the subtle incorporation of labels and formulae drawn from Scripture in the first place for common usage as weapons in political controversy (Charles I as Nimrod or Moloch, the Cavaliers as 'sons of Belial'), and returned to the original narrative carrying their accreted significations subversively back with them – making allegorical readings available but not compulsory. At the same time, through the intentional obliquity and the inevitable disparities between the stories and the political meanings we conjecture them as intending to convey, radical interpretation is constantly thwarted or veiled by opposite-seeming implications. Metaphor and the simile always by their very nature introduce extraneous and disparate elements into comparisons, importing unlikeness as a condition of likeness, and not even an intended allegory such as those of Dante or Spenser can produce uncomplicated consistency between the message and the image which is its agent.

In Milton's hands, literature became a kind of guerrilla activity. Masking its subversive intent behind the classical respectability of epic and tragic genres and the obedience of sacred art to Scripture, his later poetry used its impeccable forms and the authoritative piety of its manner as camouflage for making safe, incendiary raids on the dictatorship of institutionalised belief. Epic has traditionally been understood as a conservative and backward-looking genre, but it may also function, as Joan Webber has shown,[41] as a subversive form, generating resistance to authority through calculated obliquity of utterance. Milton's Christian epic, *Paradise Lost*, appears to take place in the walled-off and well-fortified ancient past – indeed, the most remote past of all, our prehistoric beginnings. The story feigns to be sequestered from present history and to end with the opening of history (Adam's and Eve's walk out of Eden into the landscape of our world in the last paragraph). But the narrative is not simple and linear: it is circular and multiple, making detours and excursions through a radical use of the epic apparatus into many places and epochs. The poem is cunning and manipulative in its use of insinuation, veiled threat, barbed implication and the guardedly indeterminate direction of rage and blame at persons or parties who may be recognised by readers. The personal Invocations (Books, I, III, VII, and IX) link the ancient story to Milton in the 1660s, 'on evil days . . . fallen' (VII. 26). The final two Books render a synoptic account of the cycles of human history read in the light of the first rebellion of 'King' Satan against his God. The major characters bear obscure and complex but compelling relationship to contemporary figures (Satan as demagogue/lawless monarch; the rigged 'Parliament' of Pandemonium in Book II as satire on the Parliaments of the 1650s or alternatively of Charles I's Council of State). The epic similes are corridors of subversion and espionage, down which the narrator darts to link the immemorial with the historical. Other traditional epic devices such as the use of mythological allusion (anything but 'ornamental' in Milton's strenuous adaptation) and even the epic catalogue are easily readable as acts of literary sabotage. Readers have been known to skip the catalogue of fallen angels which interrupts – or seems to interrupt – the story in Book I. But the epic catalogue is simply the first of the poem's many thrusts forward into history, not breaking but transposing the narrative into another time-scale, or scales. The descriptions of the false gods and idols bristles with innuendo:

> First Moloch, horrid king besmeared with blood
> Of human sacrifice
> ....
>   Next came one
> Who mourned in earnest, when the captive ark
> Maimed his brute image, head and hands lopped off
> In his own temple, on the groundsel edge,
> Where he fell flat, and shamed his worshippers
> ....
> In courts and palaces he also reigns
> And in luxurious cities, where the noise
> Of riot ascends above their loftiest towers,
> And injury and outrage: and when night
> Darkens the streets, then wander forth the sons
> Of Belial, flown with insolence and wine.
>   (I. 392–3; 457–61; 497–502)

Properties in the eyes of readers can make words on a page flame up or sit flat and neutral to one another in an innocuous row. Milton's generation of republicans had known Charles I as 'that man of blood', fratricidally massacring his own people. To such a reader a reference to a 'horrid king besmeared with blood' might have stained the page a momentary red with the memories it stirred. Milton saw Charles as clothed in a bloody garment shed by his subjects:

> dipt from head to foot and staind over with the blood of thousands that were his faithfull subjects, forc'd to thir own defence against a civil Warr by him first rais'd upon them, and to receive him thus, in this goarie pickle, to all his dignities and honours, covering the ignominious and horrid purple-robe of innocent blood that sate so close about him, with the glorious purple of Royaltie and Supreme Rule . . .
>
>   (*Eikonoklastes*, CPW. III. 595)

Charles I was also commonly condemned as an idol or self-elected god, and his followers as idol-worshippers. The second quoted passage concerning Thammuz celebrates with cold relish the humiliation and toppling of a truncated idol and its worshippers: an image of punitive amputation proves the scathing efficacy of the Sword of Justice with which Milton believed God rules history. A reader in the reign of Charles II might, subliminally or consciously, recall the decapitation of the first Charles. In the third quotation, the narrative voice without warning switches from past to present tense. Belial, the 'lewd' spirit, found a permanent home in courts and palaces, where he not only reigned but reigns; at night the 'sons / Of Belial' roam the streets, arrogant, drunk, raucous and looking for trouble. The powerful impression of modernity in this image of urban life must have been all the more intense for a contemporary reader, given that the Cavaliers had been popularly known as 'sons of Belial' by the opposing faction. Their reputation for hard drinking, ferocious swearing and unrestrained amorosity and bellicosity was inherited by the hell-raisers of the Restoration court.[42]

Such interpretation, based on sharp twinges of historical recognition, is inferential, conditional upon the sense of coded meaning in poetry whose language, rooted in the immediacy of a divisive present, takes the form of absolutely devious and circuitous confession. A profoundly connotative and affective discourse opens the poem to a rich possibility of multiple interpretation, whilst withholding the expository signs which would validate radical political readings and so prevent its own publication. Milton composed in *Paradise Lost* a problematic poem capable of outwitting detection but guaranteed to needle and agitate suspicion. These politically-motivated linguistic factors combine with the other problematising factors (multiple perspective, relativism, radical grammar, the artist's cloven allegiances and mixed emotions) to free the poetry from its own monumental fixity of design, so that we are led to make and remake it with every fresh reading.

2

Before the Revolution: Fear of Failure

Let us imagine that Milton died upon his return from his Continental tour in 1639:

> News he received from *England*, that Affairs there were tending toward a Civil War; thinking it a thing unworthy in him to be taking his Pleasure in Foreign Parts, while his Countrymen at home were Fighting for their Liberty . . .[1]

If we fictionally sink his ship in the Channel on the home journey, history will be innocent of *Poems, 1645* (the collection of his early poems, including *Comus* and *Lycidas*), the prose works, *Paradise Lost, Paradise Regained* and *Samson Agonistes*. It is not unlikely that the waters of oblivion would have closed over the head of the works completed before the Civil Wars, as he so feared they might, sinking without trace like so many perishable openings to inconclusive careers, or briefly brought to the surface of our attention as rare curiosities of the day, comparable with the greatly gifted one-off jobs so familiar from the seventeenth century such as Lord Herbert of Cherbury's *Ode Upon A Question Moved* or Edmund Waller's *Song*. For there is no doubt that a canon is established by reading backwards, and that the empyrean of value set by Milton's later epic and tragic works has carried up for the reading public the earlier works, in their lower (in a traditional sense, apprentice) genres of pastoral, carol, encomium and masque. Virgil's *Eclogues* and *Georgics* awaited consummation in the *Aeneid*: *Comus* and *Lycidas* are received by us not as post-Spenserian and post-Jonsonian relics but as compositions belonging to the ripeness of a completed life's work. Blasphemous though it may appear, even the committed lover of Milton is sometimes visited by the suspicion that some of Milton's earlier works scarcely justify the linked praise and exegesis which have been lavished on them. One very salient effect of killing Milton in his thirty-second year is to reveal how little the prodigy had hazarded of himself prior to the Revolution, in a period of low life expectancy.

Milton's earlier works betray, recurrently if not invariably, a fear of failure which haunts them like a shadow. The talent from which they proceed seems blighted by its own great gifts and greater aspirations. The temperament of a pitilessly self-magnifying, self-reproving high-achiever emerges from the poems which pre-date the 1640s, a perfectionist who has set himself a task fulfilling to the ego but potentially crippling to the will. Preoccupation with Time presses upon the youthful Milton. No sooner has he attained to young manhood than he is worried by intimations of premature atrophy. A fear of immaturity as barrenness pervades the early sonnet, 'How soon hath Time'. It will be all too possible to miss opportunities that only occur once in our lifetime; inexplicably, one may fall behind in the race for the laurels of achievement. Other spirits, 'more timely-happy', do not know this premonition of ultimate sterility such as wastes the surcharged genius of a prodigy before his unique message may be made known. The phenomenon of the infant mathematician or musician burnt out in adolescence is a familiar enough phenomenon to us. In fact Milton was no such prodigy. His earliest recorded poems, written at the age of 15, are metricated versions of two Psalms (114 and 136), both of which deal with the deliverance of the Chosen People. Congregations still give rousing voice to the latter:

> Let us with a gladsome mind
> Praise the Lord, for he is kind
> > For his mercies ay endure
> > Ever faithful, ever sure.

Versified Psalms are a popular form requiring simplicity, rhythmic lilt
and vividness. Milton's Psalm 136 carried a quality of arresting
immediacy, recalling and praising Jehovah's mercies and acts of fidelity
and reassurances to the Chosen People as a sequence of brightly
imagistic mnemonics, with debts to the Elizabethans, especially Spenser, and a vernacular Bible-reader's English. At 19, he opened an elegy
to his sister Anne's dead baby, with a flourish of Spenserianism, the
unforgettable:

> O fairest flower, no sooner blown but blasted,
> Soft silken primrose, fading timelessly . . .

but the preciously mythologised allegory which follows the mellifluous
delicacy of the opening is eminently forgettable. The poet who felt
himself from an early age to be the chosen vessel of Divine inspiration
in fact seems to have experienced the condition of chosenness as
arduous and agitating, and he produced little save academic exercises
in Latin or English, until the beautiful Ode, *On The Morning of Christ's
Nativity*, written at the age of 21.

The *Ode* records a tense and complex knot of attitudes to Time in a
voice of mellifluous sweetness. It celebrates beginnings as sanctuaries
or retreats, to which the lyric voice longs to return, that it may forever
delay the necessity to exit from the benign circle of Nativity into the
crises of Time. Past and present tenses feign to accord at this moment
of breathless transition (I. 1–3); the imagined music of the angel choirs
at the Nativity, reproduced in the poet's song, permits the blessed
illusion that 'Time will run back, and fetch the age of gold' (XIV.
135). Through the concept of Christian history as a pattern of cyclical
recurrence, Milton palimpsestically imprints both Creation (the beginning of Time) and the Last Judgement (its end) on the Incarnation,
the mediatorial, liminal moment of intersection betweeen God and
man. The poem's circular structure mimetically reinforces this yearning
for simultaneity, and the sense of hush and stasis as past and future
balance upon their common centre. In the complexity of the word
now, the poet celebrates the capacity of our mental processes to
prolong or replay a single moment indefinitely:

> Now while the heaven, by the sun's team untrod,
>   Hath took no print of the approaching light,
>   And all the spangled host keep watch in squadrons bright?
>   (III. 19–21)

Now identifies a cyclical moment of eternal transition: the annual *now* of 24–25 December which transiently returns to source in the birth of the holy child; the precise *now* of Christmas Day 1629, shortly after Milton's own twenty-first birthday, as the poet watched for the dawn from his window; the reader's arbitrary *now* which recurrently appropriates the poet's in the moment of reading. The *Ode* has a tone of personal tenderness and reverence intrinsic to its neo-Spenserian music of carefully-wrought stanzas, with their elegant personifications, miniature allegories and conceits – a Spenser recollected through the austerely beautiful but essentially regressive modulations of Giles Fletcher's *Christs Victorie, and Triumph* (1610),[2] rather as we catch the spirit of Bach through C.P.E. Bach, or Mozart through Hummel, an echoing mimesis rather than the organic transformation worked by Beethoven. These musical analogies may point up the intimate closeness of Milton's poetry at this stage to a cherished source: intimations of the powerfully original music of *Paradise Lost* such as may be detected in phrasings like 'that light unsufferable' (II) are strictly retrospective. The intricate harmonies of this poem, which makes the circling music of the spheres a central theme (IX–XIV), is self-protective, sealed by the infolding concentricities of its formal organisation which seeks in multiple stanza-closures and the total cyclical structure sanctuary from the flux of history.[3] From this poem of fresh but suspended beginnings he moved, at 22 or 23, to the contemplative reclusiveness of the lovely paired *L'Allegro* and *Il Penseroso*. Here a Jonsonian classicising imagination redeems for the literature of all time a form of poetry inflicted as an exercise on every disgruntled schoolboy of Milton's age, the *encomium*, with its elaborate rules of composition. Milton demonstrates an absolute virtuosity and grace in the freedom with which he releases his octosyllabic couplets (a potentially rigid, staccato form) into fluidity, 'In notes with many a winding bout / Of linked sweetness long drawn out' (*L'Allegro*, 139–40). The twinned parallel and opposite poems reflect upon states of mind in one who exists (whether in light or dark moods) always in

67

thoughtful isolation from his kind, a constitutional outsider who is an onlooker, or, as the central images of the sequestered tower imply, a fugitive in-looker whose inmost nature remains abstrusely hidden from the curious eye of the reader:

> Towers and battlements it sees
> Bosomed high in tufted trees,
> Where perhaps some beauty lies,
> The cynosure of neighbouring eyes.
>
> Or let my lamp at midnight hour
> Be seen in some high lonely tower,
> Where I may oft outwatch the Bear,
> With thrice-great Hermes, or unsphere
> The spirit of Plato . . .
> (*L'Allegro*, 77–80; *Il Penseroso*, 85–9)

At the literal centre of each poem is an inscrutable space, taking the form in *L'Allegro* of an imaginative area of pleasurable hypothesis and in *Il Penseroso* a withdrawing-space for solitary reading and incommunicable thoughts.

Much of Milton's early poetry centres on an inspiration taken from the heart of self-doubt: he sings with sublime confidence of the difficulty of song:

> How soon hath time, the subtle thief of youth,
>   Stol'n on his wing my three and twentieth year!
>   My hasting days fly on with full career,
>   But my late spring no bud or blossom sheweth.
> Perhaps my semblance might deceive the truth,
>   That I to manhood am arrived so near,
>   And inward ripeness doth much less appear,
>   That some more timely-happy spirits endueth.
> Yet be it less or more, or soon or slow,
>   It shall be still in strictest measure even
>   To that same lot, however mean or high,
> Toward which Time leads me, and the will of Heaven;
>   All is, if I have grace to use it so,
>   As ever in my great task-master's eye.

Young manhood is the season of potency and generation, towards which the octave seems to strain. The composed, urbane manner which attunes the self to the sonnet hardly masks the jittery feeling which inspired it: an acute and apparently constitutional self-consciousness about the power to generate 'bud or blossom' implies anxiety about the sexual drive that can be an energy-source for poetry. Uncertainty about maleness in the octet is answered by the turn in the sestet. From active pursuer of his career, always running along his own wake, the Miltonic persona exchanges an inimical Time for a providential Time. He yields himself to authority, becoming an active abstainer from choice, under correction from the Omniscience that oversees all men's works. In the sestet, the wrought-up strain superficially eases, though anxiety remains. The chastened will is constrained by God the task-master. From seasonal imagery of springtime fertility, a spontaneous natural process within Nature, the sonnet has moved into a fugitive acquiescence in the Protestant work-ethic, conditional upon the Divine Authority but also conditional upon the problematic 'if I have grace to use it so'. Personal grace may or may not be forthcoming. The sonnet, which appears to resolve the issues it raises, therefore, fails to achieve inward assurance. It records a doubt about the sources of creativity which foreshadows the barren inertia of Coleridge's 'Work Without Hope' and the testament of Hopkins' 'Terrible Sonnets', with their fruitless straining after productivity:

> And I the while, the sole unbusy thing,
> Nor honey make, nor pair, nor build, nor sing.
> ('Work Without Hope', 5–6)

> Birds build – but not I build; no, but strain,
> Time's eunuch, and not breed one work that wakes.
> Mine, O thou lord of Life, send my roots rain.
> ('Thou Art Indeed Just', 12–14)[4]

But Coleridge and Hopkins were both in middle age when they struggled with this sense of impotence; Milton, galvanised by the eye of a great task-master far more forbidding than encouraging, is one of the gelded elect in the prime of his life. He is unique in composing his valedictory *before the event*.

In *Comus*, written three years later, a theme surfaces which bears upon this complex of creative anxiety. It is notable that the two most celebrated poems of Milton's earlier career, *Comus* and *Lycidas*, were both occasional and commissioned poems, the one a masque for the inauguration of the Earl of Bridgwater as President of Wales (1634), the other a contribution to the volume of Latin, Greek and English elegies *Justa Edouardo King* (1638). These works were in some sense fetched from him by an external human agency, bypassing whatever block it was that made the life sources difficult of access to the younger Milton.[5] *Comus* as a masque is also founded on generic rules and expectations, as well as theatrical and economic exigencies, the form offering the poet a stable basis of security such as the questors of his poem need to affirm: 'if this fail,' says the Elder Brother, reflecting on God's justice, 'The pillared firmament is rottenness / And earth's base built on stubble' (597–9). A secure, ceremonious and ritualised form tells a story of risk, loss of bearings and extreme vulnerability – rape providentially prevented. But the masque in Milton's hands violates its nature as surface and embellishment and turns inwards and upwards for its energies. The masque had a royalist pedigree and a traditionally sumptuous and expensive material splendour. Milton smashes this flattering gilded mirror, producing what was in effect a contradiction in terms: a sacred masque. The Puritan masque as testament of inwardness sets in dynamic motion a *psychomachia* of Chastity against Fecundity, Temperance against Excess, which displays on either side elements of the Miltonic struggle.

The subject of the masque was undoubtedly fathered upon Milton by his employers, the Egerton family, the choice of Chastity as a topic being possibly related to the Castlehaven scandal which had darkened the illustrious family name with the imputation of sexual crime.[6] But it was a subject which had an unusual personal significance to Milton, who gives us to understand that he remained a virgin until his marriage in 1642, when he was 34. In an age when female chastity was obligatory but male chastity a joke, Milton from 'a certaine nicenesse of nature, an honest haughtinesse, and self-esteem, either of what I was or what I might be' affirmed an intense personal commitment to sexual restraint in a male, in whom unchastity 'must, though commonly not so thought, be much more deflouring and dishonourable' than in the female (*An Apology for Smectymnuus*, *CPW*. I. 891, 892).

The grounds of this assertion lie in the Scripturally endorsed superiority of the male as being fashioned in the direct image of God. *Comus*, earlier by eight years than this disclosure, presents a female embodiment of this virtue in the Spenserian personification of the Lady. Milton himself, Aubrey records, was as a young man 'so faire y^t they called him the Lady of X^{ts} coll.'[7] This delicate, soft-faced person, who thought that the author of poetry 'ought himself to bee a true Poem' (*ibid.*, 890) invested in the security of his own inviolacy of more-than-womanly emotional capital. He seems to have suspected that there was a woman lurking somewhere within him: a worrying and aggressively denied but perhaps secretly valuable intimation of androgynous wholeness of being.[8] Modern feminist readings of the vitriolic rage manifested by the male agonists of his later works – especially the Adam of *Paradise Lost* and the hero of *Samson Agonistes* – have read this misogynistic ire as a hypermasculinity which 'would unveil its infantile source in its identification with a Father who appears, as always to a child, all-mighty'.[9] Something of the savage anguish of *Samson Agonistes*, that monument to male infirmity, I shall see as generated by the need to extrude a female who is named as Dalila but experienced as an intrinsic part of the suffering self.

In the period of the earlier poetry that power to express rage which becomes such an important constituent of Milton's mature narrative voice has not been catalysed. Sleek couplets, dancing Spenserian measures, classicist urbanity and a harmonically subtle blank verse inherited from Renaissance dramatic poets, especially Shakespeare, are the resourceful vehicles for an emotion tempered to the measure of a superb rhetorical control. Aubrey does not record Milton's reaction to his label 'Lady' although Milton seems to accept the designation in Prolusion 6. In *Comus*, the Lady carries the full weight and value of Milton's eremitical repression and sublimation of his sexual desires. She is the Father's true child, obedient to the great task-master in withholding and hoarding her vital instincts. The arguments she advances in favour of the 'holy dictate of spare temperance' (766) extend the conception of personal chastity in the direction of public Temperance, the executive to Justice's legislature in the social world. Repression of the individual's inordinate desire in the interests of a corporate social good is unanswerably urged through an argument which stands in direct line from the socialistic Christianity of *King*

Lear. It is an extraordinary moment in the work of an author almost entirely sequestered in the privileged tower of thought from the economic predicament of the people of England whose cause he was to plead in the 1640s:

> If every just man that now pines with want
> Had but a moderate and beseeming share
> Of that which lewdly pampered Luxury
> Now heaps upon some few with vast excess,
> Nature's full blessings would be well-dispensed
> In unsuperfluous even proportion,
> And she no whit encumbered with her store,
> And then the giver be better thanked,
> His praise due paid, for swinish gluttony
> Ne'er looks to heav'n amid his gorgeous feast,
> But with besotted base ingratitude
> Crams, and blasphemes his Feeder. Shall I go on?
> Or have I said enough?
>
> (768–80)

Even so, we note that the Miltonic expression of the Temperance theme which in *Lear* assimilates the king to the condition of 'Poor naked wretches, wheresoe'er you are' (III. iv. 28), represents a fastidious and caste-bound narrowing of the scope of the Christian message. Milton never endorsed the injunctions:

> Take physic, Pomp;
> Expose thyself to feel what wretches feel,
> That thou mayst shake the superflux to them,
> And show the Heavens more just.
>
> (*King Lear*, III. iv. 33–6)

> So distribution should undo excess,
> And each man have enough.
>
> (IV. i. 69–70)

Milton never showed that he cared about the material good of the common people. He belonged to the class which persecuted, imprisoned and on occasions tortured the Levellers and Diggers who sought a system whereby the poor would be fed, clothed and housed. It is significant that the Lady's political programme does not direct attention precisely to the beggars, outcasts and wretches apostrophised by Lear without distinction of person but according to need regardless of deserts. Milton cannot get through the eye of that needle. The Lady's concern is for 'every *just* man that now pines with want' (emphasis added): the mute inglorious Miltons reduced to a calamitous destitution rather than the roaming bands of vagabonds, beggars, squatters on waste or common land, forest-dwellers, tramps, gipsies and the tens of thousands of those whom society in a phase of violent economic transition had turned into rejects. These victims of eviction and enclosure formed the basis of the community on behalf of which the Levellers and Diggers of the late 1640s and early 1650s – Walwyn, Winstanley, Overton, Wildman – were to question the basis of property-society as founded on legalised theft:

> If any man can say that he makes Corn or Cattle, he may say, That is mine: But if the Lord makes these for the use of his Creation, surely then the earth was made by the Lord, to be a common Treasury for all, not a particular Treasury for some.[10]

The communistic idea of the earth as a 'common Treasury' is not so far removed from Milton's Lady's vision of a society in which the few gorge themselves 'with vast excess' to the detriment of the majority. But the Lady (the representative of an aristocratic, propertied family) implies less a social programme than an ideal of Temperance, with something of a classicist utopianism. In her well-measured speech, she speaks decorously on behalf of a frugal Mother Nature who exhibits those virtues dear to middle-class puritanism: thrift, moderation, hard work and self-restraint. Milton's emphasis on the right of 'every *just* man' to a fair share of natural resources reminds us at once of his concern for 'the people' and his (typically seventeenth-century) interpretation of 'the people' as either the nation *minus* the working class and servant class, or (a complex variation on this theme) the élite of the saints *minus* all reprobated persons, a classification which depends on the prejudices and sympathies of the individual.[11] Milton's presentation of social justice as a by-product of Chastity in the masque asserts the just to be the chaste – an elect defended by mystical powers.

73

Justice is an aspect of that sexual self-restraint upon which Milton prided himself, and with which he no doubt to some degree crippled himself throughout the period of early manhood. *Comus* testifies at once to the gains and the dangers of such self-preservation.

The Lady's excellent sobriety is countered in *Comus* by what readers gloss as sexual libertinism. But Comus' attitude is, strictly speaking, no easy alternative to the Lady's strenuous frugality with herself. Rather, the tempter offers a kind of dazzling cautionary nightmare based on the ill effects of surcharge. His temptation to the Lady in the original form of the acting manuscript omitted the conventional *carpe diem* message inserted in the 1645 version ('List, lady, be not coy . . .' [736–55]) which owes so much to Jonson, Marlowe and Donne. The focus of Comus' seduction-speech seems to this reader to draw power from the activation of a constitutional Miltonic anxiety, which can be located at every stage of his development, but which must have been peculiarly agitating in the phase of early manhood. It is a fear lest a fertility which is held back, in the body and by implication in the heart and spirit, of the creative personality, should go bad. Superabundant potency, unexpressed, will choke the whole being in a monstrous thrusting out of the denied life-force. Milton's nightmare is a kind of parallel opposite to the modern well-founded fear of the death of our planet from pollution and over-exploitation: and it is equally well-founded. Milton could not be freed from this terror until the process of stigmatisation that occurred during the 1650s and 1660s had freed his will from the baffling fear of failure, by ensuring that he had – in an all but literal sense – nothing left to lose. In *Comus*, the fear is still enthralling:

> if all the world
> Should in a pet of temperance feed on pulse,
> Drink the clear stream, and nothing wear but frieze,
> Th'all-giver would be unthanked, would be unpraised,
> Not half his riches known, and yet despised,
> And we should serve him as a grudging master,
> As a penurious niggard of his wealth,
> And live like Nature's bastards, not her sons,
> Who would be quite surcharged with her own weight,
> And strangled with her waste fertility;
> The earth cumbered, and the winged air darked with plumes;

The herds would over-multitude their lords,
The sea o'erfraught would swell, and the unsought diamonds
Would so emblaze the forehead of the deep,
And so bestud with stars, that they below
Would grow inured to light, and come at last
To gaze upon the sun with shameless brows.

(719–35)

Line 731, in a metrical revelation of the imagery it must but cannot contain, bursts its own confines by expansion from orthodox pentameter extended by elision and feminine ending. If we imagine 'Nature' as a figure of speech for the inner cosmos of the psyche, we encounter a nightmare of excess productivity, in which generation in the fullest sense (of articulation, ridding oneself of latency) is precluded. The *Comus* neurosis concerns the bounding of the illimitable within a limited universe, infinity bottled in the finite: the womb teeming with undisclosable conceptions. In this pre-temporal enclosure, nothing can die because nothing has been truly born. The failure to expel and disperse the earth-darkening clouds of birds ('the winged air darked with plumes') which have become sinister merely by virtue of their multitudinousness; the saturnalian rout of order by the swollen numbers of the lower creatures; the crazy multiplication of diamonds that replicate the light of Heaven to the inhabitants of Hell, present a kind of Malthusian psychology of creativity. Two opposing concepts of Nature are invoked by the antagonists of *Comus*: the Lady's *lex natura*, Comus' *natura naturans*. Her world is inscribed by immortal laws; his is mortal and generative, but robbed of the blessed capacity to die. The natural processes of ripening and decay make room for new lives. Milton disturbs his reader with a vision of plenitude which serves as a figure for the mind unrelieved of its 'waste fertility', the virgin body tense with unexpressed libido. The prime of life has come for the poet (as in 'How soon hath Time'), the appropriate time for the discharge of energy, but the self secretes its promise, and finds no vessel extrinsic to itself generous enough to receive the potentiality it hoards.

In his later life, Milton was heard jokingly to assimilate the creative process with that of animal nature in its lactatory function (see page 4 above). He would awaken early and lie waiting for his amanuensis to rise and take dictation of the poetry which the replenishment of sleep and dream had allowed to accumulate overnight. Being entirely blind, he could not commit this 'good Stock of Verses' to paper independently, and hence would grumble at his secretary's belatedness, 'Saying, *hee wanted to bee milkd*'.[12] By this time, the writer's block was years in the past: composition had taken on the form of a natural compensatory activity in a mind confident in its life-sources and allegiances. The poet of *Comus* allocates sexual and sensual pleasure and spontaneous fertility to the demonic powers. Natural growth is suspect as implying an organic uncontrollability as devouring to contemplate as a whole oak-forest struggling in an acorn, silkworms by the million undoing themselves into expensive human vesture. The nightmare of excess fertility is implicitly linked (perhaps through an implied pun on *spend*, male ejaculation which is accounted 'The expense of spirit in a waste of shame')[13] with a nightmare of capitalism. Nature is an industrial system producing a vast surplus of commodities:

> Wherefore did Nature pour her bounties forth,
> With such a full and unwithdrawing hand,
> Covering the earth with odours, fruits, and flocks,
> Thronging the seas with spawn innumerable,
> But all to please, and sate the curious taste?
> And set to work millions of spinning worms,
> That in their green shops weave the smooth-haired silk
> To deck her sons; and that no corner might
> Be vacant of her plenty, in her own loins
> She hutched the all-worshipped ore and precious gems
> To store her children with . . .
>
> (709–19)

A *hutch* was a chest or coffer for the storage of valuables. Milton's usage of the root as a transitive verb touches off a richly suggestive wordplay with *hatch*, mingling organic processes (Nature's loins busy with the secretion of gold) with mechanical. The industrious silkworms in their quaint *green shops* exemplify a world-system as a great commercial enterprise set up to gratify the hedonistic appetites of a limitlessly consumer-oriented courtly and aristocratic society. Milton may be recalling Tourneur's unforgettable interrogation of the deathshead:

> Does the silk-worm expend her yellow labours
> For thee? for thee does she undo herself?[14]

Society's rotting skeleton enrobes itself in the allure of silk. In Milton too there is emphasis on grotesque display covering intrinsic rottenness; man's exploitation of Nature turns it into a factory to produce luxury articles for the few, while the many (as the Lady will retort) starve. In the light of this vision of moral squalor, and in relation to a concept of the mercantile manufacture of unnecessary artifacts, *natura naturans* which 'pours her bounties forth' so as to cover the earth with creaturely life and fill the seas with emergent young, takes on a quality of unease amounting to threat.[15]

Three decades later, the poet of *Paradise Lost* was able to pass the materials of creativity, so deeply suspect in *Comus*, from his left hand over to his right. Sexuality is presented in Books IV and V as sacramental: touch and taste are the divine enjoyments of Eden. Superabundant love calls for generous physical expression, and the language is available to articulate this productive delight:

> Our Maker bids increase; who bids abstain
> But our destroyer, foe to God and man?
> Hail, wedded love . . .
>
> (IV. 748–50)

Paradise Lost is a married poem, celebrating sexual intimacy. Adam and Eve are 'Imparadised in one another's arms' (IV. 506). The poem's defences are all down. Fertility in the great hexaemeral Book VII is liberated from the suspicion under which it lay of belonging to the Devil's party. Here it is celebrated as a principle which manifests the Divine Good. The Book is a song of Becoming, each creature making the fullest possible expression of its potential for selfhood in a world in which there is more than enough space for all variables. In this plenitude without over-crowding, Milton transfers Comus' phrasings nearly verbatim from the demonic to the divine. Comus' 'Thronging the seas with spawn innumerable' (713) becomes the innocent earth's response to the Divine Fiat:

Forthwith the sounds and seas, each creek and bay
With fry innumerable swarm . . .

(VII. 399–400)

In this dream of origins, prodigal abundance is trusted as 'unsuper-fluous': the creative personality has confidence in a Divine power to bring its conceptions to birth, and permits them to ripen to maturity.

The last major English poem Milton composed before the nearly twenty-year silence was *Lycidas*. He was now nearly 29 years-old, and had engaged himself to lament the death of a 25 year-old contemporary, Edward King, a fellow-graduate of Christ's College, Cambridge, who had been drowned in a shipwreck in the Irish Sea. King emerges in the course of the poem as a kind of twin, double or alter ego for the elegist, upon whom to project the shadow of his own sense of unfulfilled endeavour. The theme of blighted prematurity ironically called forth his ripest powers. At least since the *Lament for Bion*, attributed to Moschus, the pastoral elegy had issued a generic invitation to the practitioner to mourn *as a poet* another poet's death, and to draw from this identification of twinned writing selves reflections upon the function of poetry in a mortal universe:

> Thrice-beloved, who now will play your pipe?
> Who will put your flute to his mouth?
> What man would dare? For your lips and your breath
> live on; the sound of your music still echoes
> in those reeds
>
> . . . .
>
>   For I am no stranger
> to pastoral song, but a pupil of yours,
> an heir to your Dorian style,
> honoured, when others inherited
> your wealth, to be left your music.[16]

Poetry, then, is an important subject of the pastoral elegy. Milton's *Lycidas* shares this preoccupation: it is a self-consciously scripted poem, which contemplates its own processes in the act of creation. In *Lycidas*, Milton laments himself as a survivor, who has outlived the younger promise of the drowned youth, and who pre-experiences in the recapitulation of that foregone event his own extinction. The

poem's derangement of tenses enacts the complexity of the relationship between past, present and future Time, and between narrative
and experienced Time, which haunted him throughout his career.
The elegy ties an unhappy knot out of a complication of tenses,
predicated on the violation of an early present by an anachronistically
premature future: autumn in spring, mortal sickness in bud and lamb.
Like his niece dying of a cough, and his 23-year-old self fruitless in his
prime, the poet of *Lycidas* looks back after the event at a world
waiting expectantly prior to the event: but there is no event. The
nightmare here is not of excess fertility but of the unique chance
missed.

The early paragraphs have the precipitancy which belongs to intense
frustration. There is that odd sense of circuitousness which can be
generated in us by future perfect verbs: *I shall have done*:

> Yet once more, O ye laurels, and once more
> Ye myrtles brown, with ivy never sere,
> I come to pluck your berries harsh and crude,
> And with forced fingers rude,
> Shatter your leaves before the mellowing year.
>
> (1–5)

The conjugation of Time is violated by the retaliatory actions of the
poet's hands as they rifle the vegetation which should yield the mature
crown of poetry in due course; but may not be trusted to do so. The
emotion is vengeful but also self-scorning and impotent. 'Forced fingers
rude' rape insentient Nature to no purpose: her mellifluous process of
'mellowing' is intransigently dumb to any graceless interference, sealed
as she is in the cycle of the seasons, a self-reflexive process of birth,
degeneration and renewal from which pastoral elegy has always
lamented man's apparent exclusion:

> But thing on earth that is of most availe,
> As vertues braunch and beauties budde,
> Reliven not for any good.[17]

In reading the first lines of *Lycidas*, we need to register the fact that
the act of violent trespass against Nature is a figurative description of

the writing of the poem. The laurels and myrtles are associated with Apollo (poetry) and Venus (love, fertility and, ironically, peace and concord): the honours due to the mature poet when he is ripe to win them. The poet should wait till fit time, but the Miltonic persona snatches them peremptorily. The 'forced fingers rude' are those which hold the pen to inscribe the words 'Yet once more'. They should not be writing: to do so is to dishonour his vocation by yet another unripe testimony. The oblique anger of Milton's apology for presuming to write at all is somewhat masked by the suavity and elegance of the irregular measure, rhyme and half-rhyme in which he moderates all emotion in *Lycidas*, in an impressive self-generated ritualising form. Never has there been a smoother act of 'Shattering'; nor a more composed 'disturbance'. Nevertheless, the opening imagery is revelatory of the real disturbance perceived in the sleek mirror this poem raises to the psyche of its creator. Towards the end of his seven-year period of studious seclusion at Hammersmith and Horton, the poet, still under the patronage of his father, is unsure of his capacity to realise his powers. The father whom he congratulated in *Ad Patrem* at the beginning of this apprenticeship was one who repeatedly affirmed that he 'hated' the Muses and could not see the point of poetry: in *Ad Patrem* the son wheedled, cajoled, flattered and argued all round his parent, that earthly regent of the 'great task-master'. Evidently some of the difficulty in attaining ripeness experienced by Milton consisted of the conflict of struggles, the effort to please and to present a model of filial obedience in a patriarchal family dragging against his covert need to emancipate his writing hand from the dead weight of paternal authority. What is *Areopagitica* but a call against the dominion of father, the refusal of a perpetual adolescence? Fathers and sons were to occupy Milton's imagination throughout his writing life. His self-division was to generate the dynamic antagonism of *Paradise Lost*: two sons of God, Christ the loyal heir of the licensing Father over against Satan the errant, revolutionary and free-thinking son of the Forbidding Father, who goes so far as to protest that he is 'self-begot' (V. 860). Light and dark selves, conscious and unconscious minds are released on to the page of *Paradise Lost*, to close and struggle there like primary cosmic forces. The sonship of Christ is the major theme of *Paradise Regained*; the father Manoa and the Father-God vital presences in *Samson Agonistes*. But before the 1650s this release of energy had not taken place under the catalyst of rage, desire, disillusion, blindness and the death in 1647 of his octogenarian father.

Paradise Lost is a poem Milton chose to write. *Lycidas* is one which he could still attribute to the coercion of forces beyond himself. The apology for the intemperate disturbance of the seasons by the unseasoned poet insists on 'constraint' and 'compulsion':

> Bitter *constraint*, and sad occasion dear,
> *Compels* me to disturb your season due
> ....
> He *must* not float upon his watery bier
> Unwept, and welter to the parching wind,
> Without the *meed* of some melodious tear.
> (6–7; 12–14; emphases added)

A music of aggressive turbulence has relieved itself in the course of the stanza and modulated into acquiescence in a proposal to provide a natural and compensatory tribute: the poem becomes a soft, saline 'tear', required by the occasion. From undue emotion, the elegist consents to exact from himself what is 'due', in the sense of a tribute demanded by the human community to its lost son. This structure is proleptic to the shape of the whole poem: the motion from bafflement through partial answers to a stressful composure; from harrowing sorrow at the irreconcilable to reconciliation to things as they are, have become and will be. The medium through which such adaptation is made is that of the symbolism of an archetypal sea whose corrosive waters of destruction are ultimately as purgative and medicinal in their saline bitterness as the creative tear their agency draws from the mourner. Such a tear is *meed*: necessary, decorous and civilised, just as a process of mourning is owing to the uninterred. The poem as a whole symbolically inters its subject, the body of Lycidas being glimpsed at three stages in its descent – firstly at the surface (12–14); secondly, just at vanishing-point beneath the water (50–1); thirdly (and possibly in dismembered form) 'visiting' the sea-floor (157–8). It is hence an exercise in sublimation, the reducing of pain to an unconscious location after due and fit acknowledgement of its reality. Finally, in the unexpected emergence of the 'uncouth swain' (186), the coda recounts a literal moving-away of the mourner from the source of sorrow to a healthful rededication of himself to a future tense. *Yet once more* turns to *Weep no more* (165) in the imperative and *the shepherds weep no more* (182) in obedience to that imperative. A first-person lyric voice is abandoned in favour of the detachment of third-person narrative. The present tense, with its incorporation of a sense of future perfect in its lament for the bygone, gives place to the achieved past tense. The song is consigned to the past, its status problematised and our whole reading response thrown into doubt, as if by a quotation whose first set of quotation marks has been cunningly withheld.

Lycidas, then, is mourned and consigned to the past; but the problems associated with the gifted survivor of his younger contemporary are raised rather than resolved. We have noted that the first paragraph of *Lycidas* constitutes an apology for writing at all. The second is taken up with urging himself to begin. The reluctant Muses hang back and have to be cajoled to co-operate in the enterprise. 'Begin then, sisters of the sacred well / . . . Begin . . .' (15, 17). Time, such a nervous issue in all the earlier poems, showed in the *Nativity Ode* a ductile quality which made it at once expansive and pressing:

> It was the winter wild,
> While the heaven-born child
> All meanly wrapped in the rude manger lies . . .
> (29–31)

In the cyclical moment of the Nativity, Time incarnates Eternity; the clock returns to midnight, the year to its first heart-beat, on an annual basis. The poles of tense cross in this moment of an eternal *now* and Milton, at his own life's turning, forces disparate tenses, *was* and *lies* into the momentary appearance of simultaneity. This elastic and dilating character of Time is present also in *Lycidas*, but its circularity has here contracted to a noose. The second paragraph telescopes the future to a three-line view of the poet's own attenuated life-span. He foresees himself as his own remains in a funerary vase, a terminus which another generation of poets will move beyond, just as he passes by and salutes as he goes the spent life of Lycidas:

So may some gentle muse
With lucky words favour my destined urn,
And as he passes turn,
And bid fair peace be to my sable shroud.
                    (19–22)

In this continuum of poetic tradition, the Miltonic persona stands centrally, as that which is left on earth to mark the gap made in it by his friend's passing-away; as that which will be left behind requiring the testimonial of an epitaph. To write the poem to his predecessor is to earn the tribute of his successor – in other words, a place in history. Writing *Lycidas* is in part a project to turn the author from a might-have-been to a shall-have-been. The poem, as readers have often noted,[18] is profoundly self-concerned and ego-centred, and bears witness to Milton's own hunger for 'praise' (76) and 'Fame' (78). But it is also, more affectingly, a testament to the desire for companionship which his solitary, high-principled nature was never perhaps to achieve conclusively with either man or woman. The Divorce tracts of 1643–5 would record, during the next decade, the condition of 'God-forbidd'n loneliness', 'unkindly solitarines', 'polluting sadnes' which Milton was to undergo in his search for 'the mutual enjoyment of that which the wanting soul needfully seeks' (*The Doctrine and Discipline of Divorce*, *CPW*. II. 247, 251, 258, 252). Lycidas also reflects, in the more subtle and glossy artifice of its mirror, the state of being uncompanionate. The mind of the poem in its solitude casts around over all time and over all geography – Anglesey, Lesbos, Sicily, Italy, Cambridge, Galilee, the Hebrides, Cornwall, Spain, the New Jerusalem – for security amongst these volatile seas of thought. The final Consolation secures the baptismally purged Lycidas in a companionate world, where there is sharing and reciprocity. This state is really a new version of the first, lost world. Twinned at source, Lycidas and the elegist were 'nursed upon the self-same hill' (23), with its intimation of maternal nurture. In the next world, the youth is, as it were, weaned into a community of friendliness: 'sweet societies / That sing, and singing in their glory move' (179–80). Milton's vision of his own quietus referred to a 'destined urn' which is to be greeted transiently by the equally isolated passer-by. The passer-by hardly has time to turn before he too vanishes: 'And as he passes turn', the double caesura seeming to mark the first moment of noticing the urn and the brief diversion from his own quest which is all he has time within the deftly placed and composed short line to accomplish. The final Consolation works by cancelling the estrangement of the isolated victim of Time and assimilating him to the continuum of sociable life that circles on, like an eternal present participle – 'sing, *and singing*' – perpetually.

The concern expressed in *Lycidas* over the lack of a confirming companion spirit is endorsed in the succeeding poems which pre-date the Civil Wars. In *Mansus* (1638), a Latin poem written in Naples commemorating the venerable friend and benefactor of Tasso and Marino, whom Milton met on his Continental tour, the poet announces his decision to compose an Arthurian epic. Immediately this revelation has been made, the poem searches round for reinforcement and confirmation in the task. Manso's 'old age is green with lingering blossoms' (74–5), the enabling opposite of the contradictory season of unbudding spring recorded in 'How soon hath Time'. Milton longs for a patron such as Manso, to speak 'lucky words' at his own deathbed, to ease the passage between worlds:

> O if my fate would grant to me such a friend, who knows well how to honour the votaries of Phoebus – if ever I shall call back into verse our native kings, and Arthur waging wars even under the earth, or shall tell of the great-hearted heroes united in the invincible fellowship of the table; and – if only inspiration to be with me – I shall break the Saxon battalions under British arms! And when at last I have measured the term of a not silent life and, full of years, I pay my debt to death, if that friend might stand with moist eyes beside my bed, I should be content if I might say to him as he stood there, 'Let me be your care.' He would see to it that my limbs, loosened by gray death, were gently laid to rest in a small urn. And perhaps he would carve my face in marble, binding my hair with leaves of Paphian myrtle or Parnassian laurel, and I should lie in perfect peace.
>
> (78–93)

This piece of classicising necrophilia shows Milton in a lachrymose mausoleum mood which is almost embarrassing to a reader, and which he never affected after 1640. The father-figure, Manso, is seen as a guarantor of safe-passage, a hierophantic figure easing his companion into the next world. The fantasy-father tends the dying poet in his final hours, lays him out and retains an image of him in the visible world in the form of commemorative statuary crowned with laurels. Thus secured, the justified spirit of the poet can depart for Olympus. *Mansus* dreams of the reparation of the state most feared in *Lycidas*: unripe death, the task incomplete, the laurels unearned. The lonely ego in the neo-classical fantasia of *Mansus* (which is so much more self-involved than celebratory of the distinguished Mansus) persuades itself to anticipate a late death, public acclamation, a place in history and a place of honour in Heaven. In Italy, Milton fed his imagination and gathered the support of Continental intellectuals for the composition of 'a British theme in native strains' (*Elegy for Damon*, 170–1). He ingratiated himself with eminent figures connected with the great age of classicising humanism as well as Protestant learning; he visited Galileo; he witnessed the art and architecture of the High Renaissance and the new baroque, a visual experience which was to influence the imaginative vision of *Paradise Lost* twenty years later. In Italy were born the Protestant internationalism and the European-mindedness which were to colour his attitude when he worked as Latin Secretary to the Interregnum government. Yet visions of world fame in 1638 only seem to have deepened Milton's malaise of self-doubt. *Mansus* betrays trepidation and uncertainty about the epic project which is to make his name illustrious. An epic involving Arthurian myth would have been archaic and Spenserian at this date: it would also have had pro-Royalist implications in an age where a version of the 'Tudor myth' with its Celtic allegiances was still patronised by the Stuart royal family, and where Anglo-Saxon studies (see page 33 above) were the province of republican antiquarians favouring the ancient Saxon institutions (understood to involve a species of Parliamentary system, a fairer code of law and the jury system) as against the 'Norman Yoke' imported by the Conqueror. In *Mansus*, Milton is still enrolled as the bard of the old world, a posthumous child of the Elizabethans preparing himself without entire conviction to sing its swansong. Only by risking himself in the Civil War pamphlet dispute does Milton crack this mould and find in that rough idiom a powerful modernity of voice. The uncertainty with which he must still in 1638–9 contemplate his future was only reaffirmed by the circumstances in which the *Elegy for Damon* originated: a repetition of the experience of untimely death in a friend far closer to him than Edward King, a mere acquaintance, had ever been.

Milton could not write in English to commemorate Charles Diodati's passing. He retreated to the elaborate artifices of pastoral elegy as it had been before he himself refashioned the tradition. This brittleness may be read as reflecting a more rather than less intense personal agitation at a blow struck so near. Diodati was his closest friend, perhaps his sole true friend, to whom he had confided his early aspirations and dedicated his poems. The Latin of the *Epitaphium Damonis* has a curious and grating incoherence at those points at which it treats of Milton's own poetic enterprise falling apart:

> 'Ah, may the herbs and plants perish, and the physician's arts, since they did not avail for their master! As for me, my pipe was sounding I know not what grand strain – it is now eleven nights and a day since then – perhaps I had set my lips to new pipes. But the fastenings broke, the pipes fell apart, and could no longer sustain the noble notes. Though I may reveal some vanity, yet I will tell the tale. Give place, woodlands.'
>
> (153–60)

And give place, Diodati. The voice that ministers to its own self-image crowds out the eponymous subject of the elegy but seems thoroughly unnerved by its own centrality. The verse swells full of itself but sounds most empty as it advertises in cosmopolitan Latin its project to 'sound forth a British theme in native strains' (170–1); emptier still as Milton accords the virgin Diodati a transcendental marriage reminiscent of the Marriage of the Lamb in *Lycidas*, but so unfortunately hybridised of classical and Christian elements that there is a sense neither of comfort nor of catharsis. The 'festal throngs' that 'revel under the thyrsus of Zion' (219) strike us as an odd mob of spectral Bacchanals, partaking neither of the sensuous conviction of classical mythology nor of the strenuous piety of Christian revelation. Milton's famous humanistic synthesis of Christian and pagan elements was never less satisfactorily achieved than here in the attribution of a thyrsus to Zion. That synthesis is, at its best, a vivid failure of reconciliation: it is characterised by dynamic stress and self-contradiction. In the *Epitaphium Damonis*, it is a cobbling job. We may feel that the visit to Italy (the grand effect of whose pictorial and architectural revelations would be registered in the *chiaroscuro*, *trompe-l'œil*, Palladian perfection of construction and baroque richness and stress of articulation two decades later in *Paradise Lost*) has in the short term done Milton nothing but poetic harm. Having enhanced his ego and ambition, it has turned his sights askance to the Continent and the clock of his imagination back to a dated, academic and fanciful mythopoeia. In the long term, the Continental journey must have contributed to Milton's attempt to internationalise English in *Paradise Lost*: without losing its Anglo-Saxon roots and structures to extend the linguistic inheritance into a kind of living Esperanto. But in the short term, it dulled his pen. Had the Wars and Commonwealth not forced him to write from the guts rather than the fingertips, we might have inherited a post-Spenserian *Arthuriad* but certainly no *Paradise Lost*.

Paradise Lost bears witness to a mind which has profoundly and passionately committed itself to the process of Time as history, experienced as a man amongst men and, moreover, a man to whom the worst that can be imagined has already happened. The inertia of self-suppression has gone because there is nothing left to fear. Its title advertises loss as its central theme: its narrator is a loser qualified by defeat to act as an authoritative spokesman for Truth in a world riddled with contradiction, disappointment, false starts, high ideals and multitudinous error. *Areopagitica* had spoken of the necessity for engagement in the processes of history and the dispute over truth: *Paradise Lost* is the testament of the 'true wayfaring / warfaring Christian' who has had to share the path of pilgrimage with many other seekers, all of whom have gone the way of bewilderment and self-doubt. Achieved failure is strength for the poet of *Paradise Lost*. To gauge the intense commitment and powerful assurance of its narrative voice, we need only remind ourselves of passages in which Milton wrestles with the relationship between past, present and future tenses in the poem: the struggle between narrative time and historical time. The mode is familiar from the earlier poems, but the mood is quite altered. Book IV focuses an emotionally highly-charged negotiation between what-might-have-been and what-shall-have-been. The Book opens with a cry of invocation from the inner depths of the epic narrative (the Invocations proper, symmetrically placed at the openings of Books I, III, VII and IX seclude themselves from the narrative as lyric exordia). This is an invocation which cannot by its very nature be answered:

> O for that warning voice, which he who saw
> The Apocalypse heard cry in heaven aloud,
> Then when the dragon, put to second rout,
> Came furious down to be revenged on men,
> *Woe to the inhabitants on earth!* that now,
> While time was, our first parents had been warned
> The coming of their secret foe, and scaped
> Haply so scaped his mortal snare; for now
> Satan, now first inflamed with rage, came down,
> The tempter ere the accuser of mankind,
> To wreck on innocent frail man his loss
> Of that first battle, and his flight to hell . . .
>
> (IV. 1–12)

For twenty years, Milton had acted as 'warning voice' to the Parliament, Commonwealth and Protectorate of England. In 1660, with the Revolution all but destroyed, on the verge of the Restoration of Charles II, Milton was maintaining that prophetic voice in a pamphlet in two editions, *The Readie and Easie Way to Establish A Free Commonwealth*. We know that he had already begun composition of *Paradise Lost* in 1657–8 and that it took until (at the latest) 1665 to complete. It is therefore not inconceivable that Milton was meditating the exordium to Book IV in 1660, around the time of composition of *The Readie and Easie Way*:

> However with all hazard I have ventur'd what I thought my duty to speak in season, and to forewarne my countrey in time. . . . What I have spoken, is the language of that which is not call'd amiss *the good Old Cause*: if it seem strange to any, it will not seem more strange, I hope, then convincing to backsliders. Thus much I should perhaps have said though I were sure I should have spoken only to trees and stones; and had none to cry to, but with the Prophet, *O earth, earth, earth!* to tell the very soil it self, what her perverse inhabitants are deaf to. Nay though what I have spoke, should happ'n (which Thou suffer not, who didst create mankinde free; nor Thou next, who didst redeem us from being servants of men!) to be the last words of our expiring libertie.
>
> (CPW. VII. 462–3)

This is perhaps the final bastion of fidelity to an ideal: to speak out an allegiance whether or not there exists anyone to hear. Milton's warning voice is operative and obligatory even in the event that the audience has totally absconded. Milton in *Mansus* and the *Epitaphium Damonis* of 1638–9 needed an élite audience to validate his utterance; in 1660, he needs to ingratiate himself with no human auditor, for his words are self-authorising. A blind man's world has to be taken on trust. The hearers might all have stolen out of the room and one be left speaking to oneself. A crucial change in Milton's attitude to language has taken place. In 1660 there was no 'ready' or 'easy' way to establish a free commonwealth. But Milton's title categorically denies this. Either Milton is ignorant of the true situation (which is unthinkable) or his language represents an affirmation which has liberated itself from the contingency of Time and Space. The prophetic word in this late pamphlet has dislocated itself from the duty of practical signification, and the blind seer speaking to deaf listeners in a language they have forgotten ('the language of . . . *the good Old Cause*') parallels Jeremiah crying in the Wilderness: 'earth, earth, earth, hear the word of the Lord' (Jeremiah 22:29).

In *Paradise Lost*, narrating the events of the earliest chapters of Genesis, the first Book of the Bible, he cries aloud for the intervention of a voice from the Book of Revelation, the last Book of the Bible. Last Things are invoked to prevent the development of a future from First Things, in terms of events which are foreknown in narrative time (the ensuing fall) by virtue of hindsight in the time established by the Scriptural pre-text (the Bible) and historical time. This exertion of desire, wish and allegiance against the intransigent facts of the narrative he must tell and the life he has undergone represents the old wrestling-match between what was, will be and shall-have-been against the might-have-been. But the charge of energy within the writing testifies to a mind which has long outgrown its hesitations and irresolutions in favour of an active engagement with areas of conflict and knots of contradiction. The virginal uncertainties as to what will transpire recorded in *Lycidas*, *Mansus* and *Damon*, yearning for a crown of Paphian myrtle or Parnassian laurel and a seat amongst the blessed 'in ethereal Olympus' (*Mansus*, 100), have given way to the blazing commitment of the Prophets and the Visionary of Patmos to utterance with or without trophies. When Milton cries 'O for that warning voice' at the opening of Book IV, the urgency of the emotion comes of the profound identification of the narrator with 'our first parents' in all their tender, vulnerable glory: the narrator is emotionally involved in their story and implicated in its outcome. He becomes one with its persons, in the sense in which Plato in the *Republic* explained mimesis in epic as an act of impersonation, a becoming or inhabiting of the person described.[19] In Milton's pre-War poems, persons had been detached, fictive, stylised: after the Revolution, his poetry presents a fusion of creative ego with imagined selves (in the case of Adam, Eve and the Son) or a more complex and dynamic conflict of affinity with repulsion (as in the case of God and Satan). The whole matter is urgent and contemporary for the narrator, such that narrative, historical and Scriptural time may in this emergency be confused utterly: 'O for that warning voice . . . that *now*, / While time was, our first parents had been warned . . . for *now* / Satan, *now* first inflamed with rage, came down' (emphases added). At such points, the relationship between narrator and characters becomes so intense (for, after all, they are blood-relations) that the narrative, on their behalf, seeks to turn round upon itself and abolish its own course.

An intimacy of address, incorporating deep 'home-felt' emotions of pity, protectiveness and concern, is a characteristic voice of *Paradise Lost* in relation to the human persons whose fall it confides. The voice of the narrator is at once public, introspectively private and occasionally turned inwards and directed at the persons of the poem themselves in deep, though unheard, communion. It guards the love-making of Adam and Eve in the unfallen Book IV behind a wall of words, apparently disclosing but actually concealing their act of love from the voyeuristic eye of the reader (IV. 744–70). We hardly notice as we read Milton's powerful defence of sexual love that we have been invited to see nothing of it, and that the narrative persona has intervened between us and his subject. The fallen imagination is not innocent but nocent, and the language of sexual exchange committed to carnal knowledge. Language itself is a mighty theme of *Paradise Lost*, especially the cardinal problem of how fallen language may simulate the Incorruptible, timebound inflections may convey the stasis of the Eternal, and knowing words communicate innocence. *Paradise Lost* is a multiform experiment with language, working on the most marginal and problematic borderlands of linguistic possibility. The indescribable delight and mutual contentment of the lovers in the

Garden are conveyed to us by an involuntary closing of our eyes in this image-teeming Book; and when we awaken it is over:

> These lulled by nightingales embracing slept,
> And on their naked limbs the flowery roof
> Showered roses, which the morn repaired. Sleep on,
> Blest pair; and O yet happiest if ye seek
> No happier state, and know to know no more.
>
> (IV. 771–5)

Know, know, no: no, no, no: no more. Read aloud, the last clause resounds an anthem of negatives, concluding with the valedictory *no more*. Here again is the 'warning voice' which *must* speak though speech is abjectly useless. The story was over long ago, 'in the beginning', and only the illusion of simultaneity set up by the telling of a narrative can beguile the narrator and the reader into imagining that the poet's voice in 1660 can affect the course of events in supposedly 4000 BC which hindsight has made to seem inevitable. We know better than to think that the narrator has any control over the history which has made him what he is, precipitating the state of knowledge in which he maintains vigilance over the unknowing human pair in their blessedly unconscious state. 'Know to know no more': the same verb, by a lamentable irony built into the confusion of tongues engendered by the fall, must do duty for opposite kinds of cognition. The first *know* implies intuitive understanding, the Solomonic wisdom to content oneself with asking for 'an understanding heart'; the second *know* represents the fatal curiosity which is a version of Lucifer's rebellion, and which we fellow-losers of Paradise *know* (in the sense of recognise) all too well as our fruitless inheritance from those sleepers over whose awakening the poet mourns. The mode of address here reflects at once the curious experience of artistic composition as well as a comment upon the nature of the language which is the poet's only available resource. In the moment of telling a story, there can be a sensation of freedom from its determinants, even if the story is foregone and its outcome fated or inevitable. An evanescent gap of suspenseful freedom opens, and into this gap the poet pours his or her anguished hopes, desires and wishes. *Paradise Lost* is full of such wishful areas, in which narrative time and historical time tensely part company. The wordplay (in a poem uniquely rich in pun, paradox, innuendo, riddle and verbal allusion) signals this opening of a window onto a vista of impossible possibility: at the same time, it shuts us in the trap of language, with its anarchic resourcefulness and confusing limitation. On the one hand, we have too many words. The language of deceit streams from Satan's lips as he tempts Eve to take the forbidden fruit: copious, sensuous, profusely argumentative. On the other hand, we do not have enough words to make necessary distinctions: *know to know no more*.

Lycidas which began *Yet once more*, concluded with the decision to *Weep no more*. The stylised Arcadian swain, pastoral poet rather than familially-related fellow-victim, is permitted release from the constraints of the elegy:

> At last he rose, and twitched his mantle blue:
> Tomorrow to fresh woods, and pastures new.
> (192–3)

The Miltonic persona of *Paradise Lost* will never be free of the narrative he is bound to tell, in whose events he is representatively implicated. 'The truest poetry,' said Touchstone, 'is the most feigning', agreeing with Sidney's 'the poet . . . never affirmeth'.[20] But *Paradise Lost* claimed to be no feigning: it was God's own Truth, in so far as the poet could hear, understand and tell it. The narrative ends with a departure: an ejection which is also a birth, into a lonely, difficult but meaningful terrain:

> They hand in hand with wandering steps and slow,
> Through Eden took their solitary way.
> (XII. 648–9)

But the theory of Time and history presented by *Paradise Lost* is cyclical and recurrent: the story of Adam and Eve, together with every one of their successors made in their image, including the poet and the reader, is never-ending – until Time itself shall have had an ending. Each person's life, and each epoch of history repeats the fall. Hence the interventions of the poet's voice in his epic are almost painfully personal to read. *Know to know no more* is to be read as a statement as

committed to ideals but as disjoined from historical possibility as the
title *The Readie and Easie Way to Establish a Free Commonwealth*: gnosis
faithfully upheld against praxis.

Paradise Lost is a testament of married love. Whatever view one
takes of the oppressive power-structure which privileges male above
female in the poem ('He for God only, she for God in him' (IV. 299)),
readers have universally responded to the intensely-felt allegiance of
the human pair bonded in the poem, from Eve's

> neither breath of morn when she ascends
> With charm of earliest birds, nor rising sun
> Or this delightful land, nor herb, fruit, flower,
> Glistering with dew, nor fragrance after showers,
> Nor grateful evening mild, nor silent night
> With this her solemn bird, nor walk by moon
> Or glittering starlight without thee is sweet.
>   (IV. 650–6)

to Adam's

> so absolute she seems
> And in herself complete . . .
>   (VIII. 547–8)

and Eve's consummation of the poem in its final declaration of human
loyalty

> But now lead on;
> In me is no delay; with thee to go,
> Is to stay here; without thee here to stay,
> Is to go hence unwilling; thou to me
> Art all things under heaven, all places thou . . .
>   (XII. 614–18)

In the larger sense, too, *Paradise Lost* is a poem which has left behind
the virginal fastidiousness of the early poetry in favour of the fullest
possible commitment to life in the flesh, the embroilments of history.
Every imaginable emotion seems released onto the page in the text's
many contending voices – from rage and doubt to tenderness and

desire, acquiescent piety and rebellious questioning – so that we feel as we close the book less as if we have seen God's ways justified than that we have witnessed Jacob's famous wrestle with God in Genesis: 'for as a prince hast thou power with God and men, and hast prevailed' (32:28).

3

Paradise Lost: The Maladaptive Eye

The narrative of *Paradise Lost* begins in electric excitement with the fall of Lucifer and his angels down the entire depth of the universe. The effect is visually reminiscent of the violent irruption of tumul-tuously falling forms in Rubens' *The Fall of the Damned into Hell* or the vertiginous dynamic of Luca Giordano's *S Michael Archangel* in which Michael, safe in the freedom of his huge outspread wings treads the toppling Lucifer down upon a heap of naked bodies plummeting into infinite space.[1] The motif speaks of the human terror of an ultimate insecurity and instability. There is no ground upon which to stand and gain bearings: only the flailing of useless limbs and tensely contorted musculature as the disempowered drop sheer down into the void. To fall is to lose face and countenance: the expressions of the damned in these visual representations are set rigid with terror and violent shock. It is to lose control: their bodies are similarly aghast, diving, rolling or tumbling head-over-heels, an arm perhaps poignantly stretched out to steady them in an involuntary panic-gesture. Victims of earthquake or air disaster must know this horror of the loss of all bearings that Rubens and Milton depict – the earth whipped out from under one's feet. Like the High Renaissance and baroque artists who treat this theme, Milton presents the fall of the angels as a turbulent brew of light and darkness, with violent chiaroscuro effects.[2] Their personal catastrophe is a tumult in the universe itself, a discharge of cosmic energy which shakes

95

Creation to its roots. The entire night sky is the theatre of action, and it is as if we were witnessing the explosions of galaxies and constellations. This association is intrinsic to the myth, where Lucifer was another name for Hesper-Vesper, the morning and evening star:

> How art thou fallen from heaven, O Lucifer, son of the morning! how art thou cut down to the ground, which didst weaken the nations!
>
> (Isaiah 14:12)

The magnificence of a remote cosmic spectacle combines with the pathos and terror of a human and personal event: a star meteorically falls; an ascendent being is ruined.

The fall of the angels begins Milton's narrative because, for Milton who accounted it an historical fact, it began all narrative: Time itself derived from this initiating event:

> Him the almighty power
> Hurled headlong flaming from the ethereal sky
> With hideous ruin and combustion down
> To bottomless perdition, there to dwell
> In adamantine chains and penal fire,
> Who durst defy the Omnipotent to arms.
>
> (I. 44–9)

The clock begins to tick and the map to unfold. With the rupture of Heaven to expel its dissidents, not only does Time in the poem come into operation but Space itself is first divulged to the poem's readers as the falling angels pass down the entire created universe, from 'the ethereal sky' to 'bottomless perdition'. The reader's eye is opened to the vast geographical perspectives of *Paradise Lost* through the penetration of Space by the vagrant consciousnesses of the angels. A God's-eye view is withheld until the third Book. The illusionist techniques which Milton shared with baroque artists are spectacularly displayed in this first account of the fall. 'Him the almighty power / Hurled headlong': normal word order is violated by inversion, so that object precedes subject. Satan's governed, helplessly passive state is pinned into his object-status in the grammar of power which rules *Paradise Lost*: he is driven along into our line of vision before the subject which impels him, like a stucco figure that seems to burst from a painted dome in the zenith of some frescoed Roman church by Gaulli, Pozzo or Bernini. Grammatical inversion mimes the downfall of the hubristic challengers to Almighty Power: 'Him . . . / Hurled headlong', where a massively alliterative patterning, reminiscent of the Anglo-Saxon stress-alliteration dynamic which Milton may have known (see page 208, n.17 below), dramatises a reversal or upending of the norm. The angels pitch headfirst into the abyss, utterly endangered, and as they fall they burn: 'Hurled headlong flaming'.

Paradise Lost was the product of the Revolution of 1641 plus the Restoration of 1660: a contradiction in terms. If Milton set out to 'assert eternal providence, / And justify the ways of God to men' (I. 25–6), this was because God's baffling, inscrutable ways were on the surface of it so in need of justification, and his Providence a turncoat. God's Providence first made way for the New Model Army, the regicide, the Commonwealth, and shortly afterwards landed Charles Stuart on the coast of Dover. Many of Milton's Puritan contemporaries lost faith and direction in the light of God's apparent betrayal of his saints. People called God a devil and a tyrant in 1659: 'he hath done that he cannot make good'; Major-General Fleetwood protested that 'The Lord had blasted them and spit in their faces'; Muggleton acknowledged that 'God did seem to be more cruel than men'.[3] Milton set out to exonerate God by stressing the fallen degeneracy of man, in whom the Satanic principle of corrupted love of power, ambition and worldly gain was too well set to make him capable of liberty; he explained the fall of man by the prior fall of the all-too-human angels. Milton's poem is written from the vantage (or disadvantage) point of one who knows the hell of falling amongst the community of his fellows as an immediate personal experience. The panorama of Rubens' picture, with its torrent of consternated, pleading forms whirling like rags upon a wind, would make a good visual guide to the feelings of Milton's party in the late 1650s and 1660s. Only an act of supreme faith could keep one balanced on the conviction that one was standing upright in this wholesale mêlée and uproar: it must have been like treading air or walking on water. *Paradise Lost* is the heroic record of Milton's attempt to steady himself in the name of his God and his cause by validating both against the worst that could be said of them in the light of the invincible moral anarchy of history. It is a testament of boundless insecurity, speaking with the courage that only utter loss can generate: 'fallen on evil days', 'In darkness, and with dangers compassed round, / And solitude' (VII. 25; 27–8). The very writing of the poem, that sacred therapy and precious consolation, is a process participating in that insecurity:

> Up led by thee
> Into the heaven of heavens I have presumed,
> An earthly guest, and drawn empyreal air,
> Thy tempering; with like safety guided down
> Return me to my native element:
> Lest from this flying steed unreined, (as once
> Bellerophon, though from a lower clime)
> Dismounted, on th'Aleian field I fall
> Erroneous there to wander and forlorn.
> (VII.12–20)

The classical, Christian and humanist prototypes for the human search for knowledge and power beyond what is taken to be our natural scope – Icarus, Bellerophon, Prometheus, Phaethon, Lucifer, Faustus, Galileo – shadow the poet's risky endeavour in composition. The 'flying steed unreined' (Pegasus) represents a power not susceptible of perfect conscious control; the instability of the language available to the aberrant fallen consciousness, with its rich capacity for fabrication and fanciful invention, makes every act of writing potentially fallacious. The passage incorporates the binary verbal oppositions which provide the dynamic of the whole poem: *up/down*; *presume/fall*. The poem is strung on the live wire of the nervous tension generated by such pairs of oppositions, whose struggle informs every part of the poem in the form of verbal recurrence within sentences, verse paragraphs and narrative episodes, and the whole of the poem in the entirety of its narrative. To an extraordinary degree, the whole is in the part and the part can stand for the whole in *Paradise Lost*. Other pairs include the *ascent/descent*, *high/low*, *above/below* polarities, knit together in patterns of grammatical intensification such as the play upon positive, comparative and superlative forms of adjectives: *high, higher, highest*: 'Highly they raged / Against the highest' (I. 666–7); 'High throned above all highth' (III. 58); 'in the lowest deep a lower deep' (IV. 76); 'high advanced / The lower still I fall' (IV. 90–1). Language is a finite system; reality, Milton's poem implies, ranges illimitably beyond it. Through this pressure on the superlative, as though in the light of an infinite perspective it must be measured only as a comparative form of something beyond the reach of our classifi-cations, Milton at once criticises language and, by sleight of hand, gestures beyond it. These polarities (which cross-bias with the *light/dark, bondage/liberty, knowledge/innocence* polarities) also indicate the hell of uncertainty to which fallen man is condemned, a condition which is at once exemplified and mediated by the riddling perplexities of language.

The basis of *Paradise Lost* is of course in considerable part proverbial and truistic: 'Pride comes before a fall', 'All that glisters is not gold'. It demonstrates the truth of a commonplace, reminding us of what everybody has always known – but seldom known how to apply or put to profit. The poem abounds in newly coined proverbs. 'Long is the way / And hard,' Satan tells his followers, 'that out of hell leads up to light' (II. 432–3); 'now I see / Peace to corrupt no less than war to waste' (XI. 783–4). These are acknowledged and consensus truths, but the poem is less interested in maintaining them than in showing their extraordinary invisibility to us when we come to the cryptic business of action and choice in the realm of practicality. There is a paradoxical and oxymoronic basis to all perception in *Paradise Lost*: the plain truth is neither easily discernible nor expressible. The means of vision in Hell is 'no light, but rather darkness visible'; in Heaven perception is dazzled into blindness: 'Dark with excessive bright thy skirts appear'; in Paradise the duplicitous serpent is a scintillating form of darkness: 'So glistered the dire snake'; the gold in Hell and earth is an oxymoronic 'Precious bane' (I. 63, III. 380, IX. 643, I. 692). The work is suffused in strange transforming lights and shades, lightscapes that convince the eye of the validity of its impressions at the same time as the narrative voice points out to us the insubstantiality of all deductions based on semblances:

> Lead then, said Eve. He leading swiftly rolled
> In tangles, and made intricate seem straight,
> To mischief swift. Hope elevates, and joy
> Brightens his crest, as when a wandering fire,

> Compact of unctuous vapour, which the night
> Condenses, and the cold environs round,
> Kindled through agitation to a flame,
> Which oft, they say, some evil spirit attends
> Hovering and blazing with delusive light,
> Misleads the amazed night-wanderer from his way
> To bogs and mires, and oft through pond or pool,
> There swallowed up and lost, from succour far.
> So glistered the dire snake, and into fraud
> Led Eve our credulous mother, to the tree
> Of prohibition, root of all our woe . . .
>
> (IX. 631–45)

The slippery, aberrant locomotion of the serpent, with its capacity to interweave with itself 'In tangles' in a pattern that is 'intricate' (from Latin *intricare*, to entangle or perplex, plus *intricari*, to play tricks), is the visual equivalent of a bad argument or a false narrative which, if believed, will lead the hearer on a mortally false trail. *Paradise Lost* is a narrative poem which is a nest of minor but crucial narratives – some of which are held by the narrative voice to be true, or as true as anything can be in a world of ubiquitous delusion; most are partial and subjective, based on hearsay, rumour (even God's mightiest agents are underinformed in *Paradise Lost*, and his messenger Raphael has to guess at what he may or may not divulge to Adam in Books V–VIII),[4] personal opinion and potentially fallacious sense impressions or memory; other narratives are fictions or lies. The poem is the testament of the modern world, a polyphonic masterpiece whose many voices cannot in the nature of things concur. The narrative voice with its peremptory judgements and insistence on the monolithic authority of the biblical subtext, seeks to commend and, indeed, enforce a single standard of interpretation, yet in the four great Invocations it confesses its own partiality and credulity, its liability to 'Erroneous' wandering (see page 98 above). The passage which compares Satan's coiling undulations as he leads Eve to disaster with the *delusive light* created by an *ignis fatuus* is, on the literal level, a description elaborating the events in Genesis: an imaginative reconstruction of an historical event. On another of the many linguistic levels on which the poem operates, it is an analysis of a mental event, a process of consciousness. The poem takes as its major theme the fall of man and a justification of God's ways. But as it undertakes this task, it must reflect on perception and cognition themselves and the medium through which understanding is achieved: language. The same language mediates (literally) physical events – the serpent leading Eve to the Tree of Knowledge – and (metaphorically) mental events – a labyrinthine tangle of suasive words which, with potent subliminal action, lead the vulnerable mind of a listener to a destination she could neither have desired nor designed for herself. Just as Milton cracks open English vocabulary to reveal its etymological roots, so also he presses on this same vocabulary so as to lay bare both the visual images buried and passing unnoted in common or abstract language, and the application of this language to the inner world of the mind. The basis of this exploration is common usage. Satan has talked Eve into demanding 'Lead then.' He has done so through false (but proleptic) autobiography, a narrative explaining how, through eating the forbidden fruit he learnt to know and speak. Now he leads her through the garden 'In tangles'. We speak of 'tangled' argument, 'intricate' ideas, of the mind 'kindling', of an account that 'misleads'. The mind itself can limitlessly 'wander', with fatal consequences, from the straight and narrow path, but also roving and straying in fascinating new directions, as in Belial's unforgettable vindication of consciousness itself as a good which is the last thing we would willingly lose:

> Sad cure; for who would lose,
> Though full of pain, this intellectual being,
> Those thoughts that *wander* through eternity . . .
> (II. 146–8)

To *wander* is a key word[5] in *Paradise Lost*: it connotes the mental dereliction of living in the fallen world, a state of queasy, undirected, circuitous and inconclusive motion – a form of mental exploration which resembles blind searching, the attempt to get the hang of a world which does not offer enough clues for perfect interpretation. The devils in Hell pursue a burlesque form of Milton's own researches both in *Paradise Lost* and his theological treatise, *Of Christian Doctrine*. But burlesque can be uncomfortably close to the real thing. Groups of fallen angels sat apart and 'reasoned high'

101

> Of providence, foreknowledge, will and fate,
> Fixed fate, free will, foreknowledge absolute,
> And found no end, in *wandering* mazes lost.
>
> (II. 559–61)

Wandering mazes lost: three keys words are here bound together. They link, in this profoundly reiterative and echoic structure, with other key words, each reinforcing the total cyclic pattern of the narrative and the intense feelings of perplexity and yearning it both expresses and engenders. *Lost* tolls its message like a passing bell from the moment we pick up the book and spell over its valedictory title; the labyrinthine *maze* of the poem's mental topography recurs in relation to the idea of wandering and the possibility of error from first to last; in prelapsarian Eden, 'four main streams / . . . *wandering* . . . / with *mazy* error' (IV. 233–39) echo the 'watery labyrinth' of Lethe in Hell (II. 584). The poet's fear of 'Erroneous . . . *wander(ing)*' (VII. 20) preludes the exilic words which complete the drama:

> The world was all before them, where to choose
> Their place of rest, and providence their guide:
> They hand in hand with *wandering* steps and slow,
> Through Eden took their solitary way.
>
> (XII. 646–9)

When Eve is led by the serpent which operates as a '*wandering* fire' she becomes the first human 'night-*wanderer*' (see page 100 above), the first of many who will be 'amazed', with its obvious suggestion of *maze*, by the specious capacity of language to delude, captivate, falsify and affect action, irreversibly. The suggestion of the poem is that language itself is the maze in which we wander. God's creating Word fashioned the universe, but human languages (deriving from the confusion of tongues with which God punished the builders of the Tower of Babel, treated by Milton in Book XII. 24–62), are shadowy, riddling guides to truth, a corporate fabrication enshrining our ignorant assumptions, sophistical devices and our wish to oppress one another.[6] The poem casts enormous doubt on what people say and believe; the narratives which count as authority to the communal mind. Some of this doubt is signalled in phrases such as 'some say', 'they relate', 'as seamen tell' (I. 205), or, as in the *ignis fatuus* passage, 'they say': 'a wandering fire . . . Which oft, they say, some evil spirit attends'. The narrative voice implies that hearsay is a superstitious guide; consensus is utterly unreliable because of the defective eyesight of human beings subject to the 'delusive light' of the fallen world. *Paradise Lost* acknowledges itself to be caught in the same double bind. It sees by the same light and is limited to the same medium of language which enthralls the race. The poem feels an obligation to record opinions and experiences with which it can neither concur nor condemn with certainty: steadfastly maintaining its obligation to attest to the lunatic state of the human optic which has no accurate instrument capable of distinguishing between what its possessor 'sees, / Or dreams he sees' (I. 783–4). Hence the poem is a tissue of false narratives and defective testimonies, reflecting man's double nature as wilful liar and gullible fool.

To write a powerful poem about the experience of insecurity is an extraordinary paradox. As the Christ of *Lycidas* walked on water, so the poet of *Paradise Lost* at once treads the inconsistencies and chaos of the unconscious mind and travels with his protagonists the most eery reaches of the cosmos, both the inner world and the macrocosm. The whole poem may be read as a *psychomachia*, a struggle within the psyche, in which the author invests himself in all the personages and situations. It is a dream-poem, which came to the poet unsought in 'nightly visitation' by a Muse who 'dictates to me slumbering, or inspires / Easy my unpremeditated verse' (IX. 23–4); and it has in common with our experience of dream the splitting of the self into an abundance of persons, linked reflections (God-Son-Michael-Raphael-Abdiel-unfallen Adam-Milton); monstrous parodies dramatising fear of the desired object (Eve/Sin); apparent opposites locked in deadly combat representing the light and dark poles of the self (Son / Satan). Milton in his experience of defiant defeat had somehow gained access to that forbidden area, the subconscious mind, onto whose submerged contents he shed an astonishing light in the first two Books and the second half of the third: the accounts of Hell and of Satan's odyssey through Creation to the world. The emphasis on dream and vision, together with the importance of dream-interpretation, is of course an aspect of the Puritan stress on direct divine inspiration, the inner light 'So much the rather thou, celestial Light / Shine inward' (III. 51–2). Bunyan's *Pilgrim's Progress* claims an identical source:

> As I walked through the wilderness of this world, I lighted on a certain
> place, where was a den; and I laid me down in that place to sleep: and as I
> slept I dreamed a dream. I dreamed, and behold I saw a man clothed with
> rags . . .[7]

The den is the gaol where Bunyan spent the better part of twelve years
after the Restoration; the dream was the way out of that stigmatised
isolation, a luminous recapitulation of the soul's journey through
unknown landscapes which must be made to disclose their meaning as
the constantly endangered but growing and literate soul learns to
outface his fears and find safety at the heart of terror. It is no accident
that these two works, *Paradise Lost* and *Pilgrim's Progress* participate in
two traditions, dream-literature and travel-literature.[8] For Milton as
for Bunyan, constraint enfranchised and inner space dilated to give
views of immensities unimaginable or invisible save to those under
lock-and-key, or the lock-and-key of blindness and disgrace. Milton's
Satan is a time-traveller and a space-explorer, taking with him the
modern telescopic eye whose implications Galileo has made so famous:
to this degree the poem's cosmic vision is a novelty of the late
Renaissance. But the poem makes clear the fact that the Hell of which
it tells is a place within, where the poet has personally been and can
give a first-hand account to a readership which only has to consult its
own experience to verify. Common parlance speaks of 'hell on earth';
when we know acute pain, we say that we are 'in hell'; our neighbour
in deep trouble is 'a poor devil'. *Paradise Lost* attests to the authenticity
of such usage. Its Puritan internalisation of theological states sucks
reality from the material world, and locates it in the interior world of
the individual with his or her almost boundless capacity to enjoy or
suffer. Inner space is a central location of *Paradise Lost*: the inner space
which fills us and from which we can never flee. Seneca and the
Elizabethan Senecans had imagined the Hell within, from Kyd's hell
of conscience:

> There is a path upon your left-hand side,
> That leadeth from a guilty conscience
> Unto a forest of distrust and fear . . .[9]

to Marlowe's Protestant conception of Hell as the profound sense of
personal loss that accompanies exile from grace, Mephistophelis':

> Why, this is hell, nor am I out of it.
> Think'st thou that I, who saw the face of God
> And tasted the eternal joys of heaven,
> Am not tormented with ten thousand hells
> In being depriv'd of everlasting bliss?[10]

Satan's racking pains of introspection on Mount Niphates bear the imprint of Mephistophelis' loneliness of bereavement, the self a meaningless vacuum which cannot see and cannot taste anything beyond the self. Troubled thoughts stir:

> The hell within him, for within him hell
> He brings, and round about him, nor from hell
> One step no more than from himself can fly
> By change of place
> . . . .
> Me miserable! which way shall I fly,
> Infinite wrath, and infinite despair?
> Which way I fly is hell; myself am hell;
> And in the lowest deep a lower deep
> Still threatening to devour me opens wide,
> To which the hell I suffer seems a heaven.
> (*Paradise Lost*, V. 20–3; 73–8)

The first quoted line mimes in its symmetrical and circular structure (chiasmus – *hell*: *within him*, *within him*: *hell*) the soliloquist's trap. The rawly incantatory style of throbbing repetition which characterises *Paradise Lost* as a whole gives here a sense of eternal emergency, a panic that can scarcely be governed but must be endured. The double *within him* presses inward to the hollow centre of the line: the double *hell* rings out like an exclamation, and continues to beat out a sequence of alarm signals through the speech that ensues ('Which way I fly is hell, myself am hell . . . the hell I suffer') which act subliminally on a reader like a hopeless cry for help from a sufferer stranded beyond the reach of aid. These lines occur in a speech which was singled out by Milton's nephew as one which Milton had originally composed for the tragic drama which was his first conception of *Paradise Lost*.[11] Few readers have been able to withhold their awed sympathy for Satan in his anguish here, even those of the 'wages-of-sin' school who do not

105

admit the poem's split allegiances. The reason for this is surely the profound humanity of Satan's experience of a hell within which everyone knows and shuns.

In *Paradise Lost*, this capacity for emotional hurt is understood as far more terrible than the physical tortures of Hell, though here too Milton is more than imaginative: the sensitive sole of the foot winces in its 'uneasy steps / Over the burning marl' (I. 295–6), 'painful steps o'er the burnt soil' (562). Loss of sight had sharpened Milton's awareness of the tender vulnerability of the human organism, from the thin-skinned sole of the foot to the ball of the eye. In *Samson Agonistes* that consciousness of frailty reaches its epitome, and extends its significance to an awareness of genital vulnerability. The strutting arrogance of phallic values in a warrior culture is placed against the absurd and terrible openness of the male to humiliation by that same gift on which he prides himself: the soft, sentient, exposed materials of which the human creature is composed. In *Paradise Lost* too, sexual pain is understood as constituting a vital part of our knowledge of Hell: jealousy is 'the injured lover's hell' (V. 449–50). Some of the deepest pain of the poem is mediated through the inability both of the patriarchal myth of Genesis, the patriarchal Adam and the patriarchal narrative voice to estimate Eve (and with her, woman) justly, and to trust her with the love she draws from a heart rendered by that love susceptible and open. The area of *Paradise Lost* that deals with sexual love is a maelstrom of contradictory emotions: it is lit with lurid flames of sexual fear and oppressive misogyny, but at the same time it is visited by what can only be called impulses of justice and right-mindedness, identifying with the figure of Eve as scapegoat and outsider because it sees her from *inside*, and, through impersonating, takes her part:

> He for God only, she for God in him:
> His fair large front and eye sublime declared
> Absolute rule . . .
>
> (IV. 299–301)

> transported I behold,
> Transported touch; here passion first I felt,
> Commotion strange, in all enjoyments else
> Superior and unmoved, here only weak
> ....

> so absolute she seems
> And in her self complete, so well to know
> Her own, that what she wills to do or say,
> Seems wisest, virtuousest, discreetest, best . . .
> (VIII. 529–32; 547–50)

> O much deceived, much failing, hapless Eve . . .
> (IX. 404)

> How can I live without thee, how forgo
> Thy sweet converse and love so dearly joined,
> To live again in these wild woods forlorn?
> (908–10)

> O why did God
> Creator wise, that peopled highest heaven
> With spirits masculine, create at last
> This novelty on earth, this fair defect
> Of nature, and not fill the world at once
> With men as angels without feminine . . .
> (X. 888–93)

These quotations from the narrative voice and from Adam's speeches adequately suggest the intensity of the sexual pain and the violence of the conflict that lies deep at the heart of the poem. The key word is perhaps *weak*.[12] The Miltonic male at once idealises and looks down on the female: his 'superior love' is gratified by her 'submissive charms' (IV. 498–9); but the power-structure he imposes as fortification to his ego is overturned in the love-relation. He finds himself yielding, dependent, adoring and 'transported', literally, taken away from himself, out of control. Sexuality violates autonomy and therefore threatens the sense of safety. *Paradise Lost* shows a double vision of sexual love: it is the nearest thing to hell a man can know, opening him to the threat of separation ('How can I live without thee?') which had been such a traumatic crux in Milton's own life when his first wife Mary Powell abandoned him in 1642. Yet it is also the nearest thing to heaven available to mortals. *Paradise Lost* contains one of the most powerful defences of married sensuality and the companionship of man and woman in the language, together with an argument reminiscent of

107

his own free-thinking divorce tracts for the importance of pleasure as a major constituent of virtue: 'Sharp we our selves distast,' he wrote in *The Doctrine and Discipline of Divorce*, 'and sweet, under whose hands we are, is scrupl'd and suspected as too lushious' (*CPW*. II. 241).

Lushious looks forward to the fruitful and delicious garden of *Paradise Lost*. That garden is called Paradise, its bounties lovingly detailed in Book IV of the poem in a rich pastoral tapestry as being measured and attuned to the senses and wishes of its human inhabitants: but the garden is not Paradise. Milton distinguishes in the poem between 'names' and 'meanings' (VII. 5). Just as hell is presented as an inner state, so Paradise is a state of mind, heart and body, where no lack or unease is known but desire is met in full and unquestionably. The hell of self-consciousness which Satan imports into Eden views with rancorous envy its unself-conscious opposite:

> aside the devil turned
> For envy, yet with jealous leer malign
> Eyed them askance, and to himself thus plained.
> Sight hateful, sight tormenting! Thus these two
> Imparadised in one another's arms
> The happier Eden, shall enjoy their fill
> Of bliss on bliss . . .
>
> (IV.502–8)

The covetous 'eyeing' with which Satan contradicts his tensely self-defensive gesture of turning-away represents a masochistic pang unknown to the lovers in the freshness and refreshment of their trance. *Imparadised* expresses the rapture of Paradise as a verb, from the Italian *Imparadisare* imported in the Renaissance and used both in love-poetry and sacred poetry, connoting a bringing *in* to a Paradisal state but, taking as it does, a past participial form, it displays the action as fulfilled, completed and confirmed. The embrace is a coming-home, a steady repose in sanctuary, a fulfilment of desire as ample as Mark Antony's breath-taking: 'Let Rome in Tiber melt, and the wide arch of the rang'd empire fall! Here is my space' (*Antony and Cleopatra*, I. i. 33–4). As against the arrogance of empire (Satan is an imperialist and aggressor on the Roman model of *imperator*), *Paradise Lost* in its prelapsarian Books IV and V locates a 'space' for man, extended from the self to the area within the circle of the arms as they embrace another person. Milton tries, perhaps unsuccessfully, to purge this enlargement of the self of coerciveness: Eve's 'Subjection' is 'required with gentle sway, / And by her yielded, by him best received' (IV. 308–9). Sexuality is a kind of power-play from the beginning. Yet the blessedness of the union between Adam and Eve is strongly felt throughout: the loving space which includes the beloved as an aspect of the self is accorded a special sanctity by Milton's poem. The 'blissful bower' (IV. 690) where Adam and Eve make love is the centre and heart of Eden, a refuge within the Refuge, 'sacred and sequestered' (706), a taboo area to the other creatures. Yet even here, in its lyrical description of the safest place in this most troubled and insecure of poems, the narrative voice betrays disturbance and a sense of threat. Eve decking her nuptial bower is 'More lovely than Pandora . . . / . . . and O too like / In sad event' (714–16). We hear in this public lamentation which invites the complicity of the male readership ('What did I tell you? We always knew, didn't we?') the voice of inner distress, fear and shame taking the safe path of strident self-righteousness and public rebuke. Milton seeks safety in numbers as he hides behind the prejudices of the patriarchal tribe. The anxieties which assimilate Eve to the numerous classical stories which corroborate Genesis by libelling woman as an inherently defective creation take refuge in the unthinking, heartless punitiveness of historical common-places: *Paradise Lost is* unthinking and heartless like this. It chokes on its own gall. Like Leontes vituperating Hermione in *The Winter's Tale* it is testimony based on the first-hand evidence of having drunk and seen the spider, and bears into the happy Garden, like Donne entering *Twicknam Garden*, 'the spider love, which transubstantiates all'.[13] Nevertheless, in blessed confusion, it opposes itself. Against the Pandora myth, reinforced by the Narcissus analogy (IV. 456–76), it invokes the beautiful Ceres myth, with its emphasis on male rapacity (Dis' abduction of Proserpina) and female nurture and fidelity (Ceres' indefatigable search; or, allegorically, the abiding of the corn in the seed through the blight of the winter months):

> Not that fair field
> Of Enna, where Proserpine gathering flowers
> Her self a fairer flower by gloomy Dis

> Was gathered, which cost Ceres all that pain
> To seek her through the world . . .
>
> (IV. 268–72)

The Pandora analogy loads Eve with blame; the Proserpina/Ceres allusion unloads it all. The garrulous miscellaneousness of Greek mythology, deriving in great part from an archaic culture in which mother-goddesses were worshipped, is unlike the monolithic Christian and Hebraic cult in providing both male and female icons of glory and power. No writer's prejudices come away quite unimpaired from that pantheistic complex resource of narratives. Both Orpheus and Ceres are types of Christ in humanistic thought. Women readers of *Paradise Lost* have testified to the fact that, with the worst will in the world, the poem's imaginative splendour is such that it can hardly avoid involuntary fits of justice to Eve, the fullest personality in the prelapsarian world and the one closest to the poet's own persona.[14]

Self-completion in another human being is always perilous: the other may die, or change, or desert the lover. Division shakes the shared interiority of Adam and Eve to its foundations in Books IX and X. The violent conflict and quarrel of these books, with the descent into carnality, sexual exploitation, marital discord and misogynistic rancour, charts the disintegration of the first shared 'Paradise within'. Ricks first showed the disruption of the linguistic field as it reflected the fall in a fragmented, contentious language.[15] The diction and the very grammar of Book X are riddled with the inflection of 'sin, that first / Distempered all things' (XI. 55–6). The hell within is transferred from the mind of Satan to the mind of Eve and Adam, who here first fall into soliloquy. Adam wrangles with his Creator, vituperates Eve and takes to name-calling ('Out of my sight, thou serpent; that name best / Befits thee' (X. 867–8)) and false etymology ('O Eve in evil hour' (IX. 1067)). Adam seeks refuge from his own dependency in the fortress of conscious superiority and autonomy: there is never again to be heard in his voice the loving openness which preceded the fall. In this testament of domestic reality in the modern world, Milton atones for the sense of sexual impairment by sacrificing Eve to Adam's frenzy. To his verbal violence, she responds with meekness and willingness to take the blame upon herself:

Forsake me not thus, Adam, witness Heaven
What love sincere, and reverence in my heart
I bear thee, and unweeting have offended,
Unhappily deceived; thy suppliant
I beg, and clasp thy knees; bereave me not
Whereon I live, thy gentle looks, thy aid,
Thy counsel in this uttermost distress,
My only strength and stay: forlorn of thee,
Whither shall I betake me, where subsist?
While yet we live, scarce one short hour perhaps,
Between us two let there be peace, both joining,
As joined in injuries, one enmity
Against a foe by doom express assigned us,
That cruel serpent: on me exercise not
Thy hatred for this misery befallen,
On me already lost, me than thy self
More miserable; both have sinned, but thou
Against God only, I against God and thee,
And to the place of judgment will return,
There with my cries importune heaven, that all
The sentence from thy head removed may light
On me, sole cause to thee of all this woe,
Me me only just object of his ire.

(X. 914–36)

Forsake . . . forlorn are modulations of the key word of the title, *Lost*.
We are reminded of Milton's condemnation of 'God-forsaken loneliness' in the divorce tracts; his memorable definition of the dignity and
blessing of marriage as being placed rather 'in the mutual enjoyment of
that which the wanting soul needfully seeks, then of that which the
plenteous body would jollily give away' (*The Doctrine and Discipline of
Divorce*, CPW. II. 252). Eve stands for 'the wanting soul' in its absolute
affliction. The speech is intensely and movingly dramatic, not only in
itself but in its context, standing against the vileness of Adam's rancour
which precedes it and his ungracious hauteur which succeeds it. In this
epic of desertion and betrayal, only Eve and the poet in his personal
invocations, with his dependence on the maternal Muse and his terror
of wandering 'Erroneous . . . and forlorn' (VII. 20) unashamedly lose
face like this. Eve's speech is panic-stricken, with a note of childlike
pleading; yet it retains a mode of address proper to Eden, a ceremonious

111

lyricism, metrical balance and right feeling, in contrast to the grating belligerence of Adam and the baleful looks with which we understand him to be favouring her. The speech derives from terror, self-recognition, contrition and finally grace. Its capacity to look upon the self as the object of one's own sentence (*me* recurs nine times, three of which open the last two lines) recalls the atoning voice of Christ offering himself in cancellation of man's debt to the punitive and legalistic Almighty:

> Behold me then, me for him, life for life
> I offer; on me let thine anger fall;
> Account me man . . .
>
> (III. 236–8)

The parallel is real, and really moving; yet it occurs within a tangle of contradictory allegiances and adverse textual strategies. Christ is, after all, a blameless pillar of rectitude. Eve is the fragile, central load-bearing factor in the human world of *Paradise Lost*, weighed down with the stress of a huge onus. The narrative voice betrays gratuitous complicity with Adam in his complacent survey of her humiliated posture at his feet: 'Creature so fair his reconcilement seeking' (X. 943). On the one hand, she exemplifies the proper posture for the human soul to adopt in relation to God: 'sorrow unfeigned, and humiliation meek' (X. 1104), the posture of humility which is achieved by both in the last line of the Book. On the other hand, she presents an icon of female mortification gratifying to the patriarchal ego; a face-saving and caste-conserving device which does service both for narrator and protagonist.

Yet it is possible to see Milton's Eve as attaining a greater stability and certainty than any other character in *Paradise Lost*. The poem is predicated upon loss and built upon a ruin. The Garden in Book XI is swept out to sea to become a barren island (830–7). Iconoclastically, Milton demolishes the idea of place as the foundation of safety. Michael's insistence that Adam's and Eve's external home will be replaced by 'a paradise within thee, happier far' (XII. 587) is corroborated by Eve's final speech which, with extraordinary simplicity and equanimity, demonstrates the necessity and possibility of abdicating external security for a balance of mutual faith and trust:

112

> but now lead on;
> In me is no delay; with thee to go,
> Is to stay here; without thee here to stay,
> Is to go hence unwilling; thou to me
> Art all things under heaven, all places thou,
> Who for my wilful crime art banished hence.
>
> (XII. 614–19)

The broken line, with its seesaw motion upon the caesura, gives us pause. It is at once an index of the irremediable division wrought at the fall, and the possibility of using that gap or break in the rhythm as a place of advantage upon which to settle a new and genuine, if makeshift and self-validating, balance. The paradoxes Eve expresses are tenuously arrayed both upon the stress of their own oppositions and by the tension set up by their placement, apportioned between lines. The breath of the urgent human voice compels union of what the form severs, and the breach between incompatibles (man and woman; desire and actuality; delinquent language and truant knowledge) all but disappears in the moment of speaking, so profound and moving is the act of faith that inspires the riddling 'to go, / Is to stay'. We believe her because this is so obviously heart's evidence: the inner truth validated by the highest authority in *Paradise Lost*, the ability to say 'I know' (610), the subjectivity of the believer. Eve knows because she has dreamed her truth (611), receiving it at the same source from which the poet derived his testament (see page 103 above). No one else has right or power to query the authenticity of the experience, which carries upon it the aura of dream so numinous that it issues in conviction and the imperative mood: 'But now lead on; / In me is no delay'. Whereas Eve had previously entrusted herself to the subtle and devious entanglements of the Serpent's thought-processes ('Lead then, said Eve', (IX. 631), now she places reliance on the light within, premonitory of the 'paradise within thee, happier far', predicted by Michael. In so far as language, which itself maintains and reinforces a code of arbitrary, blurred or complex distinctions concomitant upon the fall, can express unity and stability, Eve's language here does so. To pivot upon the break in the line is to redispose all the elements of the sentence upon that nexus. It is to emphasise dissociation; but a happy outcome (a kind of *felix culpa* in the linguistic world) is to stabilise the verb *to be* at the opening of consecutive lines in that rhetorical figure of speech which Puttenham calls 'the Crosse–copling':[16] 'Is to go . . . / Is to stay . . . / Art', the mind taking over from the wilderness as the place to be. This unanimity (literally, one mind) is reproduced in the retention of the verb in the third instance: 'thou to me / Art all things under heaven', where *thou* and *me* are joined as closely as grammar (whose laws are such that it cannot undo their difference) can secure them.

*　　　　　*　　　　　*

> The mind is its own place, and in it self
> Can make a heaven of hell, a hell of heaven.
>
> (I. 254–5)

> So much the rather thou celestial Light
> Shine inward, and the mind through all her powers
> Irradiate, there plant eyes . . .
>
> (III. 51–3)

If inner space is the true location of *Paradise Lost* and Puritan subjectivism the final arbiter of reality, what is to be said of the objective cosmos beyond the enclosure of the believer's mind? *Paradise Lost* is a poem of the modern world which tests knowledge against the findings of contemporary science, especially the sciences of optics, physics and astronomy, and finds there a relativism which reinforces its Puritan and Platonist scepticism as to what can be known for sure about reality. Modern science corroborates the findings of Milton's blind eyes. Or rather, his eyes for being blind to externals, measure reality more accurately than those cunningly made but maladaptive instruments which cause us to exclaim 'I see' when they focus some image to which they happen to be conveniently adjusted. Modern science also confirms the implications of some late Renaissance, baroque and mannerist art,[17] with its *trompe-l'œil*, illusionist's vistas, adapted to the viewing of an individual standing at a given relation to the object of vision: if he maintains an eye-line on the frescoed dome, he will get a full view of the empyrean. His eye will clamber from earth to heaven, which seems to burst down through the roof, like Gaulli's *Worship of the Holy Name*, in Il Gesu, Rome. If he steps out of line, the whole effect is lost. Now you see it; now you don't. Subjective stance determines what is understood. In baroque, the illusory technique of *quadratura* dominates: the real walls of the nave are extended upwards so that they appear to reach into the distant skies, as in Andrea Pozzo's *The Glory of St Ignatius*, the ceiling fresco at S. Ignazio, Rome. Where do the true columns of stone which uphold the building end and the 'false' columns of paint which present simulacra of the pillars of eternity begin? Milton's visit to Italy in 1638–9 seems to have opened his eyes to the terror and beauty of baroque's vertiginous dynamic.

Optics and astronomy, the visual arts and the 'new Philosophy' enhanced the suspicion that locating the truth was a game of blind-man's-buff. Perception and cognition had come into doubt. Eschewing Tycho's compromise of an earth-centred sun and a heliocentric planetary system Milton writes from an impossible position of enforced eccentricity with one foot of his compass in the Ptolemaic and earth-centred cosmology and another in the Copernican heliocentric cosmos based on observation, where planetary rotations had expanded into ellipses and planetary motion now accelerated, now slowed down, according to the body's distance from the planet.[18] The 'trepidation of the spheares' so eloquently invoked by Donne,[19] had a scientific and emotional implication in keeping with the double meaning served by the word. Trepidation and vertigo are the appropriate reaction both to Kepler's heavens and to Pozzo's ceiling. The sophisticated mathematics of perspectivism accused the viewer of being out of true to the object of vision: the perspective glass, telescope, microscope, undid the amiable relationship between the eye and the field of perception.[20] To view one's own image in the preposterous looking-glass of the period was to encounter possible shrinkage, dilation, expansion, distortion, inflation: to inhabit the inside of a nutshell (*Hamlet*, II.ii. 254–6) or seem to throw a shadow over half the globe. The perspectivism which would lead to the relativist's nightmare of Swift's Lilliput and Brobdingnag was well under way by the time Milton inherited it. The perspective picture was a popular toy in the sixteenth century – exemplified by Holbein's *The Ambassadors*, in which the strange awry ellipse at the feet of the Tudor imperialist with his icons of science and culture (globes, navigating instruments, lute) can only be interpreted if you stand at an oblique angle to the picture. It is a *memento mori*, a skull: that which is not normally perceived because we do not choose that angle of vision in life, but which alters the whole meaning of the picture once we have stood aside to recognise it. In *Richard II*, Shakespeare has Bushy refer to the perspective picture and the popular 'perspective glass', a multiplying glass whose many facets supply different images:

> For sorrow's eye, glazed with blinding tears,
> Divides one thing entire to many objects,
> Like perspectives, which, rightly gaz'd upon,
> Show nothing but confusion; ey'd awry,
> Distinguish form.
>
> (II. ii. 16–20)

To see straight, it may be necessary to stand askance from the norm. Ultimately, the magnifying lens was to throw doubt on the humanism that produced it, questioning man's relation to the world he seeks to dominate by his knowledge. Milton's friend Marvell inverted, in the wink of an eye, the relative proportions of all givens, which become, fascinatingly, variables unfixed by the roving eye of the observer. Cattle in a distant prospect, entering in at the eye become features in an art-world:

> Such, in the painted world, appeared
> D'Avenant with the universal herd.

> They seem within the polished grass
> A landskip drawn in looking-glass,
> And shrunk in the huge pasture show
> As spots, so shaped, on faces do –
> Such fleas, ere they approach the eye,
> In multiplying glasses lie.
> They feed so wide, so slowly move,
> As constellations do above.[21]

Marvell's 'multiplying glasses' are that novelty of the day, the microscope,[22] whose raids on the invisible had conjured into the range of the astonished eye a panorama of minutiae: a new world opened out on the specimen tray. The revelatory device is a work of art (Renaissance 'art' is a collective term including what we now designate as science, technology and art), as a painting, a poem or any representation or reflection is a work of art. Marvell blinks his eye, and cattle in a field from a distance appear like a mirage in a glossy mirror; the indeterminacy of the specks to which they shrink resemble the blemishes on a human face. The close-up view of a human face and the far-off view of a field (implicitly, the 'face' of Nature) create in the poem a wildly contentious frame of reference: where are we standing, at a distance or with our eyes almost on the object? And what are we seeing, Nature or Nature-through-art? Blemishes on a face now give place to fleas on a specimen tray, under a microscope not quite brought into focus; then with a sudden bound of imagination, the slow motion of these scarcely discernible specks on the horizon of vision is assimilated to the vast measure of the planetary system. This sequence of witty optical shocks reflects a world that, for Marvell's and Milton's generation, would never be the same again. The odds is gone and nothing is left remarkable except in its volatility under the shifting eye of the individual. The ratio of images: cow is to flea is to planet, carries a subliminal burden of *Angst* in its collapse of value-distinctions along with distinctions of magnitude. Both creaturely life in a Horatian agricultural setting within a safe convention such as the country house poem, and the wheeling constellations at the farthest reaches of the cosmos which is the largest extension of the human home, may be pictured as infestations. Three-quarters of a century later, Swift was to reveal to the revolted eye of Gulliver the lice crawling in the clothes of the Brobdingnagians:

> I could see distinctly the limbs of these vermin with my naked eye, much better than those of an European louse through a microscope, and their snouts with which they rooted like swine.

From the King of Brobdingnag's exalted viewpoint, it was inevitable that:

> I cannot but conclude the bulk of your natives to be the most pernicious race of little odious vermin that nature ever suffered to crawl upon the surface of the earth. [23]

117

A not incomparable scrambling of normative perspectives may be viewed through Milton's threatening lens, in a state of acute flux between close-up and bird's-eye views producing images that swell and dwindle in the one sentence, or vary impossibly between the two; his volatile narrative that telescopes or extends time, and oscillates between tenses whilst it simultaneously renders grammatical relationships ambivalent; his epic similes that invoke multifarious times and places, opening out and elaborating apparently digressive minor stories which trick the eye away from the major narrative into strange *coups d'œil* which stand in relations of extreme obliquity to the body of the text.

Only one of Milton's contemporaries is mentioned by name in *Paradise Lost*: that individual is Galileo,[24] whom Milton said he had met in the period of the blind and aged astronomer's house-arrest near Florence. The opening sentence of his book, *Siderius Nuntius* (*The Star-Messenger*) of 1610, ran:

> About ten months ago a report reached my ears that a Dutchman had constructed a telescope . . . After a little time I succeeded in making such an instrument through deep study of the laws of refraction . . . And then bringing my eye to the concave lens I saw objects large and near.[25]

Bringing his inner eye to the concave lens of the poem, Milton bends light to create a ratio for viewing the shield of Satan by viewing Galileo observing the moon through his telescope:

> He scarce had ceased when the superior fiend
> Was moving toward the shore; his ponderous shield
> Ethereal temper, massy, large, and round,
> Behind him cast; the broad circumference
> Hung on his shoulders like the moon, whose orb
> Through optic glass the Tuscan artist views
> At evening from the top of Fesole,
> Or in Valdarno, to descry new lands,
> Rivers or mountains in her spotty globe.
> His spear, to equal which the tallest pine
> Hewn on Norwegian hills, to be the mast

Of some great ammiral, were but a wand,
He walked with . . .

(I. 283–95)

Galileo is presented as part of an epic simile, whose traditional generic function is that of rhetorical magnification and elaboration. If Satan's shield is to be compared with the full moon enlarged through the telescope's lens, then it is inflated to dimensions never visible to the unaided eye. The image acts as a refractive lens to endow the warrior-figure of Satan with cosmic dimensions: it towers above us, swollen beyond what our imaginations can conceive even at full stretch, with the moon on its shoulders (a moon indeterminate between that registered by the naked eye and that distended in the 'optic glass'). Characteristically, Milton's epic similes redirect and diversify atten-tion. We are less interested in the light that is thrown on Satan than in the revolutionary thinker of taboo thoughts stigmatised by Satan's representatives on earth, the Inquisition. Attention is stolen from Satan by Galileo: Galileo as an instance of the perceiving eye and mind, and the act of perception itself. Traditional criticism has taught Milton's readers to look in his epic similes for their occult decorum:[26] to interpret them as if they constituted a perfectly self-consistent secret code of moral meanings and implications, which could all be read back into the controlling image. If the similes could be detected as being digressive, there must be something wrong with them, as Eliot held.[27] But similes may be meaningfully digressive if they contain new subjects. Many become narratives or descriptions with their own (temporary) centres of gravity: or, to alter the metaphor, they begin as offshoots from the parent story which set down new root-systems, a principle in Nature known to Milton: 'in the ground / The bended twigs take root, and daughters grow / About the mother tree' (PL. IX. 1104–6). For a short space, the narrative centralises a minor subject in preference to the major. The poem at this point is more about Galileo than about Satan. His whereabouts is problematic, 'the top of Fesole, / Or in Valdarno'. In the former place, he can be imagined at a high vantage point on the low earth, taking isolated cognisance of the nearest of the heavenly bodies. The reader has the sense of the unknown and unknowable infinity of space reaching incalculably beyond the range of his petty instrument: Galileo operates on the fringe of the created

119

universe, with night falling and his 'optic glass' to his eye, incommunicado to his fellow men. As a dweller 'in Valdarno' (the Valley of the Arno, where Florence is situated) Galileo floats in the poem not only an intimation of deep, abstracted thought reminiscent of the Platonist-Hermetic thinker in the 'high lonely tower' at the occult centre of *Il Penseroso* (86–92), but of exilic loneliness and alienation. The rivers and mountains of his native Italy are no more his home than the 'Rivers or mountains' of the moon he studies or than London or Chalfont St Giles could be home to Milton after the Restoration. They are citizens of another country. In a letter of 1666 Milton spoke of patriotism, which: 'after having allured me by her lovely name, has almost *expatriated* me, as it were . . . One's *Patria* is wherever it is well with him' (*Letter to Peter Heimbach*, 15 August 1666; *CPW*. VIII. 4). In this most personal and autobiographical of epic poems – far nearer in this sense to Wordsworth's *Prelude* than to Spenser's *The Faerie Queene* – Galileo, and Milton-in-Galileo, stand as aliens whose country is the dissident self. Milton focuses on the self in the act of perception. Revolutionary perception changes history and deranges the accustomed field of vision, substituting for the easy assumptions of consensus the anomalous relationships proposed by the interrogative mind. Milton and Galileo are researchers who have set up their experiments in Hell. Ethically wary critics have felt that by placing his first allusion to Galileo in a context close to Satan, Milton may have been questioning or implicating the lawfulness of his studies.[28] Interest does not seem to this reader to centre on the licit or illicit character of his explorations at all: it is rather on the destabilisation achieved by his findings. Galileo's observations were problematic rather than definitive: the solipsistic fixity of the old model of the cosmos is not replaced by a comfortably reorganised system. His discovery of the moons of the planets of Jupiter and Saturn opened the way to the modern science of dynamics. It solved nothing, but might well be taken to demonstrate the moral hammered home throughout *Paradise Lost*: the Socratic and Solomonic acknowledgement that all we know is that we know nothing.

Derangement of perspective is continued from the description of Satan's shield to his spear, with its rapid play of *trompe-l'œil* image-substitutions: *spear – tallest pine – mast – wand*. Place the loftiest Norwegian pine against Satan's spear and it would appear a mere wand in comparison. The optical trickery of the introduction of the mast flickeringly tempts our interest away from the relativistic mathematics involved in understanding the comparison with contemporary navigation and its problems, a major metaphor of *Paradise Lost*. Our minds slide up and down a scale of ratios whose purpose is to delude us into thinking we *can* imagine what is demonstrated to be manifestly beyond our imaginative scope. In the country of the blind, such shifting ratios may be a norm. The illusionism of the first two Books is rooted in the blind seer's enquiry as to what lens may be found to focus totality: for *Paradise Lost* is committed not just to telling a complete truth but *the* complete Truth. It searches for the *terra firma* of an objective knowledge and language through the confusion caused by the fall's prejudicing of all vision by manacling it to perspective. The epic similes are connectives between the superhuman material of the story and our human experience. But they function most pointedly to emphasise how dislocated from reality our limited vision makes us. Magnitude cannot be appraised or recognised for what it is when we stand too close, just as the planets are veiled from our scrutiny by distance. Satan prone on the flood is compared with:

> that sea-beast
> Leviathan, which God of all his works
> Created hugest that swim the ocean stream:
> Him haply slumbering on the Norway foam,
> The pilot of some small night-foundered skiff,
> Deeming some island, oft, as seamen tell,
> With fixed anchor in his scaly rind
> Moors by his side under the lee, while night
> Invests the sea, and wished morn delays . . .
> (I. 200–8)

The power and poignancy of this image depend on its apprehension of the essential disproportion between the human being and the conditions in which he must survive. Traditional criticism stresses the moral burden of the simile: 'it illustrates the delusiveness of Satan and the danger of trusting his false appearance of greatness in the early books of the poem.'[29] It may indeed have been conceived as a moral caution rooted in Job, the bestiaries and Renaissance emblem

lore, but that is far from the impact of the interpolated narrative on
a reader. What alternative has the navigator in his plight but to trust
the evidence of his senses and moor to the motionless rock, given
the fact that his boat is benighted and in danger of sinking? The
creature is 'hugest', the vessel built on a different scale, 'some small
. . . skiff'; the eyes of the pilot ill-adapted to the dark and his sense
of touch to the detection of the difference (because of the grotesque
distortion of scale) between rock and 'scaly rind'. The reader, standing at a putatively remoter distance, has a chance to see it all, in
proportion and hence to grasp the disastrous nature of the seaman's
mistake – though scarcely to criticise it. The feeling of the passage,
with its extraordinary atmosphere of foreboding, the slowing-down of
time through the vigilance of anxiety ('wished morn delays'), and the
strangeness of the dark, illimitable seascape, is surely of the order
'There, but for the grace of God, go I'. The switch of tenses from
past to present reinforces this identification, as does the sense of
insecurity both recorded and generated by *Paradise Lost* at nearly
every point in its narrative, as to where we are going and how to get
there.

The geography of *Paradise Lost* stretches out in every direction, from
'Cambalu . . . And Samarchand by Oxus . . . To Agra . . . Mosco
. . . Mombaza, and Quiloa, and Melind . . . On Europe . . . Rich
Mexico . . . El Dorado' (Adam's survey of the globe in Book XI.
388–411), from end to end of the map charted by Renaissance
explorers and traders. It is a map imperfectly known, its longitudes and
latitudes inadequately plotted, on tendentious evidence; its people and
customs often the product of European fable, fourth-hand report,
anxious or fabulous imaginings. Again, epic similes carry the burden of
this sense of an as yet unnavigable *terra incognita* surrounding the island
of the known and homely. Just as the cosmography of *Paradise Lost*
admits of no determinacy:

> The golden sun in splendour likest heaven
> Allured his eye: thither his course he bends
> Through the calm firmament; but up or down
> By centre or eccentric, hard to tell,
> Or longitude . . .
>
> (III. 572–6)

so its geography is inconclusive. Paired nouns predominate in the poem: but they are just as likely to be linked by *or* constructions as by *and*. To alternate *up* and *down*, the central dynamic of *Paradise Lost*, is to collapse the meaningfulness of the distinction. The scrupulous narrator cannot say whether Satan followed the sun's own trajectory or cut across it because he cannot claim to know whether the Ptolemaic or Copernican model of the universe is authentic. By trailing the disconnected *Or longitude* along behind the helpless shrug *hard to tell*, Milton manages to suggest that the universe (to the eye of the candid) appears less a riddle than a nonsense. Anything you like to imagine that decently saves the phenomena may (or may not) be true. Our own world is, to a different degree, a matter of guesswork. As Sin and Death in Book X prepare to erect the causeway from Hell to earth, their enterprise is described thus:

> As when two polar winds blowing adverse
> Upon the Cronian Sea, together drive
> Mountains of ice, that stop the imagined way
> Beyond Petsora eastward, to the rich
> Cathaian coast.
>
> (X. 289–93)

The imagined way: a north-eastern passage to Cathay had been investigated by Hudson in 1608 and 1609, but his route was barred by ice. The world we think we know is a patchwork of apparently verifiable data joined at the seams by conjecture, desire (gold) and corporate illusion. The pilot in the skiff mooring in the lee of Leviathan is only the first of many representative voyagers in *Paradise Lost* to become confounded on the untrustworthy sea which encompasses the margins of indistinct or partially recorded shorelines. A modern reader must disadvantage himself by throwing the imagination back to a time before aeroplane and radio in order to register the full impact of the areas of shadow around the frame of Milton's picture; the intensity of the desire for the advantage of a bird's-eye view, together with the awareness that such a view is neither available nor likely to become so. The poem is richly indebted to the Renaissance travelogues published by merchant adventurers and explorers on their return from their journeys: Purchas, Knollys, Heylyn, Hakluyt. They stress the perils, difficulties and contingencies of their quest as much as their providential successes, and Milton follows them in emphasising the susceptibility of the traveller to meteorological freaks on his obscure, pitfalled jouney. Uriel gliding on a sunbeam comes

> swift as a shooting star
> In autumn thwarts the night, when vapours fired
> Impress the air, and shows the mariner
> From what point of his compass to beware
> Impetuous winds . . .
>
> (IV. 556–60)

Momentary glimpses into the turbulent atmosphere are all the voyager can hope for in order to plot his course safely on the unpredictable surface of a world in which he is never fully at home.

Magnification and diminution of vision work alongside literal acts of metamorphosis, expansion and reduction in the course of the narrative, to express the instability of the world of *Paradise Lost*. Lucifer metamorphoses from 'Light-bearer' to 'Enemy' (the allegorical meaning of Satan) by Divine deed poll; his story is a narrative of successive transformations, from archangel to demon, to false cherub, animal and bird, Serpent, invisibility, common foot soldier. His multiform incoherency is of course a dramatisation of the Devil's legendary ability to play-act: it is given a devious rhetorical manifestation by Milton's invention of a figurative category midway between simile and metaphor, with an insinuation of literality, so that when Satan invades Paradise like a 'wolf' a sheepcote or, perching on the Tree of Life, 'Sat like a cormorant' (IV. 183, 196), or crouches at Eve's ear 'Squat like a toad' (IV. 800), readers can go away believing that they have witnessed not a similitude but another of Satan's protean shape-changes. The visual world of the fall is phantasmagorical. Apparitions rise out of the soil: Pandæmonium's magnificent golden excrescence, a masterpiece of indecorous baroque 'Rose like an exhalation' (I. 711), a sumptuous masque production, at whose gates the thronging devils suddenly shrink from their grand dimensions to miniatures of themselves – a space-saving device never dreamed of by the poet of *Comus* anxious about overcrowding:

they but now who seemed
In bigness to surpass Earth's giant sons
Now less than smallest dwarfs, in narrow room
Throng numberless, like that pygmean race
Beyond the Indian mount . . .

(I. 777–81)

Thus belittled, the lesser demons can all fit into the hall of Pandæmonium, while within 'in their own dimensions like themselves' (793) the great Seraphic Lords and Cherubim sit in conclave. *Paradise Lost* is almost never given credit for its comic vision by its sober-sided readers, though occasionally rebuked for its heavy jests – the playful elephant of Book IV (345–7); 'No fear lest dinner cool' in Book V (396) – but a comic view is necessitated by the telescopic/microscopic play of refracted light onto the subject-matter. Comedy depends for its effects upon a perceived violation of due proportion. It affords us an angle from whose advantage we can look down upon its victims. So here the buzzing multitudes of demons shrink to a size at which their palaver must seem Lilliputian to the large norm of the reader's view. The full (and serious) comic point is achieved, however, only when we have assessed the great figures of the aristocracy, erected above the *hoi poloi* by their own self-magnifying pretension, plotting in Popish 'secret conclave' our own destiny (796). This mass shrinkage is echoed in the answering Book X (our last visit to Pandæmonium) on the anti-triumph of Satan in which the demons are transformed into 'thick swarming. . . . Complicated monsters' (X. 522–3): a farcical dramatisation of the Biblical promise that 'He hath put down the mighty from their seats, and exalted them of low degree' (Luke 1:52).

Paradise Lost links vision with flight. The Renaissance was the period in which both aeroplane and spaceship were seriously mooted. Leonardo's study of aerodynamics based on the construction of the bird's wing led to designs for planes; in the allegory *Kepler's Dream*, the astronomer imagines a space-traveller as being hauled into space by a group of daemons. He is anaesthetised by opiates to evade the pain of gravitational pull:

The first getting into motion is very hard for him, for he is twisted and turned just as if, shot from a cannon, he were sailing across mountains and seas. Therefore, he must be put to sleep beforehand, with narcotics and opiates, and he must be arranged, limb by limb, so that the shock will be distributed over the individual members . . .

I define gravity as a power similar to magnetic power – a mutual attraction. The attractive force is greater in the case of two bodies that are near to each other than it is in the case of bodies that are far apart.[30]

In Kepler, the space-traveller, whose experiences are described in a gripping narrative, of great visual and imaginative scope, is a figure for the astronomer himself and his thought-processes, visiting the galaxies and penetrating their secrets in the mind's deductive eye. The seer is a flier. *Paradise Lost*, like *Faustus* seventy years before, deals with the archetypal wish for wings as the means of obtaining power over our condition. The dream insinuated into Eve by Satan in Book V culminates in an hallucination of flight: 'Forthwith up to the clouds / With him I flew, and underneath beheld / The earth outstretched immense, a prospect wide / And various' (V. 86–9). Flight in *Paradise Lost* is equated with power; and power is synonymous with vision. Eve emphasises the panoramic view her airborne perspective affords: dizzy and elated, she has achieved 'high exaltation' by flying free of partial perspective (90). Eve, Satan and the narrative persona of *Paradise Lost* all bid for the total view, equated with the 'God's-eye-view' and therefore dangerous or preposterous for mortals to attempt. The lidless eye of God's omniscience sees it all, inhumanly unmoved, from his point of advantage beyond subjectivism. Our first view of God is of an Almighty act of viewing:

> Now had the almighty Father from above,
> From the pure empyrean where he sits
> High throned above all highth, bent down his eye,
> His own works and their works at once to view . . .
> (III. 56–9)

His first words ironically call attention to the sight of Satan on his expedition: 'Only begotten Son, seest thou what rage / Transports our adversary?' (80–1). There is an intense absurdity in Omniscience consulting Omniscience as to what it can or cannot see. For how could the Son not see, and what could come as a surprise to one immunised

126

to all catastrophe through possession of the objective eye-line that can neither blink nor blur through a tear, and can see round every corner in time and space? Panoramic vision in *Paradise Lost* is both freedom and security, a compensation for the loss of all bearings initiated by the fall.

The Satanic voyage of discovery out of Hell and into the cosmos represents the subjective self's attempt to penetrate the boundaries of ignorance and claw its way out to the fullest possible view of the sum of things. As the first planetary investigator, he is the first to view the universe of *Paradise Lost* in a multiple perspective enabled by his flight, a travelling lens like Galileo's *Star Messenger*. As the voyeur of Eden, he will infiltrate with his destabilising vision the stable walled enclosure with its humanist proportions where man stands to nature as the measure of all things, like the humanist statuary of Rome and Florence. Milton's account of Satan's flight into Chaos gripped the imaginations of later, and especially Romantic painters, who – like Fuseli, Blake and Martin – sought to realise in a grammar of paint the linguistic maelstrom articulated by Milton.[31] The Miltonic Abyss is the symbolic locus of conflict in its purest form: raw, inchoate desire, will, energy, the disorderly contents of the subconscious mind left to its own devices. It contains the *prima materia* from which creation springs and the detritus which is left over when reason has taken its own counsel. Milton presents it as an area of meaningless and self-contradictory excitation and blaring noise undifferentiated into meaningful syllables, dangerous to the point of engendering suicidal thoughts. Its dark mass surges threateningly around the contours of a delicately balanced, light-clarified universe. Milton invented a language within English to denote the experience of Chaos. It is heard in Books I and II in every Devil's accent but reaches its apotheosis in Satan's proposals to explore the cosmos beyond hell-gates:

> Who shall tempt with wandering feet
> The dark unbottomed infinite abyss
> And through the palpable obscure find out
> His uncouth way, or spread his airy flight
> Upborne with indefatigable wings
> Over the vast abrupt, ere he arrive
> The happy isle . . .
>
> (II. 404–10)

127

It is a linguistic world dense with epithet and connotation but empty of noun and denotation. Adjectives massively predominate in this evocation of a horror more potent than that of Hell because it is without ground or limit: *wandering, dark, unbottomed, infinite, palpable, uncouth, airy, indefatigable, vast, happy*. Over a quarter of the diction takes the form of epithet, so that in line 405 the definite article which opens the line is kept waiting for its noun until the end, and at line 408, the six-syllabled *in-de-fat-ig-ab-le* strives out its way along the metre to fill more than half the blank verse line. Adjectives are by their very nature dependent forms of speech which are structurally dispensable. To ground your sense upon an adjective would be to try to lean on a colour or walk on a sound. Chaos in *Paradise Lost* is a sea of adjectives. The imagined 'wandering feet' of Satan plunge straight through them in search of a foundation on which to rest – a fruitless search, as the rhetoric ironically insists: for, on close inspection, the array of adjectives seems to be tending towards the negative: *dark* is absence of light, *un*bottomed opens out a vertiginous drop and *in*finite knows no boundaries; *un*couth maps out a directionless path and *in*defatigable implies the unslackening continuity of exertion demanded by absence of resting-places. Yet even this undermining by negation cannot express the peculiar restlessness with which the Miltonic language of Chaos is charged. Some profound struggle and discord is to be witnessed within the grammar itself, which wrestles with the very conditions on which it depends in order to discriminate meaning. The grammatical status of words, phrases, clauses and ultimately whole sentences in *Paradise Lost* may be either plural or unsure. Here, the noun/adjective distinction has been challenged, by the incorporation of two Latin-derived adjectives-used-as-nouns, by the process known as zero-morpheme derivation, which was an attested Renaissance resource for enriching the vocabulary of English language during its period of greatest expansion (see pages 33–7 above): *the palpable obscure, the vast abrupt*, on the model of *the deep* for *the sea* a metonymic device invariably preferred by Milton. A quality is materialised, but without entirely abandoning its adjectival status. *Obscure* becomes a solid wall of darkness you can paradoxically slide right through; *abrupt*, from the Latin *ab* + *ruptus*, 'broken off', seems to be on a cliff-edge searching for its noun: the reader's voice may hang momentarily as Miltonic usage and common usage come into transient conflict.

Miltonic usage wins; but common usage does not abjectly lose: a sense of the oddness of the norm-defying illusionist's trick remains, and at the same time the shock waves reverberate throughout the total context, drawing all the qualifying adjectives fractionally further towards the condition of nouns, for if *the obscure* and *the abrupt* are possible coinages, so might be *the palpable* and *the vast*. Landslide and subsidence are principles at work within the very grammar of the journey.

Galilean magnification deranges the world of the eye in *Paradise Lost*, subverting the laws of proportion on which a communally agreed idea of what is reasonable and right depends. In the account of Satan's expedition into Chaos Milton extends the principle to the world of the ear. Blasting noise assaults Satan's ear like the siege of a city in time of war – an image classically stylised in presentation but speakingly close to the experience of the recent past in the violent siege warfare of the Civil Wars whose memory is one of the traumas recorded in *Paradise Lost* and relived not only in frequent epic similes but in the account of the War in Heaven in Books V and VI, told (many readers have felt) with a mingling of weariness and revulsion proper to the poet who admitted to being 'Not sedulous by nature to indite / Wars' (IX. 27–8). The undifferentiated noise of Chaos constitutes primal threat:

> Nor was his ear less pealed
> With noises loud and ruinous (to compare
> Great things with small) than when Bellona storms,
> With all her battering engines bent to raze
> Some capital city; or less than if this frame
> Of heaven were falling, and these elements
> In mutiny had from her axle torn
> The steadfast earth.
>
> (II. 920–7)

Milton's susceptibility to loud noise is attested by his biographers: it is the converse of his delicate and highly wrought attunement to the harmonies of music and poetry, and latterly was no doubt reinforced by the compensatory adaptation of his other senses to blindness. Sound is the material in which the poet works. Aggressive, undifferentiated noise is attended with a horror which threatens the foundations of life itself for the poet of *Paradise Lost*, as the autobiographical Invocation to Book VII makes clear. The modern world is recorded as a Bacchanalian festival of 'barbarous dissonance' (32), a phrase taken over verbatim from *Comus* (549), and a 'savage clamour' (36), capable of deranging the patterned control of the poet's song: the Restoration court and government bring in the lawless fury that impelled the Maenads to destroy Orpheus. In *Paradise Lost* as in *Samson Agonistes* there is an indelibly memorable sense of the physical helplessness and dependency of the blind poet who must rely on clues to his state of safety or endangerment through the ear alone. *Paradise Lost* with enormous dignity and pathos affirms the heroic fortitude of sitting or lying in the dark and making one's habitation in the mind; later, *Samson* would explore the humiliations of this condition. A sense of safety and bearings which cannot come through the eye, must be mediated by hearing and touch. Restoration England, which surrounded Milton with an infestation of 'evil tongues' (26) threatening to talk him into prison or execution and which sent him into hiding until pardoned by the Act of Oblivion, is presented in the epic as a Bedlam or Babel of mindless noise. In his experience of cacophonously invasive sound as in many other ways, Satan's journey through Chaos implies Milton's journey. The poem acknowledges a certain identity between the experiences of its persons and its poet:

> Thee I revisit now with bolder wing,
> Escaped the Stygian pool, though long detained
> In that obscure sojourn, while in my flight
> Through utter and through middle darkness borne
> With other notes than to the Orphean lyre
> I sung of Chaos and eternal Night,
> Taught by the heav'nly Muse to venture down
> The dark descent, and up to reascend,
> Though hard and rare . . .
>
> (III. 13–21)

This is a description of the process of composition of the poem. In his own person the narrator-voyager has undertaken the journey he has just described; he has descended into Hell and struggled up through Chaos towards the light. What Satan underwent he was forced to endure by proxy, and what Satan saw and heard he must simultaneously imagine. The very terms in which Milton figures his descent and reascent are reminiscent of Satan's 'Long is the way / And hard, that out of hell leads up to light' (II. 432–3).

Dante's visionary journey in the *Inferno* is equally personal and implicated:

> When I had journeyed half of our life's way,
> I found myself within a shadowed forest,
> for I had lost the path which does not stray.
> Ah, it is hard to speak of what it was,
> that savage forest, dense and difficult,
> Which even in recall renews my fear:
> so bitter – death is hardly more severe.[32]

Dante, accompanied by Virgil, penetrates the concentric circles of the Inferno: he suffers with those whom he sees suffer, is personally sickened and bruised by the narratives of crime together with the sights of torture he encounters. The tradition of the Christian epic as a personal journey is only perpetuated, not initiated, by Milton. 'Detained' against his will in the obscurity of Hell, he is a flying voice and eyes; rising through Chaos as a fellow-witness of what Satan sees, he has fabricated another music than 'the Orphean' – a turbulent parlance of cacophony to express the 'void profound' (II. 438), 'that abortive gulf' (441), the 'vast vacuity' (932), the 'wasteful deep' (961). The Invocation implies a passivity in a poetic role to which he is in some sense doomed and condemned by the obligation to tell the whole truth. Milton's persona is a being led and under instruction (as Dante by Virgil and Beatrice) by his Muse into the terrible vistas of the underworld. Plato records in the *Republic* the unnerving intuition that those whom in art we impersonate, by ventriloquising speech for them, we also however fleetingly become. Milton becomes as one of the damned in their immersion in 'the Stygian pool', an implicated fellow-sufferer. The empathy with the pain of the damned and the respect for courage which most readers detect in Books I and II has been attributed either to Milton's subversive unconscious complicity with the devils' mutiny against God or to a conscious triprope technique set up by God's wily poet to surprise us into tumbling into the same specious error as the justly damned devils.[33] The writer of *Paradise Lost* is, by imaginative extension, all his creations, sharing space with good and evil alike, permissively crowding all unknown gaps in experience with his own consciousness. The Invocations reveal Milton's awareness of this sharing of space, which is not exactly complicity for it belongs to a factor in the artistic process which I would identify as a-theological. The swooping arc of the mimesis enacted in line 20, which plunges our imaginations down and brings them soaring up in a matter of ten syllables ('The dark descent, and up to reascend'), replays the apparently endless fluctuation of risings and fallings which constitute the oscillating narrative structure of *Paradise Lost* in such a way as to imply that the act of writing itself has been an experience of falling (as we say we 'fall' asleep or 'fall' into a bad dream and know, in the moment of dreaming, no alternative to the experience in which we are submerged). The passage operates as an ironic critique of the dream of freewill. Sailing into space in Book II, Satan buoyantly manages the elements only to take a mighty plunge: 'Fluttering his pennons vain plumb down he drops' – a magnificent bathos rhythmically contrived of dactylic flutterings succeeded by a precipitous rush of stressed monosyllables. Satan in Chaos performs in the comic key a grotesque parody of the endurance test undergone by the epic hero and epic poet:

> nigh foundered on he fares,
> Treading the crude consistence, half on foot,
> Half flying; behoves him now both oar and sail
> ....
> so eagerly the fiend
> O'er bog or steep, through strait, rough, dense, or rare,
> With head, hands, wings, or feet pursues his way,
> And swims, or sinks, or wades, or creeps, or flies:
> At length a universal hubbub wild
> Of stunning sounds and voices all confused,
> Borne through the hollow dark assaults his ear
> With loudest vehemence . . .
>
> (II. 940–2; 947–54)

The inchoate expenditure of prodigious energy is implied by the bravura images and rhythms: Milton handed the mock-heroic mode to Pope ready-made:

> As when a dab-chick waddles thro' the copse
> On feet and wings, and flies, and wades, and hops;
> So lab'ring on, with shoulders, hands and head,
> Wide as a wind-mill all his figures spread . . .[34]

Milton's rhetorical display subjects Satan to a status somewhat beneath that of a foolishly waddling dab-chick. Some furiously persistent hybrid like a fish (swims), like a serpent or insect (creeps), like a bird or bat (flies), struggles in a fluctuating medium to which it is entirely maladaptive. The cruelly detached eye of the narrator peruses him from a distance proper to the view we might take of an insect's plight, mocking the substandard technology with which the creature is supplied for its adventure: 'behoves him now both oar and sail'. In this freakish terrain a craft such as those in which the symbolic navigators of *Paradise Lost*'s epic similes confront the great seas of the world would be of use; or such as in a picturesque telescopic image in Book III Milton presents of human adaptation to surroundings when he pictures the plains of Sericana 'where Chineses drive / With sails and wind their cany wagons light' (438–9). This brief glimpse of the curious custom of land-sailing represents an intelligent adaptation to and hence benign reconciliation with the inimical environment, which is hard-won and rare in *Paradise Lost*. The tumult and confusion in which Satan welters form a brew which not only menacingly surrounds the delicately-balanced Creation but enters with him as an aspect of consciousness itself.

In Satan's deliverance from Chaos at the end of Book II we approach with him a calm realm in which a quiet and tempered poetic music enacts the blessing of measure, proportion and reason to one whose nerves have been unstrung by disproportion:

> But now at last the sacred influence
> Of light appears, and from the walls of heaven
> Shoots far into the bosom of dim Night
> A glimmering dawn . . .
>
> (II. 1034–7)

Influence means 'flowing in': it suggests at once the visual effect of light raying from its fountain in the sun and (ironically) the influence

133

sanctity might exert upon a turbulent breast. Our earth is now located by Satan's eye, tiny and remote:

> And fast by hanging in a golden chain
> This pendant world, in bigness as a star
> Of smallest magnitude close by the moon.
>   (II. 1051–3)

The marvel of Miltonic perspectivism is never more clear than in this peaceful, threatened moment. Like a watch on a chain the world is 'pendant' and dependent on the Heaven from which its security derives. If it loses such security it will drop straight down into the black vault below. Milton's imagination has leapt beyond the furthest reach of Galileo's telescope to train his lens with wonder and poignancy back upon the world which is man's inheritance and his place of confinement. The Satanic eye-line therefore brings a means of self-examination, revealing poise, equivalence and balance aligned with absolute frailty; but that eye-line itself is fraught with menace. An image seen at this remote perspective is diminished enough to be assimilated into the eye of the voyeur in its totality. The eye engrosses and corrupts its object. That feeding eye in its rapacity is, of course a commonplace of Renaissance doctrine, generally in the context of sexual rapacity but it may extend to all forms of cupidity and coveting.[35] In the savage final lines, Satan rushes along the path of his eye-line toward full possession of what has already entered him through the retina:

> Thither full fraught with mischievous revenge,
> Accursed, and in a cursed hour, he hies.
>   (II. 1054–5)

*   *   *

In Book III, the reader first encounters Milton's God. The presentation of God is the most problematic area of *Paradise Lost*, the one which has aroused readers to passions of denunciation (the most memorable being Shelley's and Empson's) and of justification arguing (often from Milton's theological tract, *Of Christian Doctrine*) that if you view it from the right angle the God of the poem could not in conscience have behaved otherwise than he did.[36] Milton's God has been

vituperated by readers in the post-Romantic and post-Christian era as
a potentate with a sarcastic tongue and a killing eye, setting up a test
his children were bound to fail and then judging them mercilessly for
their error. Christian readers are moved by the poem's quality of
personal witness, the strenuousness of its ethics and the sense of prayer
that often breathes from it with a lyricism whose beauty attaches to its
perception of God as light and love. There is no doubt that in
interpreting the thoughts and acts of God to us on the page, Milton
sets God up for our judgement. He weighs him in the scales of the
poem, bringing him into question, but also – most dangerously –
bringing himself into question. No area of the poem testifies more
emphatically to the fact that the reading-lamp we are constrained to
play upon this text is the self, with all its allegiances, quarrels and
uncertainties: a self which, agitated into a state of acute responsiveness
by the inflammatory nature of the material, colours what is seen in the
moment of perception. 'The text' says George Eliot, 'whether of
prophet or of poet, expands for whatever we can put into it, and even
his bad grammar is sublime.'[37] The dilation of the text at this crucial
point owes something to our determination to find here what we
expressly came to look for, whether for the pleasures of assent or
dissent; but as much to the necessary indeterminacy or indefiniteness
of God, and, secondly, to the binary and contradictory representation
which Milton undertook to make of him. God is the unknown, the
unintelligible, by his very nature beyond our linguistic system and our
capacities of scientific computation. He is beyond reason. He is also
(Lutherans and Calvinists felt no compunction or embarrassment in
admitting) beyond good and evil, in the terms understood and practised
by merely human beings:

> Thus God hides his eternal goodness and mercy under eternal wrath, his
> righteousness under iniquity. This is the highest degree of faith, to believe
> him merciful when he saves so few and damns so many, and to believe him
> righteous when by his own will he makes us necessarily damnable, so that
> he seems, according to Erasmus, to delight in the torments of the wretched
> and to be worthy of hatred rather than love.[38]

Luther's God is not only beyond our understanding, he is anathema to
right reason and to good feeling and utterly absurd from our point of

view. If we were to emulate the Almighty's behaviour, we should be rightly hanged for our crimes. If you will believe that the iniquitous God is good and merciful, you will believe anything. But you are required to believe it. Such a faith in the incredible is a test of election. The paradox Luther puts forward with such fierce relish is not unlike the quandary in which Milton and his Puritan generation found themselves after the Restoration. *Paradise Lost* conveys much of that sense of unknowability and incommensurability and something of the stressful sense of absurdity generated by the semantic and moral schism documented by Luther. Our evil may be his good: ethical vocabulary parts company with itself. That absurdity is intensified by the necessity of incorporating the unknown Omnipotent into an epic poem which must humanise all its participants in a drama of speech and action. The fictional vehicle can, by its very nature, have nothing to do with the reality it is supposed to represent. Only an imaginative collusion on the part of author and reader can cover this astounding gap between the tenor and the vehicle. The makeshift contrivance provided by the doctrine of accommodation tentatively propounded by Raphael in Book V covers as a link between those divorced parties, language and meaning. Raphael is pondering how to tell Adam the story of the War in Heaven:

> what if earth
> Be but the shadow of heaven, and things therein
> Each to other like, more than on earth is thought?
> (V. 574–6)

The *what if?* strategy is a familiar one in the poem. It represents a mental process which is a norm in Hell, where successions of *what if?*s catalogue the instability of an unknown future in which furore could break out at any time:

> *What if* the breath that kindled those grim fires
> Awaked should blow them into sevenfold rage
> And plunge us in the flames? Or from above
> Should intermitted vengeance arm again
> His red right hand to plague us? *What if* all
> Her stores were opened . . .
> (II. 170–5; emphases added; and see page 19 f. above)

What if? denotes uncertainty and discloses fear: rhetorical questions wincingly display susceptibility to holocaust and an openness to infinite alternatives, none of which can be closed off. *What if?* is a gesture of ignorance endured by all who lack the God's-eye view in the poem, not excluding the narrative persona and the mediating angels who bear God's messages but seldom seem quite certain of the facts of the matter, the language to be used or what it is permissible to say. *Paradise Lost* tells a tale which hopes to bear the relation of a 'shadow' to a substance, a Platonist mirroring at two removes, necessarily fallacious. It confesses the limitations of its medium to conjure into the immanence of words the transcendence of a God who can only be approached by way of negatives:

> Thee Father first they sung omnipotent,
> Immutable, immortal, infinite . . .
>
> (III. 372–3)

> Great are thy works, Jehovah, infinite
> Thy power; what thought can measure thee or tongue
> Relate thee . . .
>
> (VII. 602–4)

The periodic hymns of the angels focus on the *unutterable* character of the Divinity: the fact that his nature cannot be communicated because it is not like ours and not like anything we can know.

In order to make the accommodation between the inscrutable Deity and the decipherable fiction, Milton resorted to a number of poetic methods, none quite commensurate with the others. These methods vary from the mystical and visionary to the ratiocinative and theological. Each is rooted in profound paradox and dubiety, the one feigning that the Invisible can be 'seen', the other that the opposites within the Divine Nature can be consistently personified and satisfactorily resolved. In this dilemma, the multiple perspectivism and *trompe-l'œil* techniques by means of which Milton could focus the complexities of fallen experience are of minimal use. There is an overwhelming problem of vision, as the Invocation to Book III makes clear, greeting a God who cannot be named, viewed directly or addressed confidently:

> Hail, holy Light, offspring of Heaven first-born,
> Or of the eternal coeternal beam
> May I express thee unblamed? since God is light,
> And never but in unapproached light
> Dwelt from eternity, dwelt then in thee,
> Bright effluence of bright essence increate.
> Or hear'st thou rather pure ethereal stream,
> Whose fountain who shall tell?
>
> (III. 1–8)

This luminous Invocation explodes upon a reader's eye with gorgeous incandescence: yet for most readers (and to judge by the learned laboriousness of their expositions, even the most doctrinally learned of readers) the lines remain abstruse and opaque. They insist upon a fine scrupulosity of theological distinction, offering in a condensed and convoluted sentence construction three possible explanations for the origin of Light: (in simplified form) Light was the first creation of God; Light was uncreated and an aspect of the Father; Light's origin remains unknown. These possibilities remain entirely open, unanswered and unanswerable, in the form of rhetorical questions. The fact is that Milton candidly does not know exactly what he is invoking, though he knows the symbolism in which it has traditionally been clothed and the implications of such symbolism (notably, the neo-Platonist image of Light as a fountain pouring from the Eternal Source, an *effluence* or flowing-out of an essence).[39] He knows and here repeats the major questions that have been pondered for sixteen centuries since the making of the Gospels, but he does not know and cannot claim to know the answers: he refuses to advance a preferred theory. Furthermore, and more critically for the author of a sacred poem, he acknowledges his quandary as to what may or may not be said without blasphemy about subjects so holy: 'May I express thee *unblamed*?', 'Or hear'st thou rather?' God knows how he wishes to be addressed but he has not vouchsafed to transmit this information to us – even to the inspired poet filled to the brim from the fountain of Light. There is a problem here, then, not only of inaccuracy, but also of possible trespass and impiety. Who is being invoked? The poetic persona can neither see nor say. He is on very dangerous ground. Insufficient light has been granted by which to work, it seems, but monumental prohibitions and penalties operate within this obscurity.

Yet this very disadvantage – the inadequacy of the creature to apprehend the Creator – is paradoxically a needle's eye through which beams of intuition may scan the unknown. In the infernal and earthly sections of the poem, the special quality of Milton's vision depends on the maladaptiveness of the eye to the shifting semblances of reality. In the heavenly part of the poem it is again disproportion that signals a meaning words cannot label nor the eye confine: to express the transcendent stability of the Divine, Milton focuses on the maladaptiveness of the creaturely eye to its object of perception. The angelic choir rounds off the first half of Book III with a hymn of praise to God perceived as:

> Fountain of light, thy self invisible,
> Amidst the glorious brightness where thou sitt'st,
> Throned inaccessible, but when thou shadest
> The full blaze of thy beams, and through a cloud
> Drawn round about thee like a radiant shrine,
> Dark with excessive bright thy skirts appear,
> Yet dazzle heav'n, that brightest seraphim
> Approach not, but with both wings veil their eyes.
>   (III. 375–82)

The passage is a mesh of Scriptural allusions, all insistent on the invisibility of God to the human eye. On Mount Sinai God spoke from a cloud which resembled 'devouring fire' (Exodus 24:17). To see God's face, Jahweh later told Moses, was death (33:20): Moses' theophany consisted solely in the viewing of 'the back parts' of God (23). Isaiah's theophany included a vision of the six-winged Seraphim who covered their faces with one pair of wings (Isaiah 6:2). Our senses determine the limits of perception. But what if there exists in meaningful relation to us a percept beyond our sensory system? The poem's hypothesis is that there may be means of imagining it if we take as it were a back view, through adapting language and imagery (themselves dependent on sense experience) to a state of affairs which is *almost* completely nonsense to them or makes nonsense of them. Oxymoron and paradox at once question language and commonsense by insisting on self-contradiction and have some recognisable basis in the complexity of life as we know it, in the senses. Light cannot be darkness, nor

139

darkness light, without abolishing significant distinctions altogether: but it is open to anyone to make an imaginative guess at the experience of a light so severely intense that it can register as its own opposite. The shrill light that bores a hole in the optic nerve is part of the experience of anyone who has inadvertently glanced straight into the sun and carried away an afterglare which he is unable to blink off his field of vision. The afterglare is perceived as a spot of darkness when the eye is open but as light when the eye is closed. Migrainous auras and eye disturbances may yield comparable witness. So, of course, did the long-drawn-out process of blindness in Milton's tortured eyes, which recorded a phantasmagoria of light, colour and even sound effects, traumatically destroying the distinctions between light and dark so that he fell into the estrangement of 'darkness visible': 'but now, pure black, marked as if with extinguished or ashy light, and as if interwoven with it, pours forth' (*Letter to Philaras*, 1654, quoted more fully page 18 above). So light may be *known* as darkness and darkness as light. In transmitting an impression of the appearance of the clouded Deity as 'Dark with excessive bright', Milton calls upon the powers of the linguistic system at its full stretch, at that point at which the only authentic account must be a self-contradiction, and upon our imaginative resources by focusing as a stable reality a condition that is only freakishly or deviantly apparent in our world of sense-impressions. The obliquity of the presentation is the most dazzling and numinous stroke of all: we witness the most clear-sighted inmost order of angels, the Seraphim, in the act of being unable to witness the object of their adoration.

This 'visionary' method coexists in *Paradise Lost* with discrepant methods of portrayal: dramatic, theological and ratiocinative. *Paradise Lost* was first projected as a play and vestiges of the theatrical dynamic linger at several points in the text. The dramatic mode is the vehicle of the theological since in personifying God it represents two of the three persons of the Trinity. God the Father and God the Son are manifested as distinct persons so that the Divine is from the first viewed as twofold and binary: a schism which, however, is held to contain within itself all the principles of synthesis. I have no wish to participate in the issue as to whether Milton was or was not a follower of the Arian heresy (the subordination of Son to Father) and as to how the poem may be read as evidence of that or any other consistent theological position. It is the kind of debate which only makes sense if one considers a poem to be reducible to a collection of theological tenets – versified dogma. But poetry exposes, perplexes and betrays to doubt the fixities and definites that are brought to it, through the rich ambivalences of the language on which it must draw in order to be a poem. The fictionalising tendency of *Paradise Lost* is always to transmute the abstract 'persons' of God and the Son into that less coherent but challenging and arousing identity which we associate with 'personality'. The poem declares its human preferences and, in Heaven as on earth, these often run against the bias of the theological imperatives notionally underpinning *Paradise Lost*. For Milton, the Son was always more approachable and less sublimely inimical than his Father: a heavenly *alter ego* in whom the embarrassing invisibility of the Almighty was made blessedly 'conspicuous' (III. 385). The lovingly intercessive Son mitigated the deplorable and preposterous attitudes and actions of his terrible Father, as the New Testament tempered the Old, often by outright opposition. The Son stood nearer to us, as the father of a family (X. 216) who would in the course of time be incarnated as a human child at the Nativity. Book III presents a dynamic God at odds with himself, in a state of profound division. Lieb has called this a function of Milton's 'dialogic imagination', appropriating a phrase from Bakhtin, which extends 'the frontiers of drama to a point at which the very theology upon which *Paradise Lost* is founded threatens to undermine its own cause':[40] threatens, but in the view of Lieb's reading of the poem, does not. However, it should be possible to assent to a creative disintegration in the text without a sense that the poem is thereby impaired or devalued. The debate in Book III between God the Father and God the Son relates to the medieval tradition of dispute between 'the four daughters of God', allegorising Psalm 85:10: 'Mercy and truth are met together; righteousness and peace have kissed each other.' The Cambridge manuscript shows that a dialogue between the figures of 'Justice, Mercie, and Wisdome' had been an initial feature of Milton's projected drama, 'debating what should become of man if he fall'. Neo-Spenserian personifications of God's attributes, however, give way in the epic poem to the more provocative disagreement of God within himself. In other words, Milton drops the face-saving device of abstraction and allegory. He involves himself, with characteristically reckless probity, in the face-exposing method of direct dramatic confrontation.

The principle of quarrel at work in the whole feuding cosmos of *Paradise Lost* is therefore located also within the unity of the Godhead itself. The punitive voice of the Father is raised against his newly-created children in a hectic tone of indignation which would seem profoundly offensive in a human father: offensive, or psychopathic, for man has as yet done nothing to merit the vituperation the Almighty hurls at him. Naked, sinless and vulnerable, Adam and Eve are still loving one another, praising their Maker and tending his garden in prelapsarian bliss, unaware of the approach of the mortal enemy God has permitted to assail them:

> so will fall,
> He and his faithless progeny: whose fault?
> Whose but his own? Ingrate, he had of me
> All he could have; I made him just and right,
> Sufficient to have stood, though free to fall.
> (III. 95–9)

In human terms, this rancorously brutal voice is impossible to justify. It is a versification of the odious vindictiveness all of us have heard and disliked either in our own parentally scolding voices or those of our own parents: 'Don't you come whining to me – I told you so.' Should we threaten to visit the punishment of death upon our unhappy offspring in the foreseeable if not inevitable event of their transgressing our prohibition, we should certainly be adjudged unfit parents. Milton's God now goes on to extenuate his inhumanity by pointing out that though he foreknows, he does not predestine (a priority being set on 'freedom') and that he himself is bound by sovereign law and decree. He ends with a better-tempered pronouncement that because man is not self-tempted, he will find grace and that 'mercy first and last shall brightest shine' (134). Traditionally, two approaches have been favoured by readers. Apologists claim that God is not as bad as he seems and that he only *seems* as bad as he does because to portray him as a person is to constrain his mystery and infinity to the crudities of our finite language; that he is a better God than most since he goes out of his way to show an anti-Calvinist concern with the dignity of man as a free individual. Antagonists label the portrayal as a central 'failure' of the poem, for the reasons sketched above.[41] I would read it as an area of profound conflict and tension in which Milton's twin but incompatible impulses – to defend his God by resort to every trick in the rhetorical book and to expose him with brutal honesty to heretical judgement – fight it out on the page.

Book III opens God's nature to debate by subjecting him to criticism, rebuke and admonition. Against the peremptory voice of the Father he sets the lovable voice of the Son, which plays an intercessive, supplicating music against the vehement ratiocinations of his parent:

> For should man finally be lost, should man
> Thy creature late so loved, thy youngest son,
> Fall circumvented thus by fraud, though joined
> With his own folly? That be from thee far,
> That far be from thee, Father, who art judge
> Of all things made, and judgest only right.
> ....
> So should thy goodness and thy greatness both
> Be questioned and blasphemed without defence.
> (III. 150–5; 165–6)

A tissue of half-rhymes, alliterative echoes (*lost, late, loved; finally, fall, fraud, folly, from . . . far, far . . . from, Father*) and rhetorical duplications (*should man . . . should man; thy creature . . . thy . . . son*), together with chiastic reversal characteristic of the Son's speech-patterns (153–4), woos the Father with melodious eloquence to remember who he is and where his allegiances should lie. Judged in human terms, as the fictionalising techniques render inevitable, the Son emerges as an expert strategist, determined to oppose his father's punitive tendencies in terms that are softly and appeasingly tactful. As the speech develops, his method becomes more directly confrontational, pointing out to him that he does not want to play into his Adversary's hands. If the Father pursues his retributive logic, he will so far open himself to 'question' and 'blasphemy' as to make such attacks on his nature a matter of duty rather than of apostasy. In the event, the only possible resolution is the promise of the Atonement, the Son's quitting of the debt God must (to remain himself) exact:

'The rigid satisfaction, death for death' (212). *Paradise Lost*, which commends itself as a 'justification' of God's ways to men in fact operates far more explosively as an argumentative probing of those ways. Milton could take refuge in Scriptural authority for such attacks on God's obvious injustices. The Son's words derive from Abraham's challenging of the justice of God's decision to destroy Sodom:

> That be far from thee to do after this manner, to slay the righteous with the wicked: and that the righteous should be as the wicked, that be far from thee: Shall not the Judge of all the earth do right?
>
> (Genesis 18:25)

God seems to see the point, for he backs down. If there are fifty righteous men in the city, he will not eliminate it. Forty-five, asks Abraham? Forty? Thirty? Twenty? He finally succeeds in beating down God to ten. This tradition of the human corrective supplied to Divine inequity is to be found in Moses, Job, Jeremiah and the Psalmist. When we recall the very close connection Milton habitually made between the Son and ourselves as sons of God, the personal charge which informs the tension of the debate becomes evident. How is God to be loved, given the extent of his responsibility for things as they are, and how is he to be exonerated from the atrocity of his indifferent or persecuting behaviour to good and evil alike? These are the questions which Milton sets out and for which he seeks resolution. It is clear that part of Milton (and it might be a great part) does love and honour his God, but another part is aroused to baffled hostility.

The disputatious Godhead of Book III is cloven into two parts: righteous Anger and absolving Love, which the dialogue seeks to synthesise by intimating that at the end of time all power-relations will be abdicated, the schismatic universe and the cleft deity being assimilated into one: 'God shall be all in all' (341). That such unification is abstruse and mysterious in the extreme and not susceptible of incorporation in the drama of the poem is attested by the laborious scholarly grapplings which the text has provoked here. *Paradise Lost* is supremely unstable at this point. It gives way as the poem develops to a different kind of instability. The dichotomy it establishes between the persons of the Deity is not sustained consistently beyond this Book: dramatic characterisation is no sooner attained than it is dropped. Milton's theological vision of the Son as a reflection of the Father seems to have forbidden integrity to the psychology of the character. We read the characters of Satan, Adam, Eve, the poetic persona himself, as we read one another's characters: but the Son does not even appear to conform with himself. In Book III Milton's fictional fabrication extends and elaborates the mercy in God's nature with such keen intensity that it all but splinters off into challenging individua-tion. In Book VI, however (the account of the War in Heaven), the Son is reassimilated and becomes no more – in dramatic terms – than the executive and military arm of the Father's legislature:

> But whom thou hatest, I hate, and can put on
> Thy terrors, as I put thy mildness on,
> Image of thee in all things . . .
>
> (VI. 734–6)

In the arresting image of the Chariot of Paternal Deity, with its wheels made of Cherubim, whose balefully staring eyes reduce the rebellious angels into a state of mind cravenly effete, Milton presents with evident relish the gracious Messiah as an avenging warrior purging Heaven of its dissidents. The denomination as 'Messiah' rather than the more usual 'Son' is a coded hint that we are to supply to the reading of these military exploits a saving and remedial function (the three-day War in Heaven is often read as an allegory of the Crucifixion and resurrection)[42] but to the ear and heart of most readers, surface and symbol must be unanimous for a stable meaning to be determined. The surface of the episode is violent and punitive: its message is not Love but the delighted accomplishment of a revenge all the more savoured because it has been postponed. The mighty Son drove his adversaries before him 'as a herd / Of goats or timorous flock together thronged' to the rim of Heaven:

> the monstrous sight
> Strook them with horror backward, but far worse
> Urged them behind; headlong themselves they threw
> Down from the verge of heaven, eternal wrath
> Burnt after them to the bottomless pit.
>
> (VI. 856–7; 862–6)

The tone of this passage is unmistakably orgiastic and assumes that the reader's response will be unreflectingly complicit. Such complacency is always poetically dangerous. Here it lets in the subversive pastoralism of the image of a herd of domesticated animals driven in panic to a sheer drop: before them terror, behind them terror more colossal. The poet may have expected us to recall the story of the Gadarene swine and to hear the resonance of the Apocalyptic Last Judgement here (the separation of souls into the sheep and the goats) but you cannot convert a creaturely life into a walking allegory just by wishing to, and a 'timorous flock' inevitably implies the deep-rooted Scriptural and pastoral associations of sheep with innocence, helplessness and symbiotic relation to the community. The narrative voice glories in the Son's vengeance, both its ruthless violence and its combustible effects, but (as we are often repelled by fantasies of retribution even as they excite and satisfy us) the poem cannot compel its reader to the same merciless attitude. Indeed, it would be possible to argue that it puts out a hand to save us from falling into its own worst excesses by the inadvertency of the pastoral image, together with the compassionate sense it stirs of the rebel angels' predicament wavering between the Devil (God) and the deep blue sea (the Abyss).

The previous two decades had seen nothing but unsuccessful Puritan purges, accompanied by the fallacious prediction of the imminence of the Second Coming and the end of the world. Parliament purged the body politic of Strafford, Laud, Charles I; Charles II with the English court fled to France. Pride's Purge decimated the Long Parliament. The New Model Army purged itself of its Agitators and Levellers. 'Whoremasters! . . . It is not fit that you should sit as a Parliament any longer,' Cromwell roared at the Rump.[43] Ultimately every attempt to expel the foreign bodies within the state recoiled upon itself. It seemed impossible to dissect away the implicated from the unimplicated because, in the end, the whole organism was riddled with original sin. Milton's passionate millenarianism wilted under the disillusioning impact of history. In Book VI of *Paradise Lost* he focuses a violently successful purge outside Time in a Messianic compensatory myth which theologically implies a threefold chronological application: set at the beginning of Time, it foreshadows the triumph of the resurrection on Easter Day and looks forward to the vindication of Christ and his saints in victory over their common enemies. The Son in his role as warrior vindicates the stigmatised Milton, at the very centre of the poem. His magnificent glorification of the retributive power-politics of the Christian God again shamelessly exposes the paradox at the heart of the myth: redemptive Love as ruthless power; tyranny raising the banner of freedom. The assertiveness and candour of Milton's account opened these paradoxes to the heretical questionings of later generations of readers. If this is how Heaven is governed, we are better out of it: Blake's *Milton*, Byron's Mystery Plays and Emily Brontë's *Wuthering Heights* are denunciations of the Miltonic vision of the Expulsion: 'heaven did not seem to be my home,' says Catherine Earnshaw, 'and I broke my heart with weeping to come back to earth; and the angels were so angry that they flung me out, into the middle of the heath on the top of Wuthering Heights, where I woke sobbing for joy.'[44] Emily Brontë rewrites Milton: a woman cannot be at home in the coercive transcendental patriarchy of a Heaven which is a contradiction in terms, for how can it be Heaven if its inhabitants are liable to punitive rage? The fortunate fall or *felix culpa* which Milton uses judiciously as an exonerating device for the actions of his God becomes centralised in the reversed theology of the Romantic reaction. It is not absolutely indecorous to the testing, challenging spirit of his work to suggest that he himself prepared the way for this radical revisionism.

At the double centre of *Paradise Lost* (the dyptych composed of Books VI and VII), the Son's nature is displayed as a paradox, in which destruction gives way to creation, a higher value being placed on the latter:

> thee that day
> Thy thunders magnified; but to create
> Is greater than created to destroy.
> (VII. 605–7)

In the hexaemeral Book VII, lyrically and descriptively the highest point in the poem for many readers, the Son is the creative Logos diffusing love into the universe: 'creator him they sung' (259). Later again, after the fall of man, he appears in Eden to bestow the Father's curse on the abashed and grieving human pair. He comes to them in a double nature, as 'Man's friend, his mediator' (X. 60), 'the mild judge and intercessor both' (96):

> So judged he man, both judge and saviour sent,
> And the instant stroke of death denounced that day
> Removed far off; then pitying how they stood
> Before him naked to the air, that now
> Must suffer change, disdained not to begin
> Thenceforth the form of servant to assume,
> As when he washed his servants' feet so now
> As father of his family he clad
> Their nakedness with skins of beasts, or slain,
> Or as the snake with youthful coat repaid;
> And thought not much to clothe his enemies.
> Nor he their outward only with the skins
> Of beasts, but inward nakedness, much more
> Opprobrious, with his robe of righteousness,
> Arraying, covered from his Father's sight.
>
> (X. 209–23)

The beautiful plainsong of the narrative marks a return to the measured lyricism of the pleading Son of Book III (which is symmetrically echoed and answered by Book X, standing three books from the close of the epic and dealing with issues first raised in Book III). The theme is pity: a pity merited by the desperate plight of the human pair, even under a mitigated view of the sentence. The pastoral idyll is over, and intimations of the ferocity of seasonal variation together with the descent of the animal species into predatory rapacity are insisted upon. Christ's posture of humility strives to moderate the abjectness of the humiliation into which they have been betrayed. The Gospel reference to Christ as the suffering servant who washes the disciples' feet prior to his own sacrifice is an explicit signal to the reader to take the New Testament as governing pre-text. To wash the disciples' feet, Christ had of course to kneel: divesting himself of high office as 'Lord' and 'Master', he bends to a menial task which acts as a comment on all power-relations. To wash the disciples' feet is at once to cleanse and to comfort. These ministrations are paralleled in Milton's text in the act of clothing Adam and Eve, charitably warming them (on the physical level of the action) from the air that 'now must suffer change', *suffer* bearing the meaning not only of 'undergo' but the more profound sense of 'enduring pain', as if the whole of creation had been abandoned to a condition of aching sentience. The passage is relatively clear of grammatical convolution or of elaborate rhetorical mannerism. Its mainly Anglo-Saxon-derived diction is bare and simple in its exposure of their absolute lack to his absolute (though in practice limited) care. The very air, which formerly embraced them, is turning into their inimical enemy, and Christ stands with them, not adverse, seeming to share (for *pity*, like the Latin-derived *compassion* and the Greek-derived *sympathy* – 'suffering with' – implies identification) in their extremity. Both the Incarnation and the Atonement are implied by this identification, as is the almost diffident unpretentiousness of some of the phrasing: 'and thought not much to clothe his enemies' with gentle tact shrugs off commendation in a verbal gesture of humane modesty. Throughout the passage a keen awareness of the psychological implications of Adam's and Eve's fall from innocence into self-consciousness is transmitted in the insistence on their state of embarrassed vulnerability: *naked to the air, their nakedness, inward nakedness*. Milton's humanised Christ occupies the protective middle ground between their physical and spiritual vulnerability and the inclemency not only of the seasons but also of God. As he will be arrayed in human form, so now he arrays them in 'his robe of righteousness', clothes them, that is, in himself. Throughout the poem, vision has been equated with power. The 'inward nakedness, much more / Opprobrious' to which the fall condemns God's youngest children is seen as total and unbearable exposure to that lidless eye which like a searchlight pierces every private recess of the guilty mind. The narrative is sensitive to the profound psychological disturbance generated by the penetration of Omniscience into human frailty. We cannot bear to be seen through. As 'father of his family', Christ hides his children from 'his Father's sight'. In context, the action comes across as almost subversive, an implicit criticism on the part of one kind of fatherhood (tender, temperate, forgiving) of another kind (that jealous Patriarch, Jehovah). The mesmerising difficulty arises from the fact that we have only the one word for both, and the poem implies that Christ would have to be disinherited from the Divine Family to become an authentic member of the human family. The beauty of his behaviour in this passage, and the mediatorial office he performs, therefore makes shift to cover a gap of confidence which the theologically unconvinced reader may find herself at some pains to resolve. But the poetry of the passage, austere, quiet in tone and stripped of poetic excrescence hauntingly prefigures the Puritan music of *Paradise Regained*.

*   *   *

This chapter has dwelt largely upon the turbulent and complex dynamics of *Paradise Lost*: an inclination which reflects the fascination of modern reading-habits with the inchoate and discrepant, at the expense of the harmonious and complete. Milton still lived on the cusp of a mental climate which favoured the *concordia discors* and the *coincidentia oppositorum*: he brought this inheritance up to the perspective-glass of a more modernistic dubiety but the perspective-glass was not fully operative. There is a Spenserian and Elizabethan aspect to his lyric poetry in *Paradise Lost* (especially the Edenic sections) which maintains the reader's sense of the concordant resolvability of paradox. The academic readership has largely forgotten how to read for beauty and harmony: but the Milton of *Paradise Lost* calls for and calls out to such a reader. The sense of the holy breathes to us from the tranquil pastoralism of prelapsarian Eden, as for instance in this nocturnal in Book IV:

> Now came still evening on, and twilight grey
> Had in her sober livery all things clad;
> Silence accompanied, for beast and bird,
> They to their grassy couch, these to their nests
> Were slunk, all but the wakeful nightingale;
> She all night long her amorous descant sung;
> Silence was pleased: now glowed the firmament
> With living sapphires: Hesperus that led
> The starry host, rode brightest, till the moon
> Rising in clouded majesty, at length
> Apparent queen unveiled her peerless light,
> And o'er the dark her silver mantle threw . . .
> (IV. 598–609)

The hushed scene glows dimly with an aura of phosphorescent beauty, which is partly a matter of changing light effects, as evening deepens into night; more still of sound effects or their withdrawal (the silencing of the stir of creaturely life and the poignant lifting-up of the nightingale's voice); still more, of the shift from human and angelic characterisation into the mode of personification. Background becomes foreground; the minor key prevails. The feminine and lunar take the place of the dominant masculine and solar, in a universe which is viewed not through the lens of the Galilean telescope but through the anthropomorphising eye of animistic classicism which personalised the cosmos as Father Sun, Mother Earth and Mother Moon. In the slumbrous night-world, the theatre of amorous action is the time of Eve and her symbol, the regnant moon. A dense cluster of personifications (Evening, Twilight, Silence, the nightingale, Hesperus, the moon) remembers the manner of Milton's early poetry, including *Il Penseroso* and *Comus*, but especially the concluding paragraph of *Lycidas*: 'the still morn went out with sandals grey' (187) and looks forward to a modulation of *Paradise Regained*: 'Morning fair / Came forth with pilgrim steps in amice grey' (IV. 426–7). Each of these hallowed moments represents the measured crossing of a threshold in time, a passage of initiation into a new beginning or an alternative world.[45] Sobriety and inwardness can seldom have been made to seem as beautiful. The grave and meditative Puritan Spenserianism of the companion figures of 'twilight grey' and Silence blend sensuous sweetness with seemliness and propriety. Where morning in *Paradise Regained* will be dressed as if for pilgrimage, the evening world of *Paradise Lost* is dressed in sign of allegiance ('sober livery'): dressed in light, suffusive and indistinct, which invests the world in strangeness. Expectancy is aroused, together with a paradoxically dignified reverentialness in Nature as it awaits an advent. The passage is less a set piece than a moving piece, transacted between personifications which move like thoughts that pass across the field of our inner vision, with a quality of contemplative reflection. As so often in Milton, a mental process seems nearly as much the subject of the narrative as an outer event, and a post-Spenserian poetry in conjuring that process of inner quietening and receptive arousal which one might identify as leading to the state of 'reverie' may also be read as pre-Romantic. We witness the birth of Keats' Nightingale and a prelude to Coleridge's nocturnals. Garish colour is resolved into monochrome and contrapuntal voices are cancelled in the solo of the nightingale, recalling *Il Penseroso* ('Most musical, most melancholy' (62)) and always, for Milton, a figure for the mind in process of creation:

151

> Then feed on thoughts, that voluntary move
> Harmonious numbers, as the wakeful bird
> Sings darkling, and in shadiest covert hid
> Tunes her nocturnal note.
>
> (III. 37–40)

The music of *Paradise Lost* impersonates the eternal aria of the nightingale, and indeed it is a nocturnal, for it was conceived at night and dictated in the blindest dark. This evensong, which does not conflict with silence ('Silence was pleased') is already in a real sense the Platonistic 'unheard' music of Keats. As the jewelled constellations ascend the heavens, the passage intensifies its suspenseful heralding, abiding time like the Milton of the *Nativity Ode*, travelling patiently towards consummation: 'Now . . . now . . . at length'. With the unveiling of the moon's naked light there is completion and assuagement of the climbing sense of 'something evermore about to be' in a moment of luminous revelation: the triumph of the minor key as it sweeps into its own orbit the major themes of the orchestration – light, sovereignty, the visionary universe of *Paradise Lost*.

4

Paradise Regained: A Language of Interiority

The first word of *Paradise Regained* is 'I': 'I who erewhile the happy garden sung, / . . . now sing / Recovered Paradise' (1–3). That 'I' advertises itself as John Milton the author of *Paradise Lost* and explicitly encourages the reader to interpret the poem as a sequel to the uninhibited intensities of eloquence in the preceding work. Milton was baffled and irritated that his readers felt a sense of let-down when they came to *Paradise Regained*: rather as Beethoven might have felt if a lover of his Third Symphony had disparaged a late piano sonata. This is a poem which is preoccupied with questions of individual identity: it investigates its own first word, pondering 'I', a double 'I' consisting in the personal pronoun as articulated by the narrative voice and as projected into the person of God's Son, the narrative subject. Though the poem's measured tone claims an emotionally safe and unimplicated distance from the material of the story, *Paradise Regained* is at least as much as *Paradise Lost* a personal and confessional narrative. A four-book 'brief epic' modelled on the Book of Job, its style is a middle-register Georgic, mid-way between pastoral and epic.[1] Its theme, the Son's temptation in the wilderness, is a non-event, a refusal of or abstention from action. Its hero is solitary and isolated from the community. If he speaks, he must address a phantasmal adversary (Satan) or talk to himself. He has neither the proximity of family, friends nor political party. An archetype of passive resistance, his claim to heroism is the radical refusal to act at all. The poem celebrates quietism and repression, and rests its sole hope of sublimity on a triumph of sublimation. Like *Comus* and *Samson Agonistes*, it celebrates the crucial moment of moral choice which expresses and endorses the integrity of the self in its fullness: choice understood here as veto, saying 'no' to intrusive or alluring voices. To say 'no' in the temptation scenarios of Milton's poetry is the individual's first and final triumph. 'No' shores up the fortress of autonomy by pure act of will, though at the cost of desires and needs commonly considered legitimate or healthy. In *Paradise Regained* the Son's 'no' represents a herculean resistance to authority, a denial of the senses and a condemnation of reason, witnessing the fact that some of the denials the ego feels the need to make appear to others as arbitrary or senseless.

The aberrant 'no' of *Paradise Regained* is the power of Thermopylae in Christian terms: the keeping of one's own counsel, holding one's peace, holding one's own against the aggressive invasiveness of the appropriative outside world. In the course of the four-book narrative, the Son refuses the temptations of bodily sustenance, wealth, glory, classical culture and literature and the self-display solicited by Satan's suggestion that he leap from the tower to prove his divinity. Persistent negation, especially when raised to the power of an overriding principle, is a quality neither amiable nor compelling in a character. *Paradise Regained* was held from the first to be an unattractive poem, a falling-off from the gorgeous eloquence of *Paradise Lost*: Milton testily resented the slight.[2] *Paradise Regained* makes not the slightest effort to attract. It is perhaps the most extraordinary linguistic experiment of this limitlessly self-extending poet who changed every literary genre he touched and who touched every available genre. In *Paradise Regained* Milton researched a language of pure interiority: a private code to address the truth of the inner life. He meditated an English purged of excrescences and ornamentation, pruned and pared down to a naked-ness which might bring it as close as possible to the spirit which underlies but is betrayed by the letter. The task was impossible and *Paradise Regained* constitutes a profound critique of language itself. Nevertheless, it advances through the maze (its own metaphor) of dubieties systematised in the riddling and figurative language which is our inheritance, in search of an appropriate plainness that will at once do justice to the enigmatic complexity of things and anatomise out a path through irregular appearances to the fine simplicities of truth-to-self. This is a soliloquist's narrative, exilic from the corporate body of language as the exchange in which we trade with one another in the community. The Son in the wilderness has parted company with the community, ceasing to communicate with the tribe: his disciples and his mother (representing his party in that tribe) are left in a mirroring state of anxious and puzzled soliloquy, revolving in their minds the meaning of his absence. Their resolution must wait upon what he is capable of discovering in his quest. Renewed communication between persons will depend upon the results obtained by communing within oneself. *Paradise Regained* invents and records a language of communing and communion. It was this *andante* language rather than the *fortissimo* of *Paradise Lost* which Wordsworth took as the staple for his *Prelude* when he internalised the poet's epic journey: *Paradise Regained* is the link between the public wanderings of Homer's Odysseus and the private journey of the Wordsworthian hill-walker.

There are events to which the telltale imagination can be the only human witness. Privacy by its very name and nature cannot be known: it is the ulterior space or no man's land which allows no fellow-participant. It is the mute index of a withheld meaning, best signified by silence. *Paradise Regained* articulates a language to cover that gap of silence.[3] From the first, the text insists on the secrecy and privacy of its material. Covering the period between Christ's Baptism (when God proclaimed him as Son) and his self-proclamation on the pinnacle, Milton chooses to centre in a reclusive hiatus in history, the liminal edge between the Old Testament and New Testament cultures: a gap which bears no historical inscription to stabilise it in the minds of readers. Milton will

> tell of deeds
> Above heroic, though in secret done,
> And unrecorded left through many an age,
> Worthy t'have not remained so long unsung.
> (I. 14–17)

The emphasis is on transcribing the undocumented; supplying an eloquence to the unheard and unseen, for which no memorial exists. The quietism of the ethic (a Job-like fortitude raised to transcendent status 'Above heroic') is matched by the guarded sobriety of the middle-register Georgic style which composes the whole poem in the minor key, as if vigilantly repressing the extravagances of the earlier work. A plainsong of negatives begins to unfold in the record of Jesus' coming to the Baptism 'obscure, / Unmarked, unknown' (I. 24–5). The poem will guess out a story of how the unknown becomes known, how from obscurity and enigma may be elicited a confirmed sense of identity. The expanses of barren, hungry silence at the centre of the Son's wilderness are an apt figure for the silencing of the radicals in the 1660s. In the heady days of the Interregnum, Radical sects had proclaimed that we were all 'sons of God'; that Christ was come again, Christ-within-us, so that each one incorporated the Second Coming. In 1656, James Nayler rode into Bristol on a donkey, before whose path women strewed palms: not an act of megalomania but a symbolic statement that it was possible for a man – any man – to achieve Christ's perfection and perform Christ's works. Christ was here and now, in us and in society. Nayler was savagely tortured into recanting.[4] The Restoration chased Christ out of the public world and onto the margins: Christ had, as it were, gone out of us, absconding to the wilderness. Like the Quakers, the disappointment of whose millenarian hopes led to the formulation of the peace-principle, and withdrawal from political action, Milton proclaims a subversive quietism as the most potent form of dissent. The Son in the Wilderness is a persecuted minority of one. The poem records the difficulty for the minority of attaining the possibility of certainty and stability where all givens have come into question and all possible avenues of action are blocked. The minority, either of one or of scattered handfuls, aborted to the fringe of the community, is condemned to a passive life of invisibility and inaudibility, condemned to inhabit the interior of the self as its only home. *Paradise Regained* shows that home to be inalienable. Beginning in the unknown and unrecorded, ('in secret done'), it ends in the unwitnessed: 'he unobserved / Home to his mother's house private returned' (IV. 638–9). This is rightly celebrated as one of Milton's exquisitely tempered 'quiet endings'. But at the heart of its law-abiding quietism burns fiercely revolutionary paradox and irony. Going home was the unobtrusive and innocuous act of a private citizen, a person of no account. Nobody would take much notice of an act so commonplace in a man so unremarkable. But Jesus' home-coming is subversive camouflage. When he goes indoors and is seen no more in the course of the poem, it is as Son of God that he returns to his human and domestic world: the New Testament and world history take over from here. Because of his vigilant patience, whole empires will convulse and the map of the world will change. The recessive Christ in repudiating every icon of worldly power and pleasure has played *Eikonoklastes* to the whole of processive history. The testimony to the fact of this cataclysmic latching of the door on the past is the paradoxical witness borne by the poem to that which was unwitnessed at the time 'he *unobserved* . . . private returned'. Christ's subdued life's radiating influence transformed posterity into gazing bystanders. Poet and reader have together observed this advent and been privy to the Son's secret, as if we were somehow (with the light of hindsight) more contemporary than the Son's contemporaries, and stood looking over the backs of the oblivious crowds in the street. What is foreground and what background in life? How shall we determine what events are real and significant and which trivial and transient? *Paradise Regained* shares a modernist line on the marginal. Considerations of state and empire dwindle to small account. The real event may go past us in the street like an unread message, unrecognised, while we meditate the throes of world events. Centrality is attributed by the poem to the eccentric, off the map of culture altogether and out of its confining circle.

Christ, and Milton-in-Christ, detach themselves from implication in the earthly kingdom, and liberationist politics are allocated to Satan, to be exerted as a temptation, to free Israel from its conquerors and (in the fourth Book) to lead the Romans in rebellion against the despot Tiberius:

> with what ease
> . . . .
> Might'st thou expel this monster from his throne,
> Now made a sty, and in his place ascending
> A victor people free from servile yoke!
> (IV. 97; 100–2)

The Son's contempt for the people 'victor once, now vile and base, / Deservedly made vassal' (132–3) registers the Miltonic superciliousness for the degenerate body politic which voluntarily welcomed slavery in the person of Charles II: which, vouchsafed a unique chance to establish the Kingdom of God on earth, wasted that chance and lost credibility forever. In its scorn for *all* worldly power, *Paradise Regained* offers an enabling myth for the disempowered 'sons of God' under Restoration persecution: it becomes a voice for the silent, in their recessive, hidden life, to all intents and purposes beaten and degraded, offering a mirror in which they may grow to discern a prodigious and gathering might. This might is to be used to *do* or *act* nothing at all, for 'Who best / Can suffer best can do'.[5] To suffer composedly is to win back that basic trust which, lost with the fall, causes the insecurity which *Paradise Lost* massively orchestrated as a central theme. The capacity to drop the voice, speak collectedly and understate – even to the point of bathos ('I never liked thy talk, thy offers less' (IV. 171); 'Me worse than wet thou find'st not' (486)) – is an index not only of the Son's inflexible uprightness but also of that posture of trust which for Milton as for all readers is so hard won on the shifting planes of time. The dynamic paradigm of *Paradise Lost* was the opposition between rising and falling (see page 98 above); the paradigm for *Paradise Regained* is the tension between *standing* and *falling*. Our language knows the intrinsic connection between personal safety and moral comprehension: we speak of understanding, withstanding, long-standing relationships, and of moral uprightness. To stand in a high place without vertigo is always an act of trust: if you look down, the knowledge of danger is a temptation to fall. This feat of confidence is at the centre equally of Christ's safety and his virtue in *Paradise Regained*. It is understood as the supremely filial act of a Son to his Father: as the child who stands on his own feet trusts both his own sense of balance and the presence of the abiding parent who has let him go. The poem's successive temptations build towards the climax of the temptation on the pinnacle, where Satan challenges him to prove his divinity by casting himself down:

> To whom thus Jesus: 'Also it is written,
> "Tempt not the Lord thy God."' He said, and stood.
> But Satan smitten with amazement fell.
>
> (IV. 560–2)

'He said, and stood.' Whereas the crucial act of *Paradise Lost* was the plucking of the fatal fruit, 'she plucked, she ate', proleptically foreshadowed in feints of imaginary arms reaching for imaginary fruit (V. 65;

VIII. 308; IX. 781) – i.e. the act of falling – the crisis of *Paradise Regained* is this non-act and non-event of standing and doing nothing, the historical and theological reversal of the first. The Son's feat of maintaining balance has a theatricality in proportion as it approximates to a condition of stasis: his dazzling tightrope-walker's certainty is supported by the Scriptural text from Deuteronomy which he quotes at his adversary. Thus, the correctly chosen words are the source of his stability and of Satan's dumbfounded and inchoate collapse into loss of self. Language is presented as the riddling problem of *Paradise Regained*. But the right words, presented in the form of a riddle, are the key to that problem. The epic simile of the Sphinx which follows Satan's fall emphasises the jurisdiction of the Son as the solution of a retributive riddle.[6] The Son's quotation from Deuteronomy is also an act of interpretation, for it reapplies the words of Holy Writ and hence changes their perceived meaning. Old Testament becomes New Testament; prophecy is succeeded by the emergence of the prophesied, and with that act of interpretation the old world ends. Interpretation can never be pure paraphrase. To interpret is to shift meaning. Christ acts obediently in doing no more than quote the Old Testament – but he transacts the old words in a revolutionary sense. In his mouth, they obtain new focus and potency in the riddlingly ironic and oblique disclosure of his divine status. Satan falls when he reads the text accurately, caught off balance by the shock of undesired meaning.

The dramatic impact of the Son's standing is created by the laconically elliptical telling of Satan's fall, in a six-word blank verse sentence. Satan seems to peel off like a shadow and to void himself suddenly and abortively into the pit of space. This of course comes as no surprise to the reader of *Paradise Regained*: Satan's time (as we are told from the beginning) has come, and his character lives in this poem only as a sort of spectral vestige of the passionately rebellious energy he represented in *Paradise Lost*. The surprise is only in the telling: the flat declension from the free-standing person of Christ. The Son in *Paradise Regained* is impregnable: a triumph, therefore, of manliness over the effeminacy Milton detected as endemic to the human race after the fall, and throughout his lifetime feared in himself. In *Paradise Lost* the admonitory Archangel had found occasion to rebuke Adam's growling misogyny:

> But still I see the tenor of man's woe
> Holds on the same, from woman to begin . . .

with the displaced misogyny of 'From man's effeminate slackness it begins' (XI. 632–4). Symbolically, the Son's 'standing' on the pinnacle may also be read as a phallic standing, the erect superiority of one whose desire has not dissipated itself in response to the enticements of the world of sense. To 'slacken' would be to lose firmness and autonomy: to give the self, to yield, to be taken over is perhaps the profoundest of all Miltonic terrors. *Paradise Regained* tolerates a woman character as a significant carrier of virtue in a way rare in Milton's poems, but it can do this because the Virgin Mary is by her nature desexualised and therefore unthreatening, an icon of motherhood abstracted from the devices and desires of the flesh. *Paradise Regained* has no time for sexuality. Satan knows enough about the Son's stony intransigence to pour scorn on Belial's suggestion in Book II that the Son be subjected to the challenge of Eros:

> Such object hath the power to soften and tame
> Severest temper, smooth the rugged'st brow,
> Enerve, and with voluptuous hope dissolve,
> Draw out with credulous desire, and lead
> At will the manliest, resolutest breast,
> As the magnetic hardest iron draws.
>
> (II. 163–8)

The diction of Belial's speech bristles with intimations of Miltonic and patriarchal dread: *soften, tame, smooth, Enerve, voluptuous, dissolve, Draw out, lead.* If 'they' draw 'us' out of our *severe, rugged, manly, resolute* and indeed *iron* fortification, we shall lie meltingly open to invasion by our enemies. In *Samson Agonistes*, that male terror of invasive entry finds haunting voice in Samson's prolonged scream of enraged helplessness. But *Paradise Regained* repudiates the allure of women with fastidious contempt. The Son, as Satan knows, is neither penetrable nor pregnable by that 'trivial toy', female Beauty (II. 223). For Milton's Son, as portrayed in *Paradise Regained*, cannot love. The Christ of this poem is sheer power, raised to that standing posture. It is non-aggressive in part because it does not choose to expend any portion of that might, hardened and consolidated through a succession of withholdings. To 'stand' thus is to avoid the necessity to 'die' or to 'spend' oneself, both familiar Renaissance *double entendres* for orgasm, which comment with saddening eloquence on the system of assumptions underlying *Paradise Regained*.

That the Miltonic Christ of *Paradise Regained* shows little capacity for tenderness is harrowing. Not only has the ravishing eroticism of *Paradise Lost* been quenched, but so has the quality of warm endearment in that impassioned epic. *Lycidas* resolved its griefs in 'the *dear might* of him that walked the waves' (173; my emphases), emphasising in that near-oxymoron the gentle benignity of the powerful Saviour, who may be said to love Lycidas as the poet loves him, humanly and personally. *Paradise Lost* presented the face of the Son as expressive in visible form of 'Divine compassion . . . / Love without end, and without measure grace' (III. 141–2). But what theologically innocent reader could come to *Paradise Regained* and learn from reading it that the message of the Gospels is Love? This is a Christ curiously lacking the tenderly profound dialect that would go on to speak the Sermon on the Mount; would draw young children to him, pity the sick and compassionate the woman taken in adultery; would ponder the lilies of the field and, on his cross, pray 'Father, forgive them, for they know not what they do.' The rigid, rigorous Son of Milton's brief epic knows nothing of this. Milton had presented him in *Paradise Lost* as to some degree a feminised figure, equated with the female personifications of Wisdom (VII. 9–10), the Muse Urania and the classical Ceres, the mother-goddess in her loving quest for her lost child (IV. 271–2). He stands against God the rampant patriarch rather as the female conventionally stands up against the male in a family grouping, taking the children's side against his punitiveness. But the Son of *Paradise Regained* has been shaven of this emotional dimension: the poem's persistent movement is towards a fuller identification between Son and Father. The very grammar of the poem tends to contract the gap between the two. The Son's telling of the Baptism story recalls that John proclaimed 'Me him . . . / Me him' (I. 276–7) and the Father's voice pronounced 'me his, / Me his beloved Son' (284–5). The first double compression identifies man and God, flesh and spirit, in a joint accusative, a corporate sharing of grammatical space; the second ('me his') couples the accusative with a genitive in assertion of intrinsic dependency; the third ('Me his beloved Son') extends this genitive to incorporate direct biblical quotation: 'This is my beloved Son, in whom I am well pleased' (Matthew 3:17). This sign of paternal approbation is amplified in Milton's version to 'Me his beloved Son, in whom *alone* / He was well pleased' (I. 285–6; my emphases). It is this meritorious singularity, the elect character of the Son, which fascinates Milton and which absorbs his poetic energies to the near-eclipse of variant preoccupations, in a vacuum of sterile emotion. When one compares Milton's reserved account of the Baptism with the passionate beauty of St John's narrative of the same event, one is struck by the paucity – almost, the depression – of Milton's telling (John 1: 27–9). It is not the same Christ: but an old man's young man, who breathes thin air on a barren plateau, at the end of the world.

This is the norm, but not the unbroken rule. Moments of endearment break the blank surface of this poem, like transient and half-voluntary expressions of tenderness which pass across a studiously self-defensive face. The narrative voice expresses its endearedness in rare images which show all the more exquisitely on the generally imageless plane of the poem: 'So spake our morning star then in his rise' (I. 294), remembering Revelation: 'I am the root and the offspring of David, and the bright and morning star' (22:16) and recording in the possessive *our* its trust that Christ is on our side. But this personal and Gospel voice is so fugitive that one must have brought one's copy of the New Testament right up to the text of *Paradise Regained* to catch its reverberations. A comparable effect is achieved in Book IV when the narrative voice mourns retrospectively the exposure of Christ to the torments of the night: 'ill wast thou shrouded then, / O patient Son of God' (419–20), which seems to gesture forward to Gethsemane and Calvary. But Milton's feelings for the Passion were always meagre or blocked (his early poem on the Passion remained incomplete), and the effect of this compassionate invocation, with its human fellow-feeling, is all but cancelled in the forthcoming insistence that 'thou / Sat'st unappalled in calm and sinless peace' (424–5), an image of immunity which has its own inhuman beauty as an icon of quietism. Other loving moments in the work are mediated in the accounts of the disciples' and Mary's poignant lamentations in Book II, but most affectingly in the baffled and forlorn yearning of Satan towards an adversary he cannot conquer but rather needs to love:

My error was my error, and my crime
My crime, whatever for itself condemned,
And will alike be punished, whether thou
Reign or reign not; though to that gentle brow
Willingly I could fly, and hope thy reign,
From that placid aspect and meek regard,
Rather than aggravate my evil state,
Would stand between me and thy Father's ire
(Whose ire I dread more than the fire of hell)
A shelter and a kind of shading cool
Interposition, as a summer's cloud.

                                        (III. 212–22)

The Satan of *Paradise Regained* is a bruised, jaded and saddened remnant of the towering, machinating self of *Paradise Lost*. He bears about with him a pain at once archaic and chronic. He has seen through himself long ago, and his temptations come with hollow ring as if he recognised at the moment of speaking the futility of anything he might fabricate to shake the rock-like foundations of this adamantine adversary. In this poem of reversals, the victim is the victor. The Son wanders the wilderness, prey to hallucinations, but Satan the showman is helplessly lost. 'My error was my error':tautology, with its flat inflectionlessness, announces a fruitless self-recognition, most wearily. The old devil-may-care arrogant stoicism has subsided to a loveless affiliation to grief and hopelessness. The word *lost* in association with Satan tolls through the poem, indicating somewhat more than his own mastery of the rhetoric of pathos and self-dramatisation ('though I have *lost* / Much lustre . . . *lost* / To be beloved . . . I have not *lost* / To love' (I. 377–80): it dramatises a psychology, one might say, a mass-psychology – prevalent in the 1660s – a desultory and clueless aftermath to the Revolution. This blank-faced and uneasy state of incomprehension afflicts Satan to a pathological degree. Christ's repression arrogates and stores power: Satan's depression implies a drop into a nerveless inertia so deep that he only goes through the motions of seeking to affect events. From this position of self-mourning, Satan's recognition of the protective beauty of Christ's mild expression is all the more tantalising: 'to that gentle brow / Willingly I could fly'. We remember the Psalmist's 'As the hart panteth after the water brooks' (Psalm 42:1). In the moving image of the

163

mediatorial character of the Son as 'A shelter and a kind of shading cool / Interposition, as a summer's cloud', Satan has intuited Christ's mission of standing between God's red-hot wrath manifest in the traditional symbol of the intolerable sun, and thin-skinned humanity, scorching in his glare. Christ's 'Ĭntĕrpŏsĭtĭon' metrically blocks the line with its flurry of unstressed syllables, forcing a caesura with that compositional nicety of polysyllable placement which made such a complex rhythmic mimesis of *Paradise Lost*. *Paradise Regained* deals not with one Son of God, but with twin figures, the light and dark Sons, the outcast and the invoked.[7] Their struggle is a dynamic unity: 'my rising is thy fall', says Christ (III. 201). The poem is a pair of scales that weighs them in the balance, justifying the one and neutralising the other. In this poem of repression and sublimation, Satan represents the sublimated material, insisting to the bitter end on the fact of his kinship with the Son and worrying away at the riddle which preoccupies both protagonist and antagonist as the ground of their difference throughout the narrative. Within fifty lines of his fall, Satan argues his identity with Christ, through questioning the meaning of the title 'Son of God':

> which bears no single sense;
> The Son of God I also am, or was,
> And if I was, I am; relation stands;
> All men are Sons of God . . .
> (IV. 517–20)

The truly unbearable – almost unthinkable – penalty, for Milton the patriarch, would have been paternal disinheritance. As the elder son of his father, he bore the identical name, passing it down to his own son who died at the age of six weeks: John Milton son of John Milton son of John Milton. In *Paradise Lost* when God disinherits the rebel angels, their names are eliminated, leaving 'no memorial, blotted out and razed / . . . from the Books of Life' (I. 362–3): relation definitively does *not* stand for these rejects of divine Paternity. Censored and nameless, the desperados unloosed from their allegiance in Heaven invented new names and conjured their own stories into being as the false gods of the Israelites. The Satan of *Paradise Regained* is an orphan longing for home and comfort; a prodigal incapable of being forgiven but querulously asserting his disclaimed right as a sibling to share the nest from which he has been ousted: 'The Son of God I also am'. Ironically the only relation that stands for him in the poem is the paradigm of his alterity to the victorious sibling-rival: the rising gain made by the Son is dependent upon his descending forfeit. Without a qualm the poem secures the surviving 'brother' in his fratricidal right to the parental nest by literally toppling out the unfit rival. Such regressive fantasy-patterns not greatly to our credit dominate more than infantile life: they lie deep in our culture and mores, and it is not surprising to find a purified disguised Cain-and-Abel myth as an energy source for a religious poem. The Miltonic playing-over of this 'cuckoo' theme is at once cathartically vengeful for the author and imaginatively haunting in its ability to render, however unconsciously, a vicarious compassion for the loser.

Paradise Regained is a product of the post-humanist world, indicting the Latin-based culture in which Milton had been educated and in which he had tutored his nephews and based his tract *Of Education*, in favour of an ethics which has neither time nor energy to spare for the erroneous beauty of a superseded world-view. The Son's asperity as he demolishes the whole corpus of Greek philosophy and culture sounds a voice of fanaticism characteristic of Puritan zealots but not of the Milton who owed such a precious debt to Hellenic thought and language, though he had consistently registered doubts and tensions about his syncretism. The barbarous philistinism of the attitudes professed here have repelled or puzzled many readers, and left almost all in a quandary. When we consider the Christian historical debt to Hellenism, it is easy to understand both the readerly reaction that sees Milton's poem as the product of elderly cantankerousness and life-denying sour grapes, and that dogged devotion of the confirmed Miltonist that seeks to save the poet's face by explaining that he did not mean exactly what seems to be said, or only in a certain sense.[8] In the Son's rebuke to Athenian philosophy, Milton performs a self-mutilation, to placate his Maker and to express a certain stream of recalcitrant self-denial in the cause of upbraiding others – always a factor (though seldom *the* factor) in the complex self-justifying apparatus of his psyche. It is no wonder that the Son's reply to the temptation to profane learning sounds so tetchily irascible:

165

> Think not but that I know these things, or think
> I know them not; not therefore am I short
> Of knowing what I ought. He who receives
> Light from above, from the fountain of light,
> No other doctrine needs, though granted true;
> But these are false, or little else but dreams,
> Conjecture, fancies, built on nothing firm.
> The first and wisest of them all professed
> To know this only, that he nothing knew;
> The next to fabling fell and smooth conceits;
> A third sort doubted all things, though plain sense . . .
>
> (IV. 286–96)

The awkwardness of the opening self-justification ties the speaker in a knot of embarrassing disclaimers: 'Think not . . . know . . . think . . . know . . . not; not . . . knowing'. Milton, in extricating himself from the knowledge and thought that are part of himself at his heart's core, betrays unhappiness at the amputation he sees fit to perform. This is barely compensated by the sense of self-righteousness which rewards it. On the other hand, the Bible to the blind Milton was a fully internalised book: it constituted throughout the dark decades *the* source of nourishment and comfort which was always at hand. His *Christian Doctrine*, written concurrently with *Paradise Lost*, comprised a total of 7,000 Scriptural proof-texts, taken no doubt from memory; *Paradise Lost* is a work of biblical assimilation from which Milton's poetry effloresces and the quick root to which it endlessly returns for vitality. The Bible was staple, necessary food. In extremity, the luxury of world-literature would have to go. The 'Fountain of Light' is an inclusive wisdom based on the touchstone of *Paradise Regained*: solidity, which leaves all other doctrines at best supernumerary, at worst fallacious, 'built on nothing firm'. The Son's flippant dismissal of pagan philosophers (two lines to Socrates, one to Plato, one to the Sceptics, etc.) does not deign to take the wisdom of the world seriously. Omniscience becomes the province of the single-minded know-all – and his derision has been met with the answering derision of a more liberal readership.

We are liberal if we can afford to be. Milton's Christ cannot afford it. This is a poem which shares a preoccupation with Shakespeare's *King Lear* (though not its solutions): need. It asks, what do we – as sons of God exiled to a wilderness – really need? What sustains us and what can or ought we to do without? It also concerns (along with *Lear*) a knowledge of hunger which is deeply bound up with its analysis of need and value. From the perspective of a total fast (the bodily equivalent of Milton's spiritual state in the 1660s), radical transvaluation occurs. The temptations of *Paradise Regained* concocted by Satan (especially the banquet, which Milton adds to the Gospel specifications) have the filmic allure of those visions of desire thrown up by the hallucinating mind under pressure of fasting. But the really biting hunger of *Paradise Regained* is towards those staple things we need, and need them *now*, for life to proceed: good bread and fresh water, and their equivalent, the Bible.[9] In contrast to *Areopagitica* with its buoyantly eclectic welcome to literature of nearly every persuasion and to an omnivorous readership, *Paradise Regained* discourages the reading of books as a redundant or decadent activity, which neither adds to the reader nor develops his moral being. Milton by the time of writing the poem has noted that our reading tends both to feed our egos and increase our confusions:

> However many books
> Wise men have said are wearisome; who reads
> Incessantly, and to his reading brings not
> A spirit and judgment equal or superior
> (And what he brings, what needs he elsewhere seek?)
> Uncertain and unsettled still remains,
> Deep-versed in books and shallow in himself,
> Crude or intoxicate, collecting toys,
> And trifles for choice matters, worth a sponge,
> As children gathering pebbles on the shore.
> (IV. 321–30)

It is as if the elder Milton contumaciously rebuked the younger Milton. Desire to read is frowned on as a form of concupiscence: it involves the libido and arouses the senses. Surely the truly revealing word is *toys*. It was the word with which Satan disparaged Belial's crude suggestion that the Son be baited with women: 'None are, thou think'st, but taken with such toys' (II. 177). Toys are playthings for idle moments, the vestiges of childhood where the realm of play was at once the most enthralling and the realest world available: our *toys* and *trifles* and the very *pebbles on the shore* were instinct with meaning. One of the saddest things about *Paradise Regained* is that it evicts poetry from this revelrous area of play, where it most truly belongs, and insists that we put away childish things. We must reshelve *Paradise Lost* where Paradise was the play-area of Adam and Eve: love-play in its central bower, gardening work which never became labour, those living toys their fellow-creatures whose sole task was to amuse them:

> Sporting the lion ramped, and in his paw
> Dandled the kid; bears, tigers, ounces, pards,
> Gamboled before them, th'unwieldy elephant
> To make them mirth used all his might, and wreathed
> His lithe proboscis . . .
>
> (IV. 343–7)

This joyously comic line on Isaiah's vision of the Age of Peace (Isaiah 11) is the measure of *Paradise Lost*'s celebration of play: one of its central insights (shared with *Areopagitica* and the divorce tracts) is that delight and virtue are mutually intrinsic. But *Paradise Regained* is sobersidedly Pauline: 'when I became a man, I put away childish things' (I Cor. 13:11).

The link between the Son's rejection of classical learning and the narrative's contempt for sexuality is recorded in the double sense of the noun *toy*: its meanings as 'thing of no value' and 'object made for a child to play with' are amplified in Renaissance usage by its sexual meaning as 'amorous sport, light caress'. Touch in *Paradise Regained* is disparaged as both infantine and erotically threatening, and classical learning (which Milton had loved only just on this side of idolatry) is somehow relegated to this world of regressive distraction – the women's world, which the growing boy is required by the tribe to abdicate. Culture, as expounded by Satan in his temptation, is a matriarchy, just as the Tree of Knowledge where the fatal fruit hung was greeted as 'Mother of science' (*PL*. IX. 680): 'Athens the eye of Greece, mother of arts / And eloquence' (*PR*. IV. 240–1). The Athenian world, the source of Renaissance humanism, on whose wisdoms, mythology and poetic traditions Milton had lavishly drawn, must be viewed in the light of the anxious virility of *Paradise Regained* as an aspect of

168

voluptuousness: the mind's mother who must be abandoned in favour
of its Father. Curious echoes of Milton's earliest poetry occur in Satan's
temptation to visit:

> the olive-grove of Academe,
> Plato's retirement, where the Attic bird
> Trills her thick-warbled notes the summer long
>
> ....
>
> There thou shalt hear and learn the secret power
> Of harmony in tones and numbers hit
> By voice or hand . . .
>
> (IV. 244–6; 254–6)

The sweet studiousness and enjoying solitariness of *L'Allegro* and *Il
Penseroso* drift into mind, with their 'Sweet bird . . . / Most musical,
most melancholy'; the high tower where the reclusive contemplative
may 'unsphere / The spirit of Plato' (*Il Penseroso*, 61–2, 88–9); the
Lydian music 'Untwisting all the chains that tie / The hidden soul of
harmony' (*L'Allegro*, 143–4). The young Milton of thirty-five years
ago has his toys thrown away in the interests of a harsher poetic
affiliation, for all that is soft, delicate and compelling, especially in the
way of language (the 'resistless eloquence' of the Sophists, the 'Mellifluous streams' of the oracle (IV. 268, 277) is a hazard to the hard-won
erect stance of one whose sole task is to stand alone. *Paradise Regained*
is above all on its guard against the appetitive attractions of language,
the taste of the word in the mouth.

A language of English Hebraism would stand as a masculine language
against the effeminacies of Greek and Latin. The poem presents a
critique of language which may be read alongside Hobbes' attack on
metaphor on the one hand, and alongside the Puritan search for a
plain style on the other. Its post-humanist taste evidences a disgust for
all that is not plain-spoken as common daylight. Because it detects
even in the plainest English a riddling openness of interpretation it is
all the more severe on the richly ambiguous language which actively
encourages such plurality of suggestion. The fresh copiousness of
diction and variegation of grammatical effect which dominated the
Renaissance and found its ultimate statement in *Paradise Lost* is avoided
as otiose; oratorical power is suspected as sophistical. The Bible is

centralised in *Paradise Regained* as a textbook for style: the Psalms to be our source-book for song (IV. 334–7), the Prophets with their 'majestic unaffected style' for rules of government, which in them is 'plainest taught' (359, 361). *Paradise Regained* may be compared with Socrates' feud with the word-mongering sophists who traded in linguistic skills:[10] the poem battles for control of the medium by which mankind gains or loses access to truth. Satan is the Sophist of *Paradise Regained*, using language as he adopts variant disguises, to conceal and deceive. In the Platonic dialogues, words are the area of dispute. The dialectic is a psychological weapon which forces its victim to define exactly what he means by what he says, with the frequent baffling effect of disclosing that he has said the opposite of what he thought he meant, so the dialogue in *Paradise Regained* is a Christian dialectic whose first aim is to cut excrescence from speech in order to reveal the simplest, most original and least obfuscated meanings. *Paradise Regained* is as bare of elaborate metaphor as it is rich in plain axiomatic statement, often leaning towards tautology. Often tautology is the nearest language can approach to Truth: a tautology which returns to God's classic 'I am that I am'. The Son is brought into deeper understanding of the fact of being himself through his recognition that he is not Satan: 'Knowing who I am, as I know who thou art' (I. 356). Tautology, with its circular self-reflexiveness, trespasses in its commitment to honourable exactitude, on the domain of the meaningless, and this is always a danger in Milton's puristic experiment with language:

> the persuasive rhetoric
> That sleeked his tongue, and won so much on Eve,
> So little here, nay lost; but Eve was Eve . . .
> (IV. 4–6)

It would not be entirely frivolous to suggest that *Paradise Regained* is committed to nothing more or less than the demonstration of the truth of tautology: that Eve was Eve, Satan was Satan and the Son was the Son.

Rhetorical patterns of repetition, both linear and (especially) circular, proliferate. The voice gravitates always towards the rationally prosaic and the poetically pedestrian: towards the clearest and cleanest statement that can be made about a given question, yet with a sense that behind the plainest statement may lie worlds of meaning more profound than the human tongue is capable of articulating. This sense of divine background to the superficies of human language is one of the major literary features of *Paradise Regained*. It is why the low style of plainness and simplicity has the paradoxical effect of presenting a sense of riddle and of subtly fugitive implication. Its language is liminal between human denotation and Divine intimation: eschewing meta-phorical ambivalences, it anatomises out a plainness paradoxically instinct with the mysteries of the creating Word. In a poem which locates its major speaker in famine conditions, the steady equation of language with food is an index of the emergency importance accorded to words, and the finding and digesting of the right words. 'For lying,' as the Son retorts to Satan, 'is thy sustenance, thy food' (I. 429): and what we eat we become. The wrong words, like the meal of forbidden fruit 'engorged' in Eden (*PL*. IX. 791), bears mortal poison. Milton characteristically picks up an equation intrinsic to the language itself and expands it to maximum extension: we speak of 'cooking up a story' or 'feeding someone a lie' which is then 'swallowed' by the victim; conversely, of being nourished and sustained by another's words. Behind the poem rests the Scriptural admonition, 'Man shall not live by bread alone, but by every word that proceedeth out of the mouth of God' (Matthew 4:4). *Paradise Regained* registers an enquiry as to where we shall find this bread of language and by what means distinguish it from the adulterated speech which passes current in the shifting maze of the linguistic code.

Of all other linguistic modes, Christ throws doubt on metaphor, that bugbear of Hobbes: 'And, on the contrary, metaphors, and senseless and ambiguous words, are like *ignes fatui*, and reasoning upon them is wandering amongst innumerable absurdities; and their end, contention and sedition, or contempt.'[11] But though the poem shows some sign of the contemporary rationalist critique of language, its purism is more closely identifiable with the Protestant quarrel with verbal artifice which had animated, for instance, Herbert's posture in the 'Jordan' poems on the practice of 'Curling with metaphors a plain intention':

> Who sayes that fictions onely and false hair
> Become a verse? Is there in truth no beautie?
> Is all good structure in a winding stair? . . .[12]

The bewigged profanities of an idle courtly mannerism are ridiculed by the Protestant poetics as time-wasting follies: the watchword is *plain*, and plainness is the touchstone of *Paradise Regained*. Book I ends with the Son's assault on the pagan oracles, those riddling arbiters of foreign policy throughout the pagan world:

> that hath been thy craft,
> By mixing somewhat true to vent more lies.
> But what have been thy answers, what but dark
> Ambiguous and with double sense deluding,
> Which they who asked have seldom understood,
> And not well understood, as good not known?
> (I. 432–7)

Double meaning is of the Devil, whose mastery of *double entendre*, open-ended pun, quibbles and indeterminate language with several possible fields of reference (in short, *poesis*) is the index of language's fall from grace. *Paradise Regained* here focuses itself as a radical experiment to refine language down to a single non-connotative discourse. This discourse will be the domain of the new 'living Oracle', the Holy Spirit, which will find lodging in each pious heart as 'an inward oracle' (460; 463).

Paradise Regained's plain style, then, is understood as the language of oracular intuition. It is a style implying circularity rather than linear progression. The poem does not have anywhere to go except home. It proceeds in circles, repeating itself palimpsestically (there are, for example, three accounts of the Baptism in Book I) like the circulation of thoughts in a questioning mind. The very title, *Paradise Regained*, with its suffix *Re-*, indicative of the completion of a cycle in return to source, implies this structure. That suffix is repeated in an insistent pattern of verbs of return, from the declaration of the subject as to be *Recovered* at line 3, through repetitions of *revolve, reveal, return, restored, rejoice, relapse, retire, resume, repine, recall, refresh*, with the concluding word the final closure of the circle, at home in *returned*. The journey into the wilderness is a round trip which recapitulates Adam's and Eve's expulsion in Genesis, and typologically fulfils the symbolic meaning of the Israelites' forty years in the wilderness in Exodus. All that is said and done in *Paradise Regained* is repetitious, but with variations. Time has come round to a climactic moment: 'And now too soon for us the circling hours / This dreaded time have compassed' (I, 57–8) as Satan worries. To think in this solipsistic poem of sealed meditation is to *revolve*: Christ in the wilderness walked 'Musing and much revolving in his breast' (I. 185); 'straight I again revolved / The Law and prophets' (259–60). Turning things over in his mind again and again, he tours the compass of the self, and the horizons of the desert blankly encircle his eye (295–8). This area of the self is by its very nature obscure and untrodden (298) by any fellow-creature. If clues are to be found in such trackless expanses they must be elicited by the method of *revolving* thought – a creative version of the familiar negative experience of 'going round in circles'. The search is for inner revelation, the miraculous-seeming emergence of the exactly right answer. The narrative voice too is stranded in a comparable desert, in the silence of what has been left 'unrecorded' (I. 16). Areas of the narrative must be left as problematic gaps, hazarded guesswork on a purely conditional basis. Where the Son passed his forty days and nights, the narrator concedes, 'is not revealed' (307). Even Scripture is a riddling patchwork of selective records, with hiatuses and blank pages. Whereas the poet of *Paradise Lost* was accompanied by a powerful feminine Muse which filled those gaps with a plenitude of imagery, the Spirit invoked in the later poem is so internalised as to make the narrator seem so solitary as to be almost Museless.

Paradise Regained is a poem of faith which admits doubt. The doubt generated by the Son's absence from his disciples and his mother is the focus of the beautiful early passages of Book II, in which his unexplained withdrawal provokes a correspondent process of inward searching and self-examination in those whom his life has touched into a blaze of Messianic fervour. The circling of his brooding thoughts is echoed in the round of perplexities into which his followers are thrown: a quandary which mimes the insecurity of the remnant of the saints in 1660, pondering the apparent disappearance of Christ from a relapsed and recidivist history. Mary's son is perceived as a bright, solacing presence; then, in his absconding, as a source of anxious uncertainty. Milton evolves a language to cover for the sorry questionmark which is all that is left in the mind in the wake of the failure of some great hope: The disciples:

> Now missing him their joy so lately found,
> So lately found, and so abruptly gone,
> Began to doubt, and doubted many days,
> And as the days increased, increased their doubt . . .
>
> (II. 9–12)

Upon the echoing balance of these subtle half-lines, Milton registers both the disciples' mourning and the rift in their belief. The eloquent musicality of the effect depends on the adaptation of the plainsong which is *Paradise Regained*'s staple mode to the emotions of the human group left suspended in time while the central actor moves out onto the eternity of the wilderness. Half-lines weave a bond with their successors through duplication ('so lately found, / So lately found') and cut it through antithesis ('so abruptly gone'), the deeply-felt *so* as elsewhere in Milton, being an elegiac sign for the personal mourning of some passing (as with Eve: 'from her best prop so far and storm so nigh', *PL*. IX. 433). Duplication and alliteration now extend the state of doubt in time: *doubt . . . doubted . . . days . . . days increased . . . increased . . . doubt*. The repetitious days accumulate and intensify the communal state of anxious incomprehension. Yet the structure of the lines retains a quality of restraint and peace: the poised poem promises in its very form to answer their queries and regain their losses. As the disciples gather, a passage of matchlessly atmospheric georgic simplicity evokes a piscatory music of common life amongst the working people beside the sacred river of Jordan. If there is an echo of the *Nativity Ode* here ('The shepherds on the lawn . . . Sat simply chatting in a rustic row' (VIII)), the Spenserian pastoral has been dragged through the net of forty years of history in which the common people have had their revolutionary say, and have more to 'chat' about than those literary rustics from a Hebrew Arcadia:

> Then on the bank of Jordan, by a creek:
> Where winds with reeds, and osiers whisp'ring play,
> Plain fishermen, no greater men them call,
> Close in a cottage low together got,
> Their unexpected loss and plaints outbreathed:
>   Alas, from what high hope to what relapse
> Unlooked for are we fallen, our eyes beheld
> Messiah certainly now come, so long

Expected of our fathers; we have heard
His words, his wisdom full of grace and truth,
Now, now, for sure, deliverance is at hand,
The kingdom shall to Israel be restored:
Thus we rejoiced, but soon our joy is turned
Into perplexity and new amaze:
For whither is he gone . . .

(II. 25–39)

The fishermen are Christ's comrades and friends. Their gathering resembles more a radical and subversive meeting of the Primitive Church (under the sign of the Fish) than a merely personal occasion. Here if anywhere in the poem we hear the voice of choric tenderness and love: but it is in the context of political faction and a corporate underground attempt to change the course of history. The minor key in which the work is composed rises here to a unique intensity, a set of variations on the key of *regain*. Six times the choric speech 'outbreathed' by the disciples circles back to its dominant theme, a chord of faith and abiding – *relapse, restore, rejoice, retire, reveal, return*, with the final line of the speech ('Soon we shall see our hope, our joy return' (57)) repairing the injury lamented at line 36 ('Thus we rejoice, but soon our joy is turned'). The *turning* of *joy* records the disruption of an inner harmony and psychic integrity which must be synthesised into *rejoicing* and *returning*. Dismembered words are reunified by act of faith. The unity achieved by the speech is one amongst several concentric circles embraced by the whole unity of the poem, for its last line prefigures the last line of the poem, which fulfils its promise 'Home to his mother's house private returned' (IV. 639) to the letter.

Milton had been a millenarian, awaiting the Second Coming along with his generation, throughout the Civil Wars and Interregnum: he expected the return of Christ *soon*: tomorrow, next month, next year. *Paradise Regained* reinterprets *soon* in the light of the interminable waiting and standing incumbent upon Christ's seventeenth-century disciples in an age when the word *restore* connoted the Restoration of Charles II and a new age of bondage and persecution. The people of God gather in a 'cottage low', subdued and camouflaged: the voice they 'outbreathe' has to be as indecipherably quiet as the natural sounds of the wind in the reeds and the 'whisp'ring' osiers. Their meditative song is a companion to that of Christ in the wilderness: 'let us wait' (49), to that of Seekers and Quakers after the failure of the Revolution, and to that of Milton years earlier under sentence of blindness: 'They also serve who only stand and wait.' This willingness to endure the passage of time with patience and equanimity – to tolerate the discomfort of uncertainty and to see it as a process towards understanding – forms the structure both of the disciples' and Mary's speech. This time-biding attitude of attendance upon circumstances and personal attunement as a means of focusing problems with lucidity represents the supreme psychological insight of *Paradise Regained*: and it is an acute one. The unconscious processes of the mind are trusted to secrete their own truths in the hidden recesses of the self. Milton explores the idea of 'sleeping on a problem'; the kind of mental exercise which Wordsworth would rename as 'wise passiveness',[13] that receptive, musing state of consciousness in which ideas can surface, so that we brighten and say 'I see it now.' The answer is experienced as naturally and passively emergent; we have neither fought for nor grasped it. This experience of involuntary assurance preoccupies Milton in the last two poems, and crucially resolves the action of *Samson Agonistes*: the 'rousing motions' of inspiration whose certitude provides the peripeteia of the tragedy.

The Mary of the Gospels is human passivity *par excellence*. She is required to do nothing but wait, receive, accept and be obedient to the summons of the active Godhead. Milton's Mary is a prototype of the time-biding mind. Meditating on her experience of her Son's life, she remembers a pattern of loss and finding, upon which she has reflected to some effect: 'what he meant I mused, / Since understand' (II. 99–100). The circling problems of interpretation which feature as a major subject of the poem are met with patience by Mary because she falls back on the mind as a 'storehouse' in which memory has 'laid up' events incomprehensible at the time (II. 103–4, and Luke 2:50–1), to be 'pondered' over time (105, and Luke 2:19). Milton's metaphor intimates perhaps a granary, where thrift ensures future nourishment; it also implies the womb. Just as in *Paradise Lost* Milton had appropriated (in a long tradition of Platonic-Christian symbolism) female creativity, so in *Paradise Regained* it is as if he had made a raid on the attitudes culturally constructed as female (passivity, receptiveness, quietism) and aggressively instated them in the territory of the male.

Christ is emphatically his mother's son in *Paradise Regained*. She is both his source and destination, and it is a version of her sustenance that he must seek in the wilderness as he 'Sole but with holiest meditations fed, / Into himself descended' (II. 110–11). But Mary's son seeks an intangible, strenuous bread which only the Father can provide. In this sense, the Son's excursion represents the ritual intitiation of the boy-child from the ample comfort of the mother-world into patriarchal law:

> Where will this end? Four times ten days I have passed
> Wandering this woody maze, and human food
> Nor tasted, nor had appetite. That fast
> To virtue I impute not, or count part
> Of what I suffer here; if nature need not,
> Or God support nature without repast
> Though needing, what praise is it to endure?
> But now I feel I hunger, which declares
> Nature hath need of what she asks; yet God
> Can satisfy that need some other way,
> Though hunger still remain; so it remain
> Without this body's wasting, I content me,
> And from the sting of famine fear no harm,
> Nor mind it, fed with better thoughts that feed
> Me hung'ring more to do my Father's will.
>
> (II. 245–59)

From the mother's natural plenitude, he passes to the Father's remorseless imposition of famine. Language loses its basis in the material world and the words dance before his famished eye like nearly meaningless counters. The 'woody maze' is also a linguistic area. The poetry mimes that almost nightmarish psychological state in which (on the edge of sleep, in illness or, as here, in great hunger) words lose stable meaning in relation to one another as well as to their referends. This state of consciousness is characterised by obsessive verbal repetition: with each repetition there is further ontological draining, so that language progressively empties the more it is subject to our interrogative stare. Such reiteration, however, is also the contemplative's route to peace and freedom: transcendental meditation depends on the repetition of a word whose sole significance is that it is barren of meaning and

177

connotation. The Son's *nature need, nature . . . needing, hunger . . . nature, need . . . hunger* is the meaning-free labyrinth which finally emancipates mind from body altogether into a transcendent lexicon which can allow in new terms: *fed . . . feed*, words which fill lack and block desire though they are attached to nothing more substantial than thoughts. *Paradise Regained* is a testament of the wilderness: it is a record of what can be said about silence and seen in blankness, where both language and vision all but die.

5

Samson Agonistes: Words Bereft of Touch or Trust

> *Samson:* A little onward lend thy guiding hand
> To these dark steps, a little further on;
> For yonder bank hath choice of sun or shade,
> There I am wont to sit, when any chance
> Relieves me from my task of servile toil,
> Daily in the common prison else enjoined me . . .
>
> *(Samson Agonistes,* 1–6)

> *Oedipus:* Tell me, Antigone – where have you come to now
> With your blind old father?
> ....
> Three masters – pain, time, and the royalty in the blood –
> Have taught me patience. Is there a resting place,
> My child, where I could sit, on common ground
> Or in some sacred close?
>
> *(Oedipus at Colonus)*[1]

In Sophocles' play the blind Oedipus, arriving at his final resting-place at Colonus (Sophocles' birth-place) is led, tended and interceded for by his daughter Antigone. Stigmatised and ostracised through incestuous and parricidal crimes committed in ignorance, he brings to Colonus the power of a resolved quietism: 'My strength has been in suffering, / Not doing' (268–9). Oedipus is paradoxically a holy man:

179

out of his impurity springs purification; from his suffering, atonement, and from his sacrificial blindness a more than human wisdom and vision. Oedipus in rags, disowned by his nation, tenant of the same blind dark as Samson, is incomparably richer than Samson. The first two lines of the plays tell us so. In being able to name Antigone, Oedipus declares his access to the assurance of a love not cryptic or strained with inner conflict, but unconditional, solacing and, literally, to hand. *Samson Agonistes* vividly remembers *Oedipus at Colonus* at its opening but there is no Antigone. The person addressed as guide is voicelessly, invisibly anonymous, metonymically reduced to the presence of a disembodied hand, cloven at the wrist, such as might reach from the arbitrary dark of any blind man's world into momentary contact, leaving the existence of the attached person eternally hypothetical. In *Samson Agonistes*, the cherishing guidance that belongs to human love, and especially to womanly love, cannot be found, and (the play suggests) should not be sought.

To whom does Samson commend himself in his need? Presumably to some fellow-slave, whose presence drops away in the course of the speech into the amorphous blank which is all that Samson can know of material reality. The tone of voice seems querulous: it supplicates, as if Samson cannot trust his bodiless attendant to remain as long as he needs his or her support. The towering Samson is reduced to helpless dependency and the pleading repetitions ('A little onward . . . a little further on') resemble the inflections of an old man: blind Gloucester led by Edgar; Oedipus groping for his resting-place. But it is a well-attested literary paradox that where nothing can be readily known and identified, meanings may range out into the illimitable. Samson's plea seems to resonate beyond the immediate theatre of action into remote areas of address: the guiding hand he reaches for may also be read as the hand of God, whose hold the hero lost before he became blind. It is God's withdrawal and man's savage sense of rejection that *Samson Agonistes* mourns, and this larger guidance that the agonist solicits. No other human hand is allowed to touch Samson in the course of the play. He exists in a vacuum of intense isolation, incarcerated and entombed in the self: 'I am gall, I am heartburn', he might have cried with the Hopkins of the Terrible Sonnets. If he could spit himself out, he would be eased. Milton's play is convulsed with hatred, self-hatred and fear which cannot be exorcised because Samson can touch no one and cannot permit himself to be touched. 'Let me approach at least, and touch thy hand,' Dalila begs. Absolute terror seems to clutch at Samson, and with it his characteristic reflex, absolute violence: 'Not for thy life, lest fierce remembrance wake / My sudden rage to tear thee joint by joint' (951–3). Samson's early career and the foundation of his glory consisted in campaigns of violence varying to atrocity against the Philistines; his utterance during the course of the play maintains an aggressive stance towards all or most comers; his cathartic action in pulling the Temple down on the Philistines is an act of demolition and massacre. To touch for Milton's Samson is to hit out. As against Oedipus' long-suffering quietism, Samson maintains an impatient passivity which breaks out in the catastrophe in an orgy of active destruction. Both Oedipus and Samson have given their names to certain sexual conflicts endemic in the psyche of the male half of the human race. About these complexes we are necessarily in the dark, since they belong to the subconscious mind, but certain narratives and myths draw up the conflict as it were by the root, for our inspection. These narratives are charged with sublimated pain and to retell them is to wrench at the quick of sexual pain at its buried nerve-endings; each retelling brings up the organic life of the tribe with the legendary shriek ascribed to the mandrake root. Hence they are public stories speaking for all, but in addition the Samson legend carried with it much that was acutely relevant to the narrative of Milton's personal life (blindness, combined with political defeat and sexual disaster). To tell the primitive story of Samson licensed the discharge of raw personal pain as poetic energy: readers have always responded to the intimate quality of the drama.[2] Both *Oedipus* and *Samson* deal with the riddle of male conflicts in relation to the mother, but whereas excess of love and attachment predominate in the Oedipus story, male fear and the sense of betrayal are the obsessive elements in the Samson narrative. Each suffers in the penalty of blindness (doubled in Samson's loss of virile hair) a symbolic castration. But Samson's story, unlike Oedipus' but like Adam's in Genesis, is an Oedipal myth which elects a scapegoat, interpreting the tragic weakness of man in terms of an alleged treacherous will to power in woman. The Greek story blames no Dalila; the Hebrew story has recourse to no Antigone. It is fatally loveless.

The essential loneliness and obscurity of Milton's *Samson* is an experience replicated in the mind of the reader, who makes no expedition from his study to join a corporate audience at the theatre in order to view this drama. Milton intended the play as a closet drama, the theatre of action being the closed interior of the reading mind, a theatre-in-the-round which impersonates the almost eventless action of the story by its dark interiority and the silence of its voices. There is neither touching nor sharing in that soliloquist's theatre of the self, rather the remorseless urgency of voices that take over from our inner dialogues, to focus conflicts equally private and just as deadlocked. The characters who speak with Samson – the Chorus, Manoa, Dalila, Harapha the Philistine champion, the Philistine officer – seem to speak at or alongside him rather than with him. The choric comfort resembles that offered to Job by the cold comforters, and the suggestions made by his visitors invariably incline Samson to do otherwise. Their voices (sound being the only contact Samson has with the world and that contact being all but completely disrupted at the beginning of the play) come to him muffled and dislocated: 'I hear the sound of words; their sense the air / Dissolves unjointed ere it reach my ear' (176–7). *Hear: their: air: ere: ear*: the multiple pararhyme seems to display the arbitrariness of the accord between meaning and sound in a world where only a sense of the ridiculous remains confirmed and fundamental. The dissolution of words in air is hauntingly enacted in the last three modulations of breath on a theme of open vowel, ending in unvoiced consonant – *air: ere: ear*. So, in a stupor of grief and depression, words reach us thinly and never truly gain our ear. Language has betrayed Samson, opening to Dalila's 'Tongue-batteries' (404) his 'fort of silence' (236), stigmatising himself 'as a blab, / The mark of fool set on his front' (495–6). Samson records a dread of consigning himself to words, expression implying the loss or abdication of the self, its secrets ceded in language. It is proverbial that speech 'gives us away'. The strong man in our culture is silent, costive, retentive, especially with woman, whose allegedly loose tongue is associated with designs on male autonomy. Loud-mouthed Samson, the cunning riddler of Judges, was also the blabbermouth who blurted out his secrets at the moment of maximum sexual weakness.

In the language of *Samson Agonistes* Milton created a potent hybrid, composed of the fusion of Greek and Hebrew, Sophocles, Euripides and Aeschylus with the Book of Judges,[3] in a language which moves between a free verse remembering the music of *Lycidas* and a driven, dynamic blank verse from *Paradise Lost*, alternating with a style that is neither of these but rather a seventeenth-century English equivalent to the argumentative lyricism of a Sophoclean chorus. A characteristic feeling of the language of *Samson* is of energy compressed, blocked and compacted into lines that, like muscles maintaining unbearable tension, present a metrical counterpart to Samson's frustrated power both to act and understand. This rhythmically varies to a simple voice of self-mourning like a solo flute:

> The sun to me is dark
> And silent as the moon,
> When she deserts the night
> Hid in her vacant interlunar cave.
>
> (86–9)

> So much I feel my genial spirits droop,
> My hopes all flat; nature within me seems
> In all her functions weary of herself;
> My race of glory run, and race of shame,
> And I shall shortly be with them that rest.
>
> (594–8)

In this elegiac and valedictory music, the feeling is again of a chemical amalgam of Hebraic and Hellenistic tragic expression: Job's 'my soul chooseth strangling, and death rather than my life' (7:15) and the Sophoclean Chorus's 'Say what you will, the greatest boon is not to be; / But, life begun, soonest to end is best' (*Oedipus at Colonus*, 1228–9). Yet the nerve-strung agitation and the torpid inertia of these two musics are psychologically one, the death-wish an inevitable corollary of the wish to kill. The plot's catastrophe enacts this unity, as Samson's release occurs through the pulling-down of the temple on his enemies *and* himself – himself his own bitterest enemy to the end.

The lamentatory style and the pugilistic outcry of the hero are equally articulations of a sense of initially incomprehensible orphanhood which penetrates the hero to the marrow. It is notable that, whereas the thirteenth chapter of Milton's source, The Book of Judges, gives a major role to Samson's mother in its description of the miraculous events preceding his conception and birth, Milton virtually deletes her from the narrative. In Judges, the angel of God appears twice to Manoa's wife, to deliver detailed instructions as to antenatal care and child-management, and she subsequently corrects her husband's pessimistic interpretation of the divine visitation (13:23). These biblical references to the mother are some of the most pregnant factors in the Christian exegesis which identified Samson as a type of Christ: Samson's mother prefigures Mary at the anunciation; his elect character as a Nazarite whose hair is not to be cut in token of his special closeness to God and role as deliverer prefigures the child of Nazareth. Milton simply eliminates direct allusion to Samson's mother from the script:

> O wherefore was my birth from Heaven foretold
> Twice by an angel, who at last in sight
> Of both my parents all in flames ascended . . .
> (23–5)

Milton abstains from saying that the angelic message was imparted initially to the mother in private. In Milton's re-imagining of the story, the father-son relationship has precedence, Manoa being the sole representative of the household to appear on the stage, lamenting and questioning his son's fall, remonstrating with his marriage-choices and subsequent lapses, compassionating him and finally inviting him home to be nursed.

This gap or silence signifying the mother is meaningful in relation to the play's presentation not only of Dalila but also of Manoa and God the Father. It is as if the play wished (as Adam explicitly did in *Paradise Lost*) that God had invented some more satisfying system of reproduction by male parthenogenesis whereby masculinity might clone its own divine image and thereby evade the moral maladies so graphically evident in Samson. Milton has made woman abdicate her maternal position as nurturer and carer: the human father and the divine Father have moved over to appropriate the vacated role. When Samson looks back to his days of infant innocence, his remembrance is of fatherly cherishing which has a curious resonance of maternity:

I was his nursling once and choice delight,
His destined from the womb,
Promised by heavenly message twice descending.
Under his special eye
Abstemious I grew up and thrived amain;
He led me on to mightiest deeds
Above the nerve of mortal arm
Against the uncircumcised, our enemies.
And now hath cast me off as never known . . .
(633–41)

The concept of God as a nursing mother is not without biblical precedent (Isaiah 49:15, Numbers 11, John 7:38) and continues through the Church Fathers from Clement to Augustine: 'He who has promised us heavenly food has nourished us on milk, having recourse to a mother's tenderness.'[4] The form of Samson's reminiscence makes it possible for a reader to attribute the breasts and womb which nurtured his infancy to God the Father rather than a human mother. The endeared and homely word 'nursling', so out of keeping with the Titanic *lexis* of *Samson Agonistes*, suggests the peace and safety of mother-love and looks back to the time of complete holding and providing which infants lose at weaning and when they are taught a language which denotes them as solitary individuals. That word is one of the most unguarded of the drama in its yearning acknowledgement of the need to depend, to be loved and to take nourishment. It confesses the primary need for touch and trust (so interrelated) which Samson elsewhere enragedly denies. Manoa offers to nurse him at home, but Samson points out with indignation that he would rather toil at the mill than become a freakshow or an object of pity (563–72). Dalila also offers 'my redoubled love and care / With nursing diligence, to me glad office' (923–4). But Samson the cast-off and reject through woman from God can never again know the primal trust that alone could assuage his anguish. The symptoms of bereavement he so movingly expounds ('faintings, swoonings of depair, / And sense of Heaven's desertion' (631–2) represent a universal experience of separation which, if it is accompanied by a conviction of betrayal by woman, can find no compensation on this side of the grave.

The story of Delilah's betrayal of Samson is a major topos of Western

visual art. One remembers Rubens' powerfully voluptuous representation with its dynamic play of light on flesh and feature. But the
tradition was much older than Rubens and the arrogant beauty of the
Renaissance theatre of paint. The infantile terrors incorporated in the
story are spelt out in a Dutch engraving of 1460 by Master E.S. which
(in contradiction to his usual practice) violates the laws of proportion
by showing Samson as a frail, slender person resembling a child resting
his sleeping head on his mother's knee, while a magnified Delilah
applies the scissors to his hair.[5] The picture has ironically absorbed
something of the Madonna-and-child configuration. Later representations incorporate elements of the typological interpretation which
equated Samson with Christ and Delilah with Judas selling the
deliverer to his enemies for ready money. Samson's humiliation typifies
the Derision of Christ; his revenge on the Philistines foreshadows the
crucifixion or the Last Judgement.[6] Such interpretation naturally
intensified the misogyny built into the narrative by conflating a
treacherous woman with the ultimate betrayal of deicide. The typological reading still enjoyed credence and currency in the seventeenth
century, Milton himself having used the figure of Samson as a type of
the English Protestant Revolution in *The Reason of Church Government*
and *Areopagitica*: 'Methinks I see in my mind a noble and puissant
Nation rousing herself like a strong man after sleep, and shaking her
invincible locks' (*CPW*. II. 557–8). This is a prelapsarian Samson who
has not succumbed to the wiles of Dalila and perhaps never will: a
Samson plucked out of the toils of his story as an image of fresh,
resurrected vigour in its potent heyday. Such is the leonine buoyancy
of the emotion invested in the renovated Samson of *Areopagitica* that
the effect is to release the hero from bondage to his own ignoble story.
As with the Truth/Osiris emblem in the same work (549–51), such is
the extravagant spirit of freedom from oppressive laws and conventions
that the story is alluded to only to be opened up and recreated: the
narrative violates its own misogynist determinants by presenting an
androgynous Samson. The Nation, gendered feminine, rouses 'herself'
like a 'strong man'. This all-permissive androgyny would go on to
create some of the most beautiful effects of *Paradise Lost*: the herma-
phroditic Dove of the first Invocation, the mingling of bisexual angels
in erotic love, the Hermetic treatment of Eden. In *Areopagitica*, the
Samson allusion is twinned to the symbolic eagle with its iconographic

association with Christ's resurrection as light and vision, the eagle being traditionally the only creature able to look straight into the sun without injury to its eyes. Milton before he loses his sight summons a visionary and liberating Samson to shake himself free of failure.

This interpretation of Samson as essentially a figure for regeneration and reawakening has been traditionally applied by critics to *Samson Agonistes*, its action being said to imply a pattern of spiritual recovery and growth in the hero, who moves from enraged alienation from God and demoralisation through a sequence of enlightenments (wrought by his visitors and strengthened by the Chorus) until he is in a state of grace, able to hear God's inner prompting and atone for his mistakes.[7] Arguments endorsing this approach stress the fact that Milton rehabilitates the hero by dropping the more primitive, ridiculous or squalid aspects of his history (the firing of the Philistine corn through the agency of three hundred foxes with burning tails (15:4–5); Samson's motive for being in Gaza – to visit a brothel (16:1); the status of Dalila as harlot, which is 'elevated' to that of wife). The Christian interpretation also lays stress on the climactic Phoenix symbol, used by the Semichorus (1687–1707) to celebrate Samson's triumph. The Phoenix, unique of its species, with its multiple regenerations from its own ashes, has a long-standing association with Christ. This reading of the play requires that we credit the opinions of Samson and possibly the Chorus with a growing wisdom and enlightenment and that we discredit those of the tempters, Manoa (well-meaning but short-sighted), Dalila (malign, mendacious and sensual) and Harapha (inane thuggery). The apocalyptically violent catastrophe is read as a prototype of the Atonement or Last Judgement.

It is possible to read *Samson Agonistes* in this light, but only with one eye closed. The play records a complex, self-contradictory attitude, a burningly active engagement with a narrative arousing to every level of the author's personality. *Samson* contains the possibility of polarised readings, just as polarised readings of the Samson story ran concurrently amongst Reformation Christians. To many Reformation teachers, Samson embodied risible mistakenness, presenting an example to be strenuously avoided rather than that of a great man stricken but glorified. Samson was a fool, a voluptuary, an evil-doer. Luther's Samson (though justified by individual election) is a figure who maintains right of vengeance, in the teeth of the contrary law:

For we read thus of Samson . . . that he said, 'As they did to me, so have I
done to them,' even though Proverbs . . . says to the contrary, 'Do not say,
I will do to him as he has done to me, and . . . adds, 'Do not say, I will
repay him his evil.'[8]

Thomas Goodwin saw Samson as a negative example; Richard Bernard
placed him as a contrast to Christ.[9] Milton's Samson is unregenerately
violent. Violence is his creed, his *crie de cœur*. The subject of the
forgiveness of one's enemies is never raised. It is never put to Samson
by anyone other than Dalila, pleading for herself, that Samson might
usefully moderate the snarling insults he lets fly at her – and indeed,
the Chorus reinforces his contempt by its summing-up of the evidence:
'She's gone, a manifest serpent by her sting / Discovered in the end,
till now concealed' (997–8) and its lengthy excursus on the inferiority
of women (1010–60). As for the bloody fate of the Philistines, no one
is sorry: they are, after all, inveterate enemies rather than fellow
humans. The play endorses those 'rousing motions' (1382) which form
the *peripeteia* of the tragic action, giving Samson the idea for his
revenge, as a direct inspiration of unquestionably divine origin, in the
Puritan tradition of direct revelation on which Milton placed supreme
value throughout his life. The 'something extraordinary' which is heard
from offstage as a murderous noise is acclaimed by the text as an
elemental cataclysm, 'O dearly-bought revenge, yet glorious!' (1660),
which may strike the reader still fresh from the portrayal of Divine
Love in *Paradise Lost* with all the incongruity of unintended irony: 'O
unexampled love, / Love nowhere to be found less than divine' (III.
410–11). For all its parallels with the Gospel story, the Samson
narrative opposes the Christian ethic and appeals to primitive psychological and tribal aggressions which Christianity, however unsuccessfully, sought to restrain or rechannel.

The murder of the Philistines is presented in a heroic and spectacular
light:

> This uttered, straining all his nerves he bowed,
> As with the force of winds and waters pent,
> When mountains tremble, those two massy pillars
> With horrible convulsion to and fro
> He tugged, he shook, till down they came and drew

The whole roof after them, with burst of thunder
Upon the heads of all who sat beneath,
Lords, ladies, captains, counsellors or priests,
Their choice nobility and flower, not only
Of this but each Philistian city round
Met from all parts to solemnize this feast.
Samson, with these immixed, inevitably
Pulled down the same destruction on himself;
The vulgar only scaped who stood without.

(1646–59)

A rare epic simile (1647–8) is introduced into the narrative to give a sense of dynamic commotion on a cosmic scale, together with other effects reminiscent of *Paradise Lost*: the 'massy pillars' with their intransigent solidity, destabilised by the 'horrible convulsion' which rocks their foundations, and the vernacular idiom and syntactic redoubling of the verbs, 'He tugged, he shook', remembering *Paradise Lost*'s critical moment of fall, 'she plucked, she ate' (IX. 781). The poetry focuses with Miltonic relish on the moment of absolute and suspenseful stress, delayed as if in the slow-motion perception that registers shock, until it affords the almost childish gratification of the sudden grammatical release of that energy: 'till down they came'. Exalted satisfaction accompanies this last self-projection of Milton as *Eikonoklastes*, smashing the idols and bringing the whole roof down on his enemies. The 'burst of thunder' which sustains the imagery of elemental cataclysm demolishing the lightweight fabrications of man-made architecture, presents an awesome soundscape to our inner ear and simultaneously implies the thunder of divine justice mediated through the human agency of Samson. The entire ruling caste of the Philistine nation is wiped out at one throw: 'Lords, ladies, captains, counsellors or priests, / Their choice nobility and flower', that is, both the aristocracy, the military, the legislature and the prelacy, with withering irony on the words 'choice', 'nobility' and 'flower'. Milton leaves unscathed the 'vulgar . . . who stood without', that is, the common people, making possible a revolutionary political reading which understands *Samson Agonistes* as a testament to a defiant resistance to Restoration dictatorship on behalf of the people of England.[10] The play celebrates revenge in festival terms: there is an air of desperate saturnalia about the catastrophe. The Chorus is quick to exempt Samson from the charge of suicide, since his death was inevitably involved in the accomplishment of retribution. But, for all the devices deflecting blame and signalling the regeneration of the hero, what we have witnessed in the course of the action towards tragic purgation cannot be called a Christocentric pattern. The play's conflicts are raw, ambiguous and psychologically primitive, as impervious to the normative emollients of good doctrine as the subconscious mind itself.

Samson Agonistes might be thought of as an artistic act of profoundly cathartic regression. In choosing a pre-Christian subject, Milton could licence his passionate need to transgress the New Testament taboo on hatred, violence and revenge. *Samson* absolved Milton from the Gospel duty of forgiveness because Samson, who lived under the old law, pre-dated the arrival of the difficult light shed by Christ on fratricidal and matricidal urges. Milton had used this device of licenced regression once before, at a moment of maximum political hatred, when he wanted to justify the regicide in *Eikonoklastes*. Charles I (or whoever impersonated his authorship in *Eikon Basilike*) had argued from the primacy of Gospel charity over Old Testament revenge, publically forgiving his murderers by quoting the crucified Christ: *'forgive them, O my Father, for they know not what they do.'*[11] Milton replied with bale by quoting the law given to Noah and the law of Moses enjoining capital punishment for murderers. He glossed over the implications of Christ's teachings by a hurried dismissal of Christ as apolitical, and by treating the New Testament as secondary in authority because it comes chronologically second to the Old Testament in the Bible: 'Next in order of time to the Laws of *Moses* are those of Christ' (*CPW*. III. 587). The political need to sanction punitive violence gives Christ the slip by reverting to an earlier law. In *Samson*, a desire on the part of the whole frustrated personality to avenge the loss of eyes, sexual peace, integrity, prestige and the certainty of God's favour, finds an outlet through comparable retreat to a world which requires of Samson every sacrifice *except* that most exacting and testing sacrifice that is love. Such a tactic also made for a true tragedy in the classic sense. There is no expectation for Samson of a life beyond the grave, and the Phoenix emblem with its connotations of rebirth refers explicitly to the new life conferred by 'fame' (1706), recurring cyclically in the here-and-now and confirmed by its re-enactment under the reader's eye, the text, reborn with every reading.

The lonely ego towers at the centre of Milton's stage, stripping itself of disguise through words which expose a profound inner distress and channel its conflicts and energies into art. Samson as a Nazarite is an embodiment of isolation. The word *Nazarite* derives from the Hebrew *nazar*, meaning 'to separate [oneself]': separate to God, the Nazarite performed feats of superhuman strength, but, joining himself to woman, he was disempowered. The name 'Samson' may have been understood by Milton to mean 'there the second time'. The play records a myth of second chances, the opportunity for Samson to re-enact his choices and to sever himself from all human bonds so that, reaffirming his singularity, he may enter again the safety of God's patronage. The Chorus remembers how, when embattled iron-bound armies hurled themselves upon him, the unarmed Samson repulsed them with contemptuous ease: 'safest he who stood aloof' (135). The separated self is a fortress, to which Samson is understood to return in the closing moments of the tragedy, 'Like that self-begotten bird' (1699). To be 'self-begotten' would be to abdicate the bond that ties man to the mother-world; but to stand aloof thus, refusing the vulnerability of that link is to die as a human being. In separating himself from the feminine, Milton's Samson may be said to go the same way as Shakespeare's Leontes, but without the possibility of purgation and atonement. Samson has been called an 'all too human character'.[12] But the essence of the hero's tragedy does not seem to this reader to lie in a comprehensive humanity; rather, it lies in the acute specificity of a nature all-too-male. The play is at once compulsive and complicit, its author being a fellow-victim of and sharer in the same drives and maladies as Samson; in addition it is diagnostic and therapeutic in the sense of using the control of art to ritualise these drives.

The original story is, as Joseph Wittreich says, pluralistic, polyse-mous and ambiguous.[13] Milton further increases its ambiguities and discontinuities in his struggle with its telling. But Wittreich, who sees in *Samson Agonistes* a radical feminist reappraisal of the Samson/Dalila relationship, underrates the primary character of the male investment in the topos.[14] Milton releases on to his page the raw agony of an unresolved and irresoluble masculine complex: a complex which is represented as proverbial and cyclical from generation to generation. For a woman reader, the horror and pity generated by the drama are perhaps doubled: all the more painful because we may be less tempted to share in the blindness of Samson, his father and the Chorus as to what the agonist really needs in order to be whole. The text is not, for such readers, a mirror but a privileged view into someone else's lived nightmare. Milton does not renovate and rehabilitate Dalila, as some kind-hearted critics have suggested,[15] though, through the imaginative licence of dramatic art to break free of the prejudices of the artist she does talk herself into some freedom from the stereotype, giving an impression of complex and inscrutable vitality. By elevating Dalila's status from that of harlot to lawful wife, Milton does not (as is traditionally assumed) improve her moral position in the text, but rather increases the odium to be cast upon her and the collusive sympathy accorded to a Samson who is presented as an honourable alternative to the barbarous sensualist of Judges. What would be venial in a prostitute is accounted opprobrious in a wife, who is paid not to gratify male appetites on a piecework basis but to satisfy his higher need for a solacing helpmeet, 'needfull . . . against all the sorrows and casualties of this life . . . an intimate and speaking help, a ready and reviving associate in marriage' (The Doctrine and Discipline of Divorce, CPW. II. 251). In Samson Milton returns to the lacerated feelings exposed in his divorce tracts and associated with the sense of his first wife's desertion: Dalila is the embodiment of female power and autonomy, and Samson of male fear of such self-containment.

*　　　　　*　　　　　*

What does Samson most fear – his blind openness to abuse and derision, God's abandonment, his loss of self-esteem, his bruised sexuality? Samson seems to shrink from none of these so wincingly as from what may be called the woman in himself. We have followed Milton's poetic career from his youth at Cambridge, 'so faire y^t they called him the Lady of X^ts coll', through his identification with the Lady in Comus, the partial but intense identification with Eve in Paradise Lost, and finally to the expulsion of sexuality in the withheld potency of a glorified male autonomy in the Christ of Paradise Regained. Samson is Milton's final agon with his sense of something feminine within himself, which was at once a source of creativity and at the same time alien and alarming. To excise that feminine self, the hero of Samson has to tear his heart out of his body. If we take Samson

Agonistes as Milton's last poem,[16] then we are at liberty to see it as a poem of old age. It dramatises the closure of a life. Old age strips men of the assets which give them value in their own eyes and raise them culturally above the status of women: physical power and autonomy; sexual vigour; honour in the tribe. Their very hair, on which Milton laid special stress in Adam's wavy (but vigorous and 'manly') locks, falls out. Impotence, baldness, decrepitude, dependency and house-bound marginality are the fate of most elderly men in our society. In other words, they are taken down from their high horse and reduced to something like the condition of women. Milton in later life was afflicted with the gout from which he was to die and (though warmly cared for by his third wife Elizabeth) confined to small living quarters within a quarrelsome female household. Eyelessness in Gaza at the mill with slaves might take on a domestic as well as a political character as a kind of house-arrest in enemy territory. There is an intensity in Samson's denunciation of the image of geriatric domestication in 'contemptible old age obscure' (572) at once vitriolic and sad. Samson's sense of emasculation, his loss of dominance and attack, are imaged in a persistent metaphor of penetration, forced entry and infiltration of his autonomous person by inimical forces. 'They' (the Philistines), or rather 'she' (Dalila), have got in to him, usurping the private space of the self. Samson's own thoughts are imaged as an invasive 'deadly swarm / Of hornets armed' which, whenever they find him alone, 'rush upon me thronging' (19–21). This remorseless stinging of diseased multitudes of bad thoughts serves to represent Samson's impairment as a form of self-division: he has turned against himself at the core of being. The reader's imagination is curdled at the thought of housing a swarm of hornets. The repulsive image has a seething invasiveness. Its obscenity is an organic extension of the Satanic figure 'Myself am hell'. 'Hornets *armed*' catch up the military context of the action in an image of malign unnaturalness.

Later, the Chorus will speak of 'The tumours of a troubled mind / . . . festered wounds' (185–6). A physiology of mind is articulated, which makes us conscious of Samson's mind as a delicately sentient organ, capable of cancer or sepsis, with the concomitant piercing of pain to the vulnerable quick of being, in just the same way as the body's organs and tissues register pain. At the end of the debate with Manoa, Samson bursts out in one of the most powerful lyric passages

193

in the play into an exclamation of mental agony that questions the entire physiological and psychological make-up of mortal man by closing the gap between body and mind. Samson is anatomised on the page, opening up to our distress the inmost body of his psyche:

> O that torment should not be confined
> To the body's wounds and sores,
> With maladies innumerable
> In heart, head, breast, and reins;
> But must secret passage find
> To the inmost mind,
> There exercise all his fierce accidents,
> And on her purest spirits prey,
> As on entrails, joints, and limbs,
> With answerable pains, but more intense,
> Though void of corporal sense.
> My griefs not only pain me
> As a lingering disease,
> But finding no redress, ferment and rage,
> Nor less than wounds immedicable
> Rankle, and fester, and gangrene,
> To black mortification.
> Thoughts, my tormentors, armed with deadly stings
> Mangle my apprehensive tenderest parts,
> Exasperate, exulcerate, and raise
> Dire inflammation which no cooling herb
> Or med'cinal liquor can assuage,
> Nor breath of vernal air from snowy alp.
> Sleep hath forsook and giv'n me o'er
> To death's benumbing opium as my only cure.
> Thence faintings, swoonings of despair,
> And sense of heav'n's desertion.
>
> (606–32)

The body of the mind, thus displayed, presents a symptomatology worthy of Burton's *Anatomy of Melancholy*. Ulcerated, festering and gangrenous, the tissue of the despairing mind is a locus of corruption and decay for which no soothing emollient or natural antidote can be found. Again, the imagery is profoundly invasive. Samson imagines a 'secret passage . . . / To the inmost mind'; his thoughts, 'armed with

stings', recall the hornets of the earlier scene, and these stings are
implanted in the most vulnerably sensitive interior of his person: 'my
apprehensive tenderest parts'. *Tender* is a suggestive word in relation
to the emotional area of violation which the sufferer exposes. It
connotes not only the capacity to feel pain but also the capacity to
receive and confer love. These hot, sore, angry places of infection
which so gall Samson crave relief: such relief is conceived in medical
terms – 'cooling herb', 'med'cinal liquor' – the administration of some
external balm with which to annoint inner wounds. In fact the only
medicine the play can apply to this body of pain is the purgative of
tragedy itself, and that Aristotelian homeopathy prescribed by Milton
in the Prologue: 'things of melancholic hue and quality are used against
melancholy, sour against sour, salt to remove salt humours'. To relieve
the violence of his malady, Samson will use (verbal) violence against
one source of disease (Dalila and himself) and physical violence against
the other (the Philistines and himself). The relief he cannot have is
the comfort of love that would both ease his pain and sustain him
alive.

If there is a 'passage' to the inmost mind, that path is opened by
sexuality and is a love-passage. In relation to Dalila, Samson is
defensive and terrified. That is why his language to her is so immoder-
ately violent. She is experienced as the destroyer of his virility at the
moment of its climax. *Samson Agonistes* plays out a familiar sexual
paradox: the male is enervated by his triumph; he is colloquially said
to 'die', his vigour 'spent'; predator becomes prey. In other words, male
sexuality opens him to effeminacy. Power-terminology is, of course, at
the very root of the language of sexual relations which records
provocation, tactics, stratagems, aggression, surrender, truce or conquest. The love/war trope which is intrinsic to Renaissance literature,
bears a crucial part in the psychological drama of *Samson Agonistes*.
Dalila, like a Trojan horse, brought into Samson's bed not one solitary
alien enemy but an ulterior version of the entire Philistine army, with
full armaments and stratagems:

> Yet the fourth time, when must'ring all her wiles,
> With blandished parleys, feminine assaults,
> Tongue-batteries, she surceased not day nor night
> To storm me over-watched, and wearied out.

195

At times when men seek most repose and rest,
I yielded, and unlocked her all my heart,
Who with a grain of manhood well resolved
Might easily have shook off all her snares:
But foul effeminacy held me yoked
Her bondslave . . .

(402–11)

A *muster* is the assembling of soldiers for inspection, prior to some action, but Dalila's soldiery consists of *wiles*, a conceit which depends for its flavour on the popular male complaint that women do not fight by the rules but wage insidious, underground campaigns of manipulation. A *parley* is an informal conference under truce, but Dalila is incapable of honourable negotiation, her tongue being always a weapon of war, besieging her victim with feminine *assaults* (the violent storming of a fortress), weakening her intimate enemy's defences by *Tongue-batteries*, artillery bombardment which she keeps up on a round-the-clock basis. The success of these stratagems depended on Samson being in an almost helpless position, desperate with insomnia and no doubt enfeebled by post-coital torpor. The mock-heroic imagery carries a burden of acute embarrassment: its suggestion of comic convention[17] intimates that Samson has taken part in a farce, and that is his tragedy. The image of a relentlessly besieged city was still in the late 1660s and early 1670s a contemporary memory and is therefore proper to the political aspects of Samson's dilemma. Additionally, the conceit has an ancient sexual application in the poetry of seduction: the lover besieges his mistress's impregnable virtue with a view to penetrating her portcullis and forcing her to yield, whereupon he will enter, 'take' and possess her.[18] A rich range of aggressive innuendo makes itself available in the trope, whose erotic pleasure is generated by the patriarchal and misogynist bias of the wit. The male is endorsed in his active wish to penetrate the passive body of the woman in a licit and complicit act of delicious violence. Donne seized and complicated the device when he represented himself as female in relation to the male Almighty:

I, like an usurpt towne, to'another due,
Labour to'admit you, but Oh, to no end
....

Take mee to you, imprison mee, for I
Except you enthrall me, never shall be free,
Nor ever chaste, except you ravish mee.[19]

The masochistic self-demotion Donne performed in divesting himself
of his male high caste and appropriating the vulnerable passivity of the
fortress-image produces a strange and wonderful sense of sacred, erotic
excitement, like the allowing of a forbidden fantasy of latent female-
ness in the male. Milton's adaptation of the figure is accompanied with
blank self-disgust. The victory of Venus over Mars, celebrated by
Renaissance Platonising poets and painters as a desirable immobilising
of uncivilised aggressions in the name of a higher ethos,[20] was recorded
by Milton in old age as a rude fall from God-given dignity. In the
political inversion of the symbolism (aggression to the female, passivity
to the male) there is a sense of savage and ugly saturnalia, the world
turned upside-down and inside-out. The male becomes penetrable and
pregnable as a passage is forced to his inmost core: 'I yielded, and
unlocked her all my heart'. This 'unlocking' is an act of 'foul
effeminacy' (410): there is a woman within him who has actively
colluded with the woman without. Samson can hardly live with the
violent comedy of his situation. It is the ridiculous, risible and foolish
aspect of his situation that most gores him. He has made a fool of
himself, but (worse) he has made a woman of himself.

In the biblical account, Samson is on his knees to Delilah: 'And she
made him sleep upon her knees; and she called for a man, and she
caused him to shave off the seven locks of his head' (Judges 16:18).
His abject posture haunts Samson throughout most of the play, for he
is imaginatively visible to himself in all his ridiculousness. This posture
is conveyed in lists of barbed negatives, as he recalls a sexual slavery
and blindness far worse than those he now suffers at the mill: 'ignoble, /
Unmanly, ignominious, infamous' (416–17). This is a play in which
adjectives are relatively few.[21] When they do appear, however, they
mass in tribes, often (as here) loading Samson with insult – as if to
exhibit and deplore his humiliation might somehow pre-empt the
laughter and (just as objectionable) pity of those others who have the
advantage over him: sight. Shame before the patriarchal fraternity
whose scorn for the cuckolded or the emasculated is a way of

maintaining caste provokes Samson to obsessive self-display in this posture of sexual humiliation:

> Then swoll'n with pride into the snare I fell
> Of fair fallacious looks, venereal trains,
> Softened with pleasure and voluptuous life;
> At length to lay my head and hallowed pledge
> Of all my strength in the lascivious lap
> Of a deceitful concubine who shore me
> Like a tame wether, all my precious fleece,
> Then turned me out ridiculous, despoiled,
> Shaven, and disarmed among my enemies.
>
> (532–40)

In this phallic version of the Icarus complex, recalling Faustus' 'swol'n with cunning, of a self-conceit' (*Doctor Faustus*, Prologue, 20), the traumatised hero replays the scene of betrayal as a sexual come-down of wincingly embarrassing proportions. The play builds up a double sense: Samson's tragedy was avoidable, and Samson's tragedy was well-nigh inevitable, given his character and the nature of things. If Samson had only acted temperately, profiting by his experience of women in the case of his first marriage . . . But there is the counter-suggestion written complicitously into this male text for a male readership: sexuality is universally threatening because it is always an *agon*, a contest between rivals with polarised interests, and because woman always inclines to take the advantage Dalila seized. Thus to be 'swoll'n with pride' belongs to sexual arousal: detumescence is as inevitable. The whole play discharges unhappy energy in the form of questionings of the sheer biology of the human animal: is this defective equipment the best our Maker could supply? The play insists on its proverbial status (Samson's bitter 'Am I not sung and proverbed for a fool?' (203) and Dalila's ironic 'I shall be named among the famousest / Of women' (982–3)). Samson's memory of his betrayal implies a bedroom scene with a blighted and lurid sensuality worthy of Rubens: alliterative adjectives crowd the spaces between nouns, overwhelming denotation with connotation in a disastrous plenitude which signals the inherent viciousness of the desirable. Samson's head in Dalila's *lascivious lap* is a barely veiled euphemism for the abandonment of his sacred phallus into the desecrating interior of her body. The adjectives with which he scourges his own folly load her with blame: *fair fallacious, softened, venereal, voluptuous, lascivious, deceitful*. Samson entrusted what was *hallowed* and *precious* to an enemy who treated the potent warrior as a sheep-shearer does a ram, dismissing him with business-like thoroughness when she had finished with him. He ends the speech in a helpless ejaculation which throbs out self-disgusted epithets: *tame, ridiculous, despoiled, Shaven . . . disarmed*. Fifteen out of seventy-six words in this sentence are adjectives, 20 per cent or double the average for the poem, and because so many are polysyllabic, their preponderance is conspicuous. They mediate the smarting hurt of Samson's remembrance of rejection and ejection in his shaven state, together with an incredulity at the heart of wrath and shame. The past participial form of *despoiled, Shaven . . . disarmed* follows a norm for the play to fix Samson in the still-life impotency of a state that has been dictated by being acted upon rather than by acting: a grammar of emasculation.

The Chorus goes on, by way of consolation, to congratulate Samson's abstemiousness with strong liquors, but Samson can take no comfort, for:

> What boots it at one gate to make defence,
> And at another to let in the foe
> Effeminately vanquished?
>
> (560–2)

In this recurrence of the usurped fortification figure, if the 'gates' are allegorisations of bodily orifices, then the well-guarded gate represents the mouth; the unguarded gate should not exist at all in man for it implies an intimate passage which allows another entry, leaving one 'Effeminately vanquished'. The final statement of this theme occurs after the debate with Dalila, during the Chorus' reflections on the inferiority of women. Even more than in Greek drama, Milton's Chorus is not omniscient: it can offer a well-meaning judgement based on common sense and common insight – an insight imperfectly adapted to the paradoxical vision towards which Samson gropes. Nevertheless, the Chorus fulfils an intercessive function, universalising the questions raised by the central *agon*, interrogating God's meanings and intentions, reflecting on the human condition and praying for light and

healing for Samson. Its verdict on the feminist issues at the centre of
the play is a conclusive statement of misogynist consensus, containing
prudent advice for the male readership in terms of a generalisation
from Samson's own experience:

> Whate'er it be, to wisest men and best
> Seeming at first all heavenly under virgin veil,
> Soft, modest, meek, demure,
> Once joined, the contrary she proves, a thorn
> Intestine, far within defensive arms
> A cleaving mischief, in his way to virtue
> Adverse and turbulent; or by her charms
> Draws him awry enslaved
> With dotage, and his sense depraved
> To folly and shameful deeds which ruin ends.
> What pilot so expert but needs must wreck,
> Embarked with such a steers-mate at the helm?
> (1034–45)

As a 'thorn/Intestine', the woman has gained false entry to the person
of her victim, uniting to him so as to become 'one flesh' in the
marriage ceremony. *Intestine* connotes civil strife, a feud within the
body of the community. The *defensive arms* which have been immobi-
lised are metaphorically the armaments which should defend a besieged
city from infiltration and the husband's arms which have (defence-
lessly) opened in an embrace, affording the enemy right of entry. The
Chorus plays bitterly on the vows undertaken in the marriage
ceremony, in which the partners pledge themselves to 'Cleave only
unto thee'. This vow of fidelity is angrily ironised in terms of the wife's
malign usurpation of the interior world of the husband (his domicile,
but more profoundly, the sacrosanct self) as a *cleaving mischief*. She
cleaves to him as parasites, thorns or stinging insects might, closely and
to his bane; she *cleaves him* as a blade might, severing him in two,
dividing him from himself. Either she makes his home a misery and
impairs his virtue by showing her true colours only when it is too late
to expel her, or she sensually corrupts a hitherto right-thinking male.
In the recurrent ship-and-pilot-imagery, the Chorus indicates the
instability that comes when one enters into intimate alliance with a

woman: shipwreck becomes almost unavoidable. One or two excep-
tions are acknowledged (1046–52) but these prove the rule that
'despotic power' (1054) of male over female is divine law.

Penetrable thus by an enemy whose nature it seems to be to address
itself to the subliminal violation of the soft interior of the self, Samson
experiences primal terror at the approach of his wife in the second
temptation: 'My wife, my traitress, let her not come near me' (725). It
is notable that heightened emotion of a complex kind emerges in
passages in *Paradise Lost* and *Samson* which show a penitent wife
throwing herself on her husband's mercy. In *Paradise Lost*, Eve 'at his
feet / Fell humble' (X. 911–12) and in deep distress begs Adam's
pardon, taking upon herself the full burden of guilt. The narrator's
tone combines a rather embarrassing mixture of pity, relish and respect,
and the narrative elevates Eve in this contrite posture by assimilating
the posture to the iconography of Christian humility. In *Samson
Agonistes*, the Chorus describes Dalila's behaviour in a dazed but
neutral tone, as if transmitting an impression of a stylised representation of grief rather than the real thing:

> Yet on she moves, now stands and eyes thee fixed,
> About t'have spoke, but now, with head declined
> Like a fair flower surcharged with dew, she weeps,
> And words addressed seem into tears dissolved,
> Wetting the borders of her silken veil:
> But now again she makes address to speak.
>
> (726–31)

At first sight the Chorus was unpersuaded as to whether Dalila was
human or some grotesquely resplendent craft dressed to kill, and sailing
amphibiously on the solid earth: ambiguous, foreign, strange and
unknowable, she navigates a territory midway between exotic mystery
and black comedy (see page 55 above). Upon closer inspection, the
Chorus can see that she is no trading vessel (although Dalila has traded
Samson for wherewithal to buy her finery) but the semblance of a
human creature, with the implication that semblance is all there is.
The flower simile with which her pose of tearfully penitent beauty is
adorned challenges the referend for pride of place: vehicle overwhelms
tenor. As against Samson's filthy rags, so self-revealing, Dalila is

covered by an expensive screen of clothing – her finery, her words, the duplicitous textures of her self-delusion. Tears that wet 'the borders of her silken veil', with its tactile sleekness, are made to seem to flow for effect, as though artistically represented upon a pictorial simulacrum of grief. The doubt Milton casts upon Dalila's integrity by viewing her penitence in terms of its effect upon her wardrobe seems to look back to the cluster of unexorcisable emotions generated by Milton's desertion by Mary Powell, and her subsequent well-orchestrated return, staged by her family and the friends of both sides:

> One time above the rest, he making his usual visit, the Wife was ready in another Room, and on a sudden he was surprised to see one whom he thought to have never seen more, making Submission and begging Pardon on her Knees before him; he might probably at first make some shew of aversion and rejection; but partly his own generous nature, more inclinable to Reconciliation than to perseverance in Anger and Revenge; and partly the strong intercession of Friends on both sides, soon brought him to an Act of Oblivion, and a firm League of Peace for the future . . .[22]

Milton's nephew stresses the theatricality of the scene, which he seems to enjoy imagining, going beyond the known facts (though possibly not beyond family tradition, based on his uncle's account) to dramatise a conflict between initial 'aversion and rejection' and innate generosity and forgiveness in Milton. The facetious figuring of the reunion in terms of Restoration politics (the Act of Oblivion) and foreign policy (League of Peace) points up the element of farce in the situation. Milton, who must subsequently on many occasions have rued the return of his first wife, was in a situation which conventionally opens a man embarrassingly to public jest.

Samson's first response to Dalila's pleading is the shriek of abhorrence of a man who has been made ridiculous: 'Out, out, hyaena!' He goes on to insist that his is not a unique plight but belongs to a tragic farce of nearly universal proportions, for Dalila's peaceful words are 'thy wonted arts, / And arts of every woman false like thee' (748–9). Two readings are possible here: either, every member of the group of women who are false has such arts, or, every woman is false and hence artful. In the course of Samson's speech, under pressure of his passionate emotion, the first meaning with its greater degree of rationality gives way to the second, and Dalila is made to appear as an Everywoman:

> Out, out, hyaena; these are thy wonted arts,
> And arts of every woman false like thee,
> To break all faith, all vows, deceive, betray;
> Then as repentant to submit, beseech,
> And reconcilement move with feigned remorse,
> Confess, and promise wonders in her change,
> Not truly penitent, but chief to try
> Her husband, how far urged his patience bears,
> His virtue or weakness which way to assail:
> Then with more cautious and instructed skill
> Again transgresses, and again submits;
> That wisest and best men full oft beguiled
> With goodness principled not to reject
> The penitent, but ever to forgive,
> Are drawn to wear out miserable days,
> Entangled with a poisonous bosom snake,
> If not by quick destruction soon cut off,
> As I by thee, to ages an example.
>
> (748–65)

The speech forsakes the second person singular for the third person singular and then plural: it becomes a rancorous meditation on men and women, husbands and wives, generalising from his particular misfortune in a wife to the proverbial ubiquity of the disparity between husbandly straightforwardness and wifely duplicity, male uprightness and female crookedness. As a 'hyaena', 'a poisonous bosom snake', Dalila is dehumanised, attributed with the less-than-human predatory rapacity of a hostile species, but a species with a more-than-human instinct for cunning. The hyena, miming the human voice, allures man only to make a meal of him; the assimilation of woman to Serpent in Christian iconography becomes in Samson's flayed imagination not a snake-in-the-grass or Serpent-in-the-Garden but a snake-in-the-bosom. This picks up the idea of infiltration and fatal implication: sexually 'entangled', the husband takes a poisonous snake to his bosom – or does he suck at her milkless poisonous breast? Here as so frequently in *Samson* the grammar is suggestively problematic, as if to show

203

through the surface gloss of consciousness the deeper hardly-admitted fears and conflicts that shake the hero.

In answer to Samson's ideological interpretation of the exemplary and proverbial meaning of his name and narrative, Dalila moves to a fall-back position which, acknowledging the weakness of women, argues that the proverbial status of the female defects of curiosity and loquacity meant that Samson must have known he was committing his secrets to a sieve:

> Nor shouldst thou have trusted that to woman's frailty
> Ere I to thee, thou to thyself wast cruel.
> Let weakness then with weakness come to parle
> So near related, or the same of kind,
> Thine forgive mine, that men may censure thine
> The gentler, if severely thou exact not
> More strength from me than in thyself was found.
>
> (783–9)

'Thine forgive mine' perhaps comes nearer to a Christian position and spirit than anything in the play. But acquiescence to such a position would be taboo for a hero committed to the separation of man from woman, Jew from Philistine, hero from populace. Samson's stance requires of him a sort of evisceration, to expel the feminine element from the self, whereas Dalila is urging upon him a full accommodation to what he perceives as the emasculating weakness he has somehow ingested from her. She asks that he stand on equal terms with woman and say the equivalent of 'Since we are alike, let us forgive one another.' His answer to her proposition is 'Such pardon therefore as I give my folly, / Take to thy wicked deed' (825–6): that is, none. For this self-divided hero, integrity can only be posthumous. It is ritually celebrated when, having heard of the murderous virtue of his final act, the Chorus pronounces a fit epitaph: 'Samson hath quit himself / Like Samson' (1709–10). The conflict activating the living sufferer is resolved into the welcome but deathly peace of static tautology. The reality of Samson has joined the sign 'Samson', at last bridging the abyss between language and what it denotes, but only through the cancellation of the unruly life that will not fit its name. Samson has become a proverb, achieving the phoenix-like status of words-in-the-mouth or marks-on-a-page, capable of endless iteration: Samson the agonist has become the text, *Samson Agonistes*.

*   *   *

Milton's work throughout his life derived from the deep stress and agitation of irresolvable conflict: its power is rooted in the probity which could not allow such conflict, a less than ambivalent resolution. Despite the legendary eloquence of the 'quiet endings' – 'Through Eden took their solitary way' (*PL*. XII. 649); 'Home to his mother's house private returned' (*PR*. IV. 639); 'And calm of mind, all passion spent' (*SA*. 1758) – the endings of his poems are paradoxically seedbeds of new beginnings. There is a sense in which Milton's *Complete Works* are unfinished, as unfinished as Schubert's symphony of that name and more so than Spenser's epic *The Faerie Queene* which terminates in 'Mutabilitie' at just over half its projected length. Whereas Spenser sought and found the temporary resolution of a vast succession of minor closures, touching home at the end of every self-sealed stanza with comforting premature finality, Milton opened up the metrical and generic forms of poetry, refusing the confinement of rhyming verse for his epic and forcing language to release its dynamic of conflict. The poetry of Milton's middle and old age is an affirmation of the ego's compulsive desires and fears as electric as anything we have in literature: the Chorus speaks of 'calm of mind' but the iconoclast Samson goes down in thunder. After the completion of every poem, Milton looked round unsatisfied for new forms of expression, an as yet untried genre to subvert and remake. At the moment when inspiration comes, he wrote in *Lycidas*, 'Comes the blind Fury with the abhorrèd shears, / And slits the thin-spun life' (75–6). That was in 1637. It was another thirty-seven years before Time caught up with him in what was still his prime and heyday: there is no reason to think that he had finished.

Notes

Introduction

1. John Phillips, *The Life of Mr John Milton*, in *The Early Lives of Milton*, ed. Helen Darbishire (London, 1932), p. 33.
2. Michel Foucault, 'What is an author?', in *Textual Strategies: Perspectives in post-structural criticism*, ed. J. V. Harari (London, 1979), p. 159.
3. Roland Barthes, 'From work to text', in Harari, *Textual Strategies*, p. 76.
4. For the idea that the 'pop culture of our times' suggests that even 'general readers may be ready for theory', see Thomas McLaughlin's Introduction to *Critical Terms for Literary Study*, ed. Frank Lentricchia and Thomas McLaughlin (Chicago, 1990); for the 'non-existence' of the common reader, see Jeremy Hawthorn, *Unlocking the Text: Fundamental issues in literary theory* (London, 1987), p. 8.
5. Catherine Belsey, *John Milton: Language, gender, power* (Oxford, 1988), p. 6.
6. A. L. Rowse, *Milton the Puritan: Portrait of a mind* (London and Basingstoke, 1977), pp. 25, 101, 159.
7. Peter du Moulin, *Regii Sanguinis Clamor ad Coelum Adversus Parricidos Anglicanos*, in *Complete Prose Works of John Milton*, general ed. Don M. Wolfe, 8 vols (New Haven, 1953–82), IV. ii, pp. 1045, 1050, 1077–8; hereafter referred to in text as *CPW*.
8. J. Milton French, *Life records of John Milton*, 4 vols (New Brunswick, 1949–58), II, p. 287.
9. See Mikhail Bakhtin, *Problems of Dostoevsky's Poetics*, ed. and tr. Caryl Emerson (Manchester, 1984); *The Dialogic Imagination: Four essays by M. M. Bakhtin*, ed. Michael Holquist, tr. Caryl Emerson and Michael Holquist (Austin, Tex., 1981). See Ferdinand de Saussure, *Course in General Linguistics*, ed. Charles Bally and Albert Sechehaye, tr. Wade Buskin (London, 1974 edn); Jonathan Culler, *On Deconstruction* (London, 1983).
10. John Aubrey, *Minutes of the Life of Mr John Milton*, in Darbishire, *Early Lives of Milton*, p. 1.
11. William Shakespeare, *King Lear*, III, vii, 81–2, ed. Kenneth Muir (London, 1972).

12. Quoted in Joseph Wittreich's exemplary reader-oriented study, *Feminist Milton* (Ithaca and London, 1987), p. 36.
13. *ibid.*, pp. 29–82, for a fuller account of the positive responses made by the female subculture of Milton's early readers.
14. Sandra M. Gilbert and Susan Gubar, *The Madwoman in the Attic: The woman writer and the nineteenth-century literary imagination* (New Haven and London, 1979).
15. Lord Byron, *Don Juan*, I. xi, in *The Poetical Works* (London, New York and Toronto, 1945 edn); Percy Bysshe Shelley, *Adonais*, 29–34, in *The Complete Poetical Works*, ed. Thomas Hutchinson (London, New York and Toronto, 1934, edn).
16. M. M. Ross, *Milton's Royalism: A study of the conflict of symbol and idea in the poems* (Ithaca, New York, 1943).
17. Christopher Hill, *Milton and the English Revolution* (London, 1977). I am indebted to the insights generated by Hill's Marxist analysis of seventeenth-century puritanism and society, and especially to the imaginative vitality of his reconstruction of persons and events, together with his 'plea for total history, across disciplines' (*The Experience of Defeat: Milton and some contemporaries* (Harmondsworth, 1984), p. 27).
18. William Blake, *The Marriage of Heaven and Hell*, in *Poetry and Prose of William Blake*, ed. Geoffrey Keynes (London, 1961 edn).
19. See Wittreich, *Feminist Milton*, Chapters 2–4, for this multiple appropriation.
20. William Kerrigan, *The Sacred Complex: On the psychogenesis of 'Paradise Lost'* (Cambridge, Mass., 1983). See also *Re-Membering Milton: Essays on the texts and traditions*, ed. Mary Nyquist and M. W. Ferguson (New York and London, 1987) where, however, psychoanalytic zeal tends to suppress literary sensitivity.
21. See C. G. Jung, *Aion*, in *The Collected Works of C. G. Jung*, ed. William McGuire, tr. R. F. C. Hull (London, New York and Princeton, 1939), IX (2) for the *anima*, and Emma Jung, *Animus and Anima* (New York, 1957). The perceptions of the Jungians on gender may be read alongside those of post-Freudian feminist psychoanalysts, e.g. Nancy Chodorow, *The Reproduction of Mothering: Psychoanalysis and the sociology of gender* (Berkeley, Cal., 1978); Dorothy Dinnerstein, *The Mermaid and the Minotaur: Sexual arrangements and the Human Malaise* (New York, 1976); D. W. Winnicot, *Playing and Reality* (New York, 1971).
22. See Charles Martindale's excellent defence of the common reader's view that the precise human situation is a legitimate part of a poem's meaning, in *John Milton and The Transformation of Ancient Epic* (London, 1986), pp. 64–6.
23. See W. B. Hunter, 'Some speculations on the nature of Milton's blindness' (1962), reprinted in *The Descent of Urania: Studies in Milton, 1946–1988* (Lewisburg, London and Toronto, 1989), for a cogent statement of the evidence for ascribing to Milton acute or narrow-angle glaucoma.

Chapter 1

1. See M. H. Nicolson, *The Breaking of the Circle: Studies in the effect of the 'New Science' upon seventeenth-century poetry* (Evanston, Ill., 1950); G. W. Whiting, *Milton and this Pendant World* (Austin, Tex., 1958), for studies of Milton's complex response to the new cosmology.
2. Francis Bacon, *The 'Novum Organum Scientiarum'*, ed. and tr. Dr Shaw (London, 1880), pp. 7, 10–11.
3. See Thomas Hobbes, *Leviathan: Or the matter, forme and power of a Commonwealth*

ecclesiasticall and civil, ed. Michael Oakeshott (New York and London, 1962), pp. 38–40.

4. The most helpful introduction to Renaissance linguistic development remains Charles Barber's *Early Modern English* (London, 1976). For the rise of the plain style, the concept of the 'philosophical language' and comparative linguistic and philological studies, see pp. 124–37. See also A. C. Partridge's *Tudor to Augustan English: A study in syntax and style from Caxton to Johnson* (London, 1969).

5. See John Aubrey, *Minutes of the Life of Mr John Milton*, in Darbishire, *Early Lives of Milton*, p. 2.

6. Edward Phillips, *The Life of Mr John Milton*, in Darbishire, *Early Lives of Milton*, pp. 60–1.

7. Quoted in C. V. Wedgwood, *The King's War, 1641–1647: The great rebellion* (London and Glasgow, 1958), p. 257.

8. On Milton's Hebraic learning, see H. F. Fletcher, *Milton's Semitic Studies and Some Manifestations of Them in his Poetry* (New York, 1966).

9. These lines are susceptible of double interpretation: that Tudor England was unlike our age in its high valuation of the New Learning; that their age, like ours, showed hostility and prejudice against learning (see *Milton's Sonnets*, ed. E. A. J. Honigmann (London and New York, 1966) pp. 125–6n.) Neither interpretation casts an imputation on King Edward.

10. John Dryden, *Mac Flecknoe*, 100–1, in *The Poems and Fables of John Dryden*, ed. James Kinsley (London, Oxford and New York, 1970).

11. See Barber, *Early Modern English*, pp. 76–98.

12. Phillips, *The Life of Mr John Milton*, in Darbishire, *Early Lives of Milton*, p. 69.

13. In his *Commonplace Book*, Milton notes that King Alfred 'turned the old laws into english . . . I would he liv'd now to rid us of this norman gibbrish' (*CPW*. I. 424). The Levellers also protested that 'its a badge of our Slavery to a Norman Conqueror to have our Laws in the French Tongue' (*A Declaration of Some Proceedings* (1648), in William Haller and Godfrey Davies (eds) *The Leveller Tracts, 1647–1653* (New York, 1944), p. 109). For the Norman Yoke, see Christopher Hill, *Puritanism and Revolution* (London, 1958), pp. 58–125.

14. See Oxford English Dictionary for fuller accounts of etymology and usage of these words. It will be noted that the list of 'vernacular' terms contains Norman-French-derived popular usage, comprising words short and idiomatic enough to have fallen through the mesh of the class net into mass usage. This vernacular assimilation emphasises the fundamental inseparability of loan-words from core-language.

15. See Christopher Hill, *God's Englishman: Oliver Cromwell and the English Revolution* (London, 1970), pp. 95–6.

16. See Barber, *Early Modern English*, pp. 91ff.

17. Milton's reactionary approach to Anglo-Saxon studies in compiling his *History of Britain*, together with the fact that no significant Anglo-Saxon texts were available until 1655 when he was totally blind, have produced a consensus conjecture that Milton was entirely unfamiliar with the Anglo-Saxon language (see *A Milton Encyclopedia*, ed. W. B. Hunter (Lewisburg, Pa., 1978–83), 9 vols, I, s.v. *Anglo-Saxon Period*). As against this, significant similarities exist between *Paradise Lost* and *Genesis A* and *B* as conflated in the Caedmon manuscript, edited by Francis Junius in 1655. For the implications of any possible debt, see J. M. Evans, '*Paradise Lost' and the Genesis Tradition* (Oxford, 1968). But linguists had been working on the roots of English for at least a century, and it is unnecessary to assume

acquaintance with the newly-published Anglo-Saxon texts to conceive of Milton as penetrating the logic of original English.

18. Jonathan Richardson, *Explanatory Notes and Remarks on Milton's 'Paradise Lost'*, in Darbishire, *Early Lives of Milton*, p. 313.

19. See Christopher Ricks, *Milton's Grand Style* (Oxford, 1963), pp. 109–17, for the concept of linguistic 'fall'. So profound is Ricks' analysis of the Miltonic language that later critics have done little more than elaborate on his principles.

20. For these theories, see D. P. Walker, *The Ancient Theology: Studies in Christian Platonism from the fifteenth to the eighteenth century* (London, 1972); Wayne Shumaker, *The Occult Sciences in the Renaissance* (Berkeley, Cal., 1972); Don Cameron Allen, *Mysteriously Meant: The rediscovery of pagan symbolism and allegorical interpretation in the Renaissance* (Baltimore and London, 1970); Stevie Davies, *The Idea of Woman in Renaissance Literature: The feminine reclaimed* (Hemel Hempstead, 1986), pp. 1–36.

21. Edmund Spenser, *The Faerie Queene*, III, vi, 47; III, xi, 46a, in *The Poetical Works*, ed. J. C. Smith and E. de Selincourt (London, New York and Toronto, 1912).

22. Aubrey, *Minutes of the Life of Mr John Milton*, in Darbishire, *Early Lives of Milton*, p. 6.

23. See Christopher Hill, *The World Turned Upside Down: Radical ideas during the English Revolution* (Harmondsworth, 1975 edn), pp. 13–18, 373, for the Revolutionary importance of the printing press.

24. See C. W. Wedgwood, *The Trial of Charles I* (London, 1964), pp. 92–3; 100–1.

25. Hill, *The World Turned Upside Down*, p. 401.

26. See C. V. Wedgwood's vivid account of Puritan iconoclasm, in *The King's War, 1641–1647*, pp. 116, 256.

27. Hill, *The World Turned Upside Down*, p. 176.

28. *ibid.*, p. 93.

29. For Milton's complex attitude to the people, see A. E. Barker, *Milton and the Puritan Dilemma, 1641–1660* (Toronto, 1942); Christopher Hill, *Milton and the English Revolution* (London, 1977), especially pp. 160–2; Don M. Wolfe, *Milton in the Puritan Revolution* (New York, 1963); Stevie Davies, *Images of Kingship in 'Paradise Lost': Milton's politics and Christian liberty* (Columbia, Miss., 1983).

30. For the tradition of anti-ecclesiastical satire, see Patrick Cullen's excellent treatment of *The Shepheardes Calendar* in *Spenser, Marvell, and Renaissance Pastoral* (Cambridge, Mass., 1970) and D. M. Rosenberg, *Oaten Reeds and Trumpets: Pastoral and epic in Virgil, Spenser, and Milton* (Lewisburg, London and Toronto, 1981), pp. 59ff.

31. George Puttenham, *The Arte of English Poesie*, ed. G. D. Willcock and Alice Walker (Cambridge, 1936), p. 191.

32. For Milton's debt to masque traditions, see J. G. Demaray, *Milton and the Masque Tradition* (Cambridge, Mass., 1968) and *Milton's Theatrical Epic: The invention and design of 'Paradise Lost'* (Cambridge, Mass. and London, 1980).

33. Quoted in Wedgwood, *The King's War, 1641–1647.*, p. 37.

34. *ibid.*, pp.35, 156, 206, 365.

35. The transcript of the Putney Debates is published as *Puritanism and Liberty: Being the army debates, 1647–9*, ed. A. S. P. Woodhouse (London, 1938). The overwhelming impression of words caught on the wing, human voices with their individual inflections, dialects, mannerisms and commitments which we receive from the Putney Debates gives an electrifying impression of the 'schismatic word' caught at the transition between the vocal and the literary, contemporary immanence and the fixity of the past.

NOTES

36. William Kerrigan, *The Sacred Complex*, pp. 152–3.
37. John Cleveland, 'The Kings Disguise', 47–8, in *The Poems of John Cleveland*, ed. Brian Morris and Eleanor Withington (Oxford, 1967).
38. Consciously hidden meanings are attributed to Milton's poetry not only by political interpretations but also (impressively) by mystical readings such as those of the numerologists, notably Fowler in his edition of *Paradise Lost* and Gunnar Qvarnström in *The Enchanted Palace: Some structural aspects of 'Paradise Lost'* (Stockholm, 1967).
39. Quoted in Richard Ollard, *Pepys: A biography* (London and Toronto, 1974), p. 265.
40. John Tolland, *The Life of John Milton*, in Darbishire, *Early Lives of Milton*, p. 180.
41. See J. M. Webber, *Milton and His Epic Tradition* (Seattle and London, 1979), p. xi and *passim*.
42. See Davies, *Images of Kingship in 'Paradise Lost'*, pp. 32–4.

Chapter 2

1. Edward Phillips, *The Life of Mr John Milton*, in Darbishire, *Early Lives of Milton*, p. 58.
2. See *Christs Victorie, and Triumph*, in *The English Spenserians: The poetry of Giles Fletcher, George Wither, Michael Drayton, Phineas Fletcher and Henry More* (Salt Lake City, Utah, 1977).
3. For the structure and iconography of the *Nativity Ode*, see *John Milton: Odes, pastorals, masques*, ed. J. B. Broadbent (London, 1975), pp. 6–44.
4. 'Work Without Hope', in *The Poems of Samuel Taylor Coleridge*, ed. E. H. Coleridge (London, New York and Toronto, 1912); 'Thou Art Indeed Just', in Gerard Manley Hopkins, *Poems and Prose*, ed. W. H. Gardener (Harmondsworth, 1953).
5. For a Freudian interpretation of the nature of this block, understood as the trauma of Oedipal submission, see William Kerrigan, *The Sacred Complex*, pp. 20ff.
6. For the details of this scandal, see Barbara Breasted, 'Comus and the Castlehaven Scandal', *MS*, 3 (1971), pp. 201–24; William B. Hunter, *Milton's 'Comus: Family piece* (Troy, New York, 1983). John Creaser's questioning of the Castlehaven relevance in 'Milton's *Comus*: the irrelevance of the Castlehaven Scandal', *Notes and Queries*, n.s. 31 (1984), pp. 307–17, and Cedric Brown's scepticism in *John Milton's Aristocratic Entertainments* (Cambridge, 1985) do not seem to me entirely convincing.
7. John Aubrey, *Minutes of the Life of Mr John Milton*, in Darbishire, *Early Lives of Milton*, p. 3.
8. See Stevie Davies, *The Idea of Woman in Renaissance Literature*, pp. 185ff., for a Jungian reading of the literary significance of Milton's apprehension of the 'woman within'.
9. Jackie DiSalvo, 'Samson's struggle with the woman within', in *Milton and the Idea of Woman*, ed. J. M. Walker (Urbana and Chicago, 1988), p. 220.
10. Gerrard Winstanley, *The New Law of Righteousnesse* (1649), in *The Works of Gerrard Winstanley, with an Appendix of Documents Relating to the Digger Movement*, ed. G. H. Sabine (New York, 1965), p. 197.
11. I am indebted to Christopher Hill's pithily aphoristic statement of the case in *The Experience of Defeat: Milton and some contemporaries* (Harmondsworth, 1984), p. 26.
12. John Phillips, *The Life of Mr John Milton*, in Darbishire, *Early Lives of Milton*, p. 33.
13. William Shakespeare, Sonnet CXXIX.

14. Cyril Tourneur (attrib.), *The Revenger's Tragedy*, III, v. 72–3, ed. R. A. Foakes (London, 1966).
15. The issues raised in this central confrontation are resolved in the intervention of Sabrina, a celebration of married fertility being presented in the Epilogue, where the Spirit's Song invokes the Spenserian *coincidentia oppositorum* in the twinned emblems of Venus/Adonis, Cupid/Psyche and Youth/Joy. Such resolution is not only merely generic and mechanical but does not take place on the earth at all but 'Up in the broad fields of the sky' (979).
16. Moschus, *Lament for Bion*, 60–4, 112–16, in *Greek Pastoral Poetry*, tr. and ed. Anthony Holden (Harmondsworth, 1974). See also *Milton's 'Lycidas': The tradition and the poem*, new and revised edn, ed. C. A. Patrides (Columbia, Miss., 1983), for an anthology of attitudes to the relationship between *Lycidas* and its antecedents, especially S. E. Fish's essay, '*Lycidas*: a poem finally anonymous', which dwells on the disruptions and dislocations of the poem.
17. Edmund Spenser, *The Shepheardes Calendar, November Eclogue* (XI), pp. 87–9.
18. See E. M. W. Tillyard, *Milton* (London, rev. edn, 1966), pp. 70–4, for the 'characteristic egotism' of Milton's manner.
19. Plato, *Republic*, 392C–398B. See F. M. Cornford's illuminating remarks on mimesis as identification in his edition of the *Republic* (London, Oxford, New York, 1941), pp. 80, 323.
20. William Shakespeare, *As You Like It*, III. iii. 16; Sir Philip Sidney, *An Apology for Poetry*, ed. Geoffrey Shepherd (London, 1965), p. 124.

Chapter 3

1. These and a rich variety of other visual analogues will be found in R. M. Frye's *Milton's Imagery and the Visual Arts: Iconographic tradition in the epic poems* (Princeton, NJ, 1978), pp. 47 and 114.
2. The most useful book on Milton's debt to baroque is still Murray Roston's *Milton and the Baroque* (London and Basingstoke, 1980).
3. See Christopher Hill, *The Experience of Defeat*, pp. 307–8.
4. The greatest exponent of the case against the Divine intelligence-system is William Empson who, in his classic *Milton's God* (London, 1965), turned the principles of Milton's iconoclasm against Milton and his theology.
5. See Christopher Ricks' *Milton's Grand Style*, pp. 109ff., for complex key words in *Paradise Lost*. I have added emphases to quotations containing *wander*.
6. For a semiotic account of the arbitrariness of the fallen sign-system, see R. A. Shoaf, *Milton, Poet of Duality. A study of semiosis in the poetry* (New Haven and London, 1985), which often tells a tall story through fertile punning excesses, but also lays bare the patterned dichotomies of Milton's lexicon.
7. John Bunyan, *The Pilgrim's Progress in the Similitude of a Dream*, ed. Roger Sharrock (Harmondsworth, 1965), p. 39.
8. For Milton's debt to travel-literature, see R. R. Cawley, *Milton and the Literature of Travel* (Princeton, NJ, 1951).
9. Thomas Kyd, *The Spanish Tragedie*, III. ix. 13–15, in *Five Elizabethan Tragedies*, ed. A. K. McIlwraith (London, Oxford and New York, 1971).
10. *Doctor Faustus*, III. iii. 78–82.
11. See Edward Phillips, *The Life of Mr John Milton*, in Darbishire, *Early Lives of Milton*, pp. 72–3.

12. For discrepant views of this conflict, see Jackie DiSalvo's exellent 'Blake encountering Milton: politics and the family in *Paradise Lost* and *The Four Zoas*', in *Milton and the Line of Vision*, ed. J. A. Wittreich (Madison, Wis., 1975), pp. 143–84, and D. K. McColley's equally excellent *Milton's Eve* (Chicago and London, 1983).

13. William Shakespeare, *The Winter's Tale*, II. i. 36–45; John Donne, 'Twicknam Garden', 6, in *The Poems of John Donne*, ed. H. J. C. Grierson, vol. I (Oxford, 1912).

14. For fuller treatment of the Eve/Ceres analogy, see Stevie Davies, *The Idea of Woman in Renaissance Literature*, pp. 231–47; for the history of the female readership, see Joseph Wittreich, *Feminist Milton*; for Eve as a personification of poetry, see Diane McColley, ' "Subsequent or precedent"? Eve as Milton's defense of poesie', in *Milton Quarterly*, 20 (1986), pp. 132–6.

15. See Ricks, *Milton's Grand Style*; see also R. L. Entzminger, *Divine Word: Milton and the redemption of language*, Duquesne Studies, Language and Literature Series, VI (Pittsburgh, Pa., 1985) for demonic and redeemed speech.

16. George Puttenham, *The Arte of English Poesie*, p. 206.

17. For the relationship between baroque and the Copernican astronomy, see Roston, *Milton and the Baroque*, pp. 7–29.

18. For Milton's problematic cosmology, see Grant McColley, 'The astronomy of *Paradise Lost*', *Studies in Philology*, 34 (1937), pp. 209–47; Kester Svendson, *Milton and Science* (Cambridge, Mass., 1956); R. M. Schwartz, *Remembering and Repeating: Biblical creation in 'Paradise Lost'* (Cambridge, New York, 1988), Chapter 2.

19. John Donne, 'A Valediction Forbidding Mourning', 11.

20. J. D. Bernal's *The Extension of Man: A history of physics before 1900* (London, 1973) offers a cogent and accessible account of developments in Renaissance optics and their implications.

21. Andrew Marvell, 'Upon Appleton House', 455–64, in *The Complete Poems*, ed. E. S. Donno (Harmondsworth, 1972).

22. Richard Hooke's *Micrographia: Or some physiological descriptions of minute bodies made by magnifying glasses* came out in 1665, two years before the publication of *Paradise Lost*. Although it was too late for Milton to have seen either magnifications or drawings of magnifications, the subject of the lens on the microscope was as much in the air as the telescope. See Vasco Ronchi, *The Nature of Light: An historical survey* tr. V. Barocas (London, 1970).

23. Jonathan Swift, *Gulliver's Travels*, in *Gulliver's Travels and Other Writings*, ed. L. A. Landa (London and Oxford, 1976), pp. 90–1, 107.

24. *Areopagitica*, *CPW*. II. 538. See M. H. Nicolson, 'Milton and the telescope', *ELH*, II (1935), pp. 1–35, for the circumstances and implications of this visit.

25. Quoted in Bernal, *The Extension of Man*, p. 169.

26. See, e.g. David Daiches, *Milton* (London, 1959), pp. 161–3; J. B. Broadbent, *Some Graver Subject: An essay on 'Paradise Lost'* (London, 1960), p. 87, for the characteristic technique of reading the epic similes 'in' to the major narrative, in implicit contradiction of Eliot's attack on Miltonic stylistic excrescence. It should now be possible to reassess the whole question in the light of the modern attention to plurality of meaning in language, not as superfluity but as superabundance.

27. T. S. Eliot, 'Milton', *Proceedings of the British Academy*, 33 (1947), pp. 74–5.

28. See A. O. Lovejoy, 'Milton's dialogue on astronomy', in *Reason and the Imagination: Studies in the history of ideas, 1600–1800*, ed. J. A. Mazzeo (New York and London, 1962), pp. 129–42; Neil Harris, 'Galileo as symbol: the "Tuscan artist" in "Paradise Lost"', *Estratto da Annali dell'Instituto e Museo di Storia della Scienza di Firenze*, 10 (1985), pp. 3–29.

29. See Alastair Fowler's edition of *Paradise Lost*, I. 200–8n.
30. John Lear, *Kepler's Dream*, with full text of *Somnium, Sive Astronomia Lunaris Joannis Kepleri*, tr. P. F. Kirkwood (Berkeley and Los Angeles, 1965), pp. 106–7.
31. See M. R. Pointon, *Milton and English Art: A study in the pictorial artist's use of a literary source* (Manchester, 1970), Chapters III and IV.
32. *The Divine Comedy of Dante Alighieri: Inferno*, I. 1–7, tr. Allen Mandelbaum (Toronto and Sydney, 1982).
33. For the latter view, see S. E. Fish, *Surprised by Sin: The reader in 'Paradise Lost'* (London and New York, 1967).
34. Alexander Pope, *The Dunciad*, II, 63–6, in *The Poems of Alexander Pope*, ed. John Butt (London, 1963).
35. See, e.g. Edmund Spenser, *The Faerie Queene*, II. vii. 4, 9; XII. 64, 68.
36. For the essence (and the scholarly best) of the theological debate, see W. B. Hunter, C. A. Patrides and J. H. Adamson, *Bright Essence: Studies in Milton's theology* (Salt Lake City, 1973).
37. George Eliot, *Middlemarch*, ed. W. J. Harvey (Harmondsworth, 1965), p. 74.
38. Martin Luther, *De Servo Arbitrio* (1525), in *Luther and Erasmus: Free will and salvation*, tr. and ed. E. Gordon Rupp and A. N. Marlow (London, 1969), pp. 206–7.
39. See Hunter, Patrides and Adamson, *Bright Essence*, for informed wrestlings with these difficulties.
40. Michael Lieb, *The Sinews of Ulysses: Form and convention in Milton's Works* (Pittsburgh, Pa., 1989), pp. 96–7. See *The Dialogic Imagination: Four essays by M. M. Bakhtin*, ed. Michael Holquist, tr. Caryl Emerson and Michael Holquist (Austin, Tex., 1981).
41. See, on the *pro* side, R. M. Frye, *God, Man, and Satan: Patterns of Christian thought and life in 'Paradise Lost', 'Pilgrim's Progress', and the great theologians* (Princeton, NJ, 1960), pp. 71ff.; on the *contra* side, John Peter, *A Critique of 'Paradise Lost'* (London, 1960), *passim*.
42. See W. B. Hunter, 'The war in heaven: the exaltation of the Son', in Hunter, Patrides and Adamson, *Bright Essence*, pp. 115–30.
43. Quoted by Antonia Fraser in *Cromwell, Our Chief of Men* (London, 1973), p. 420.
44. Emily Brontë, *Wuthering Heights*, ed. Ian Jack (Oxford, 1981), p. 80.
45. See P. A. Parker's essay, 'Milton', in *Inescapable Romance: Studies in the poetics of a mode* (Princeton, NJ, 1979), pp. 114–58, for a penetrating analysis of 'threshold' states of suspension in the poetry.

Chapter 4

1. For the genre and Milton's debt to Job, see B. K. Lewalski's definitive *Milton's Brief Epic: The genre, meaning, and art of 'Paradise Regained'* (Providence and London, 1966).
2. See Edward Phillips, *The Life of Mr John Milton*, in Darbishire, *Early Lives of Milton*, pp. 75–6.
3. On a related theme, see S. E. Fish, 'Inaction and silence: the reader in *Paradise Regained*', in *Calm of Mind: Tercentenary essays on 'Paradise Regained' and 'Samson Agonistes'*, ed. J. A. Wittreich (Cleveland, Ohio, and London, 1971), pp. 25–47.
4. See Christopher Hill, *The Experience of Defeat*, pp. 129–70.
5. For the relationship between being and action, see S. E. Fish, 'Things and actions

indifferent: the temptation of plot in *Paradise Regained*', *Milton Studies*, 17 (1983), pp. 163–85.

6. See William Kerrigan, 'The riddle of *Paradise Regained*', in *Poetic Prophecy in Western Literature*, ed. Jan Wojnik and R.-J. Frontain (Madison, Wi. and Toronto, 1984), pp. 64–80, for a Freudian reading of the 'riddle'.

7. The Freudian concept of the 'no' of primitive repression, making judgement possible by allowing the repudiated to be thought without being repressed, sheds light on this antithesis. See William Kerrigan, *The Sacred Complex*, p. 29: 'Meaning exudes its own adversary', and his treatment of *Paradise Regained*, pp. 86ff.

8. See John Carey's succinct introduction to his edition of *Paradise Regained* in the Carey and Fowler *Poems*, pp. 1063ff., for the details of the controversy.

9. See L. S. Cox, 'Food-word imagery in *Paradise Regained*', *ELH*, 28 (1961), pp. 225–43.

10. See Plato, *Republic*, 487B–497A.

11. Thomas Hobbes, *Leviathan*, p. 46.

12. 'Jordan' (II), 5; 'Jordan' (I), 1–3, in *The Poems of George Herbert*, ed. F. E. Hutchinson (London, New York and Toronto, 1961).

13. William Wordsworth, 'Expostulation and Reply', 24, in *Lyrical Ballads*, ed. R. L. Brett and A. R. Jones (London, 1963).

Chapter 5

1. Sophocles, *Oedipus at Colonus*, 1–2, 6–7, in *The Theban Plays*, tr. E. F. Watling (Harmondsworth, 1947).

2. A characteristic view will be found in J. H. Hanford's '*Samson Agonistes* and Milton in old age', reprinted in *John Milton, Poet and Humanist* (Cleveland, Ohio, 1966), pp. 264–86.

3. For an account of this fusion, see Sir R. C. Jebb, '*Samson Agonistes* and the Hellenic drama', reprinted in *Milton: 'Comus' and 'Samson Agonistes', a casebook*, ed. Julian Lovelock (London and Basingstoke, 1975), pp. 175–84.

4. See V. R. Mollenkott, *The Divine feminine: The biblical imagery of God as female* (New York, 1983); the Augustine citation is on p. 22.

5. See M. M. Kahr's adept essay 'Delilah', incorporating plates of Master E. S.'s engraving and of Rubens' *Samson* pictures, in *Feminism and Art History: Questioning the litany* ed. Norma Broude and M. D. Garrard (New York, 1982), pp. 118–45.

6. For the Revelation typology, see B. K. Lewalski, '*Samson Agonistes* and the "tragedy" of the Apocalypse', *PMLA*, 85 (1970), pp. 1050–62.

7. For the fullest, best-documented version of this viewpoint, see M. A. Radzinowicz, *Toward 'Samson Agonistes': The growth of Milton's mind* (Princeton, NJ, 1978).

8. *Luther's works*, ed. Jaroslav Pelikan and H. T. Lehman (55 vols, St Louis, 1955–76), XLV, p. 104.

9. For the problematic status of the Renaissance and Reformation Samson, see Joseph Wittreich, *Interpreting 'Samson Agonistes'* (Princeton, NJ, 1986).

10. See Christopher Hill, *Milton and the English Revolution*, pp. 428–48.

11. King Charles I (attrib.), *Eikon Basiliké: The portraiture of His Majesty Charles I*, ed. C. M. Phillimore (Oxford and London, 1879 edn), p. 62.

12. D. F. Bouchard, *Milton: A structural reading* (Montreal, 1974), p. 141.

13. Wittreich, *Interpreting 'Samson Agonistes'*, pp. xiv–xvii.

14. Wittreich, *Feminist Milton*, pp. 119–54.

15. e.g. J. C. Ulreich, Jr, 'Incident to all our sex: the tragedy of Dalila', in *Milton and the Idea of Woman*, ed. Walker, pp. 185–210, who sees Dalila as 'more nearly embod[ying] the spirit of charity' than Samson (p. 198) and makes the traditional point about the elevation of Dalila to the position of Samson's wife (p. 197).

16. Arguments for a later date seem incontrovertible. See W. B. Hunter, 'New evidence for dating *Samson Agonistes*', republished in *The Descent of Urania*, pp. 219–23.

17. See C. A. Patrides, 'The comic dimension in Greek tragedy and *Samson Agonistes*', *Milton Studies*, 10 (1977), pp. 3–21.

18. See, e.g., Shakespeare's use of the trope in *All's Well That Ends Well*, IV. ii and iii.

19. 'Batter my heart, three person'd God', 5–6; 12–14.

20. See Edgar Wind, *Pagan Mysteries in the Renaissance* (London, 1958), for this higher ethos, and especially Plates 54–7.

21. See Archie Burnett, *Milton's Style: The shorter poems, 'Paradise Regained' and 'Samson Agonistes'* (London and New York, 1981), pp. 139ff., for stylistic analysis.

22. Edward Phillips, *The Life of Mr John Milton*, in Darbishire, *Early Lives of Milton*, pp. 66–7.

Chronology

1608, 9 December	John Milton born in Bread Street, London, son of John Milton, a scrivener.
1620	Entered St Paul's School.
1625, 12 February	Matriculated at Christ's College, Cambridge.
1629, March	Took BA degree.
1629, December	Wrote *On The Morning of Christ's Nativity.*
1632, July	Took MA degree.
1632, July to 1638, April	Lived in studious retirement at Horton, preparing himself for the vocation of poetry.
1634, 29 September	*Comus* performed at Ludlow Castle.
1637, November	*Lycidas* written in memory of Edward King, drowned in shipwreck in the Irish Sea.
1638, April to 1639, August	Continental tour, cut short by news of revolutionary events in Britain. Settled in London.
1641–2.	Began pamphleteering with five anti-prelatical tracts: *Of Reformation in England; Of Prelatical Episcopacy; Animadversions; The Reason of Church Government; Apology for Smectymnuus.*
1642	Married Mary Powell, of a Royalist family, who absconded about a month later.
1643–5	*The Doctrine and Discipline of Divorce; Of Education; Areopagitica; Tetrachordon; Colasterion.*

216

1645	Return of Milton's wife. Publication of *Miscellaneous Poems*.
1649	*The Tenure of Kings and Magistrates* (February). Appointed Secretary for Foreign Tongues to the Council of State (March); *Eikonoklastes* (October).
1651	*Defensio pro Populo Anglicano*.
1652	Milton finally became totally blind. Death of his first wife.
1654	*Defensio Secunda*.
1655	*Defensio Pro Se*.
1656, November	Married Katherine Woodcock.
1658, February	Death of Katherine Woodcock. Composition of *Paradise Lost* begun.
1660, March	*The Ready and Easy Way to Establish a Free Commonwealth*, written on the eve of the Restoration of Charles II. Milton went into hiding as a candidate for the regicide list. Henceforth, despite influential friends, *persona non grata* in state.
1663	Married Elizabeth Minshull.
1667	*Paradise Lost* published.
1671	*Paradise Regained* and *Samson Agonistes* published.
1674	Second edition of *Paradise Lost*.
1674, 8 November	Died; buried in St Giles' Church, Cripplegate.

Suggestions for Further Reading

Bacon, Francis, The 'Novum Organum Scientiarum', tr. and ed. Dr Shaw (London, 1880).

Bakhtin, Mikhail, The Dialogic Imagination: Four essays by M. M. Bakhtin, ed. Michael Holquist, tr. Caryl Emerson and Michael Holquist (Austin, Tex., 1981).

Barber, Charles, Early Modern English (London, 1976).

Barker, A. E., Milton and the Puritan Dilemma, 1641–1660 (Toronto, 1942).

Belsey, Catherine, John Milton: Language, gender, power (Oxford, 1988).

Bernal, J. D., The Extension of Man: A history of physics before 1900 (London, 1973).

Bouchard, D. F., Milton: A structural reading (Montreal, 1974).

Broude, Norma and Garrard, M. D. (eds), Feminism and Art History: Questioning the litany (New York, 1982).

Charles I, King of England (attrib.), Eikon Basiliké: The portraiture of His Majesty Charles I, ed. C. M. Phillimore (Oxford and London, 1879 edn).

Chodorow, Nancy, The Reproduction of Mothering: Psychoanalysis and the sociology of gender (Berkeley, Cal., 1978).

Darbishire, Helen (ed.), The Early Lives of Milton (London, 1932).

Davies, Stevie, Images of Kingship in 'Paradise Lost': Milton's politics and Christian liberty (Columbia, Miss., 1983).

Davies, Stevie, The Idea of Woman in Renaissance Literature: The feminine reclaimed (Hemel Hempstead, 1986).

Donne, John, The Poems of John Donne, ed. H. J. C. Grierson (2 vols, Oxford, 1912).

Empson, William, Milton's God (London, 1965).

218

Frye, R. M., *Milton's Imagery and the Visual Arts: Iconographic tradition in the epic poems* (Princeton, NJ, 1978).

Harari, J. V. (ed.), *Textual Strategies: Perspectives in post-structuralist criticism.* (London, 1979).

Herbert, George, *The Poems of George Herbert*, ed. F. E. Hutchinson (London, New York and Toronto, 1961).

Hill, Christopher, *The World Turned Upside Down: Radical ideas during the English revolution* (London, 1972).

Hill, Christopher, *Milton and the English Revolution* (London, 1977).

Hill, Christopher, *The Experience of Defeat: Milton and some contemporaries* (Harmondsworth, 1984).

Hobbes, Thomas, *Leviathan. Or the matter, forme and power of a Commonwealth ecclesiastical and civil*, ed. Michael Oakeshott (New York and London, 1962).

Holden, Anthony (tr. and ed.), *Greek Pastoral Poetry* (Harmondsworth, 1974).

Hunter, W. B., with Patrides, C. A. and Adamson, J. H., *Bright Essence: Studies in Milton's theology* (Salt Lake City, 1973).

Hunter, W. B., *Milton's 'Comus': Family piece* (Troy, New York, 1983).

Hunter, W. B., *The Descent of Urania: Studies in Milton, 1946–1988* (Lewisburg, London and Toronto, 1989).

Kerrigan, William, *The Sacred Complex: On the psychogenesis of 'Paradise Lost'* (Cambridge, Mass., 1983).

Lear, John, *Kepler's Dream*, with full text of *Somnium, Sive Astronomia Lunaris Joannis Kepleri*, tr. P. F. Kirkwood (Berkeley and Los Angeles, 1965).

Lewalski, B. K., *Milton's Brief Epic: The genre, meaning, and art of 'Paradise Regained'* (Providence and London, 1966).

Lieb, Michael, *The Sinews of Ulysses: Form and convention in Milton's works* (Pittsburgh, Pa., 1989).

Luther, Martin and Erasmus, Desiderius, *Luther and Erasmus: Free will and salvation*, tr. and ed. E. Gordon Rupp and A. N. Marlow (London, 1969).

Marvell, Andrew, *The Complete Poems*, ed. E. S. Donno (Harmondsworth, 1972).

Milton, John, *Complete Prose Works of John Milton*, gen. ed. D. M. Wolfe (8 vols, New Haven, 1953–82).

Milton, John, *Milton's Sonnets*, ed. E. A. J. Honigmann (London and New York, 1966).

Milton, John, *The Poems of John Milton*, ed. John Carey and Alastair Fowler (London and New York, 1968).

Patrides, C. A. (ed.), *Milton's 'Lycidas': The tradition and the poem* (Columbia, Miss., 1983).

Puttenham, George, *The Art of English Poesie*, ed. G. D. Willcock and Alice Walker (Cambridge, 1936).

Ricks, Christopher, *Milton's Grand Style* (Oxford, 1963).

Ronchi, Vasco, *The Nature of Light: An historical survey*, tr. V. Barocas (London, 1970).

219

Roston, Murray, *Milton and the Baroque* (London and Basingstoke, 1980).

Schwartz, R. M., *Remembering and Repeating: Biblical creation in 'Paradise Lost'* (Cambridge and New York, 1988).

Shoaf, R. A., *Milton, Poet of Duality: A study of semiosis in the poetry* (New Haven and London, 1985).

Sophocles, *The Theban Plays*, tr. E. F. Watling (Harmondsworth, 1947).

Spenser, Edmund, *The Poetical Works*, ed. J. C. Smith and E. de Selincourt (London, New York and Toronto, 1912).

Walker, J. M. (ed.), *Milton and the Idea of Woman* (Urbana and Chicago, 1988).

Wedgwood, C. V., *The King's War, 1641–1647: The great rebellion* (London and Glasgow, 1958).

Winstanley, Gerrard, *The Works of Gerrard Winstanley, With an Appendix of Documents Relating to the Digger Movement*, ed. G. H. Sabine (New York, 1965).

Wittreich, Joseph (ed.), *Calm of Mind: Tercentenary essays on 'Paradise Regained' and 'Samson Agonistes'* (Cleveland, Ohio and London, 1971).

Wittreich, Joseph, (ed.), *Milton and the Line of Vision* (Madison, Wis., 1975).

Wittreich, Joseph, *Interpreting 'Samson Agonistes'* (Princeton, NJ, 1986).

Wittreich, Joseph, *Feminist Milton* (Ithaca and London, 1987).

Woodhouse, A. S. P., *Puritanism and Liberty: Being the army debates, 1647–9* (London, 1938).

Index

INDEX

Hopkins, G. M. 69, 180
Hunter, W. B. 207 n., 210 n.

Independents 49

Jonson, Ben 49, 74
Jung, C. G. 15

Keats, John 151–2
Kepler, Johannes 20, 115, 125–6
Kerrigan, William 14, 207 n., 210 n.,
    214 n.
Kyd, Thomas 104

language
    of Chaos 127 ff.
    fallibility of 22 ff., 100–3
    'philosophical' and international 22–3,
        35, 87
    plain style of 22–3, 154 ff., 169–73
    theory of 23 ff., 50, 89–90
Latin 28–35, 51, 56, 84–7, 149, 169
Levellers 40, 51, 73, 146
Lever, Ralph 32
Lieb, Michael 141
Luther, Martin 135–6, 187

Marlowe, Christopher 45, 74, 104–5,
    126, 198
Marprelate, Martin 53
Martindale, Charles 207 n.
Marvell, Andrew 116–7
masque 70, 209 n.
Milton, John, poetic works 51, 56, 65–6,
    80
    L'Allegro and Il Penseroso 49, 67, 151,
        169
    Comus 15, 53, 64, 65, 70–7, 124, 154,
        192, 211 n.
    Epitaphium Damonis 85, 86, 89
    Lycidas 54, 64, 65, 78–83, 89, 92, 103,
        183, 205
    Mansus 84–5, 89
    Nativity Ode 25, 66–7, 82, 152, 174
    Paradise Lost, passim
    Paradise Regained 16, 25, 40, 48, 49,
        56, 59, 60, 64, 151, 153–78, 192,
        205
    Samson Agonistes 12, 15, 26, 40, 48,

    49, 55, 59, 60, 64, 71, 106, 130,
        154
    Sonnets 9, 16–17, 26–8, 68–9
Milton John, prose works 8, 54, 70–1,
    101, 120, 134, 166, 186, 208 n.
    Areopagitica 20, 28–33, 38–9, 44, 47,
        52, 58, 80, 87, 167, 186
    divorce tracts 27, 36, 83, 108, 111, 192
    Eikonoklastes 41, 62, 190
    Of Education 23, 165
    Of Reformation 51–2, 54
    Readie and Easie Way 88–9
Milton, John (poet's father) 10–11, 80
Moschus 49, 78

Naylor, James 156
New Model Army 47, 49, 50, 97, 146
    and Putney Debates 58, 209 n.
newspapers 57
'Norman Yoke' and 'Tudor Myth' 28, 32,
    85

optics 114 ff.
Ovid 11

Pepys, Samuel 59
Phillips, Edward 24, 208 n, 211.,
    213 m., 215 n.
Phillips, John 206 n., 210 n.
'philosophical' and international language
    22–3, 35, 87
Plato 90, 166, 170
Platonism 35, 114, 137, 138, 152, 176,
    197
Pope, Alexander 132–3
Powell, Mary 107, 202
Presbyterians 25, 27–8, 31
'Pride's Purge' 32, 146
Protestantism 24, 27, 104
    revolutionary language of 31, 52, 53,
        57
Puritans 41, 97, 114, 136, 151
Puttenham, George 55

Quakers 40, 156, 176
Quintillian 28

Restoration 37, 40, 48, 59, 97, 130, 136,
    156, 158, 163, 167, 175–6, 189